"The book vividly retains Professor Walls's spoken lectures, concepts, emphases, and teachings on the western missionary movements. It embodies his dedication to sound scholarship in the service of church and society."

—DANIEL JEYARAJ, Oxford Centre for Religion and Public Life

"*The Missionary Movement from the West* is vintage Walls, bringing his remarkable perspective on the ebb and flow of Christian history into this fourth collection of his priceless writings. Those of us who studied under him remember his sharing these insights in the courses we had with him. Now they are published and available to all. The insights in this volume are, in many ways, the culmination of the breathtaking career of Walls who, arguably, stands as the pioneer of what is now known as 'global Christianity.'"

—TIMOTHY TENNENT, Asbury Theological Seminary

"Brian Stanley and others have rendered a great service by transforming several years' worth of lectures from Andrew Walls into a compelling monograph. The result is a feast full of the wisdom, insight, and (yes) wit so characteristic of Andrew Walls's landmark essays, but now developed as a history of the Western missionary efforts that have meant so much—though often inadvertently—for the new realities of 'world Christianity.' It is vintage Andrew Walls, and therefore a book to read, savor, ponder, and read again."

—MARK NOLL, coauthor of *Clouds of Witnesses: Christian Voices from Africa and Asia*

"Andrew Walls was a brilliant and influential interpreter of the history of Christianity as a world-wide movement. These essays demonstrate his deep knowledge, incisive prose, and lively faith. We are deeply indebted to Brian Stanley for bringing this volume to fruition. It will keep Walls's voice alive for another generation of readers and inspire scholars and practitioners alike."

—DANA L. ROBERT, Boston University

"Andrew Walls's scholarship is captivating in part because it excels in reframing existing para-digms and conventional assessments in ways that transform understanding and uncover prom-ising lines of inquiry. So, this reappraisal of the Western missionary movement is replete with penetrating insights and fascinating analyses that will galvanize fresh thinking within the study of missions and world Christianity. Typical for Walls's offerings, the intellectual force of his reasoning is belied by a simplicity of style that makes even the most profound insights readily apprehensible. Well-known historical figures, familiar narratives, and commonplace missiolog-ical themes are reinvigorated with new perspectives and presented with vivid freshness. Superb editing allows Walls's masterful erudition and splendid storytelling ability to shine through. Readers, old and new, will find in this compendium of essays an absorbing reassessment that greatly enriches the historical study of Christianity."

—JEHU J. HANCILES, Emory University

"*The Missionary Movement from the West* invites all of us interested in the fortunes of Christianity across the continents of the modern and late modern world to be informed and gripped by a master storyteller. The narrative that unfolds in *A Biography from Birth to Old Age* is a must read for anyone seeking to anticipate what the rebirth or resurrection of Christian mission on the other side of ⸻ ⸻ e should think they could imagine the possibility of e⸻ ⸻ ⸻ ₅ without first having read this book!"

—AMOS YONG, Fuller Seminary

T0244428

STUDIES IN THE HISTORY
OF CHRISTIAN MISSIONS

R. E. Frykenberg
Brian Stanley
General Editors

The Missionary Movement from the West

A Biography from Birth to Old Age

Andrew F. Walls

Edited by Brian Stanley

WILLIAM B. EERDMANS PUBLISHING COMPANY
GRAND RAPIDS, MICHIGAN

Wm. B. Eerdmans Publishing Co.
4035 Park East Court SE, Grand Rapids, Michigan 49546
www.eerdmans.com

29 28 27 26 25 24 23   1 2 3 4 5 6 7

ISBN 978-0-8028-4897-0

Library of Congress Cataloging-in-Publication Data

A catalog record for this book is available from the Library of Congress.

Unless otherwise noted, Scripture quotations are from the King James Version.
Scripture quotations labeled NIV are from the New International Version.

For Alice, most beloved granddaughter

致爱丽丝, 我最爱的孙女

"Childhood is health."

Contents

EDITOR'S PREFACE *by Brian Stanley*   xi

FOREWORD *by Gillian Mary Bediako*   xvii

PART 1
Birth and Early Years:
The Origins of Western Missions   1

1. **The Birth of the Western Missionary Movement**   3
   Christendom and the Great European Migration

2. **Puritan and Pietist Origins**   27
   Jonathan Edwards and the Missionary Significance
   of Native America

3. **A History and Geography of Christian Obedience**   44
   Early Protestant Foreign Mission Initiatives from Europe and America

4. **"Honour All Men"**   66
   The Humanitarian Strand in Early Protestant Missions

CONTENTS

PART 2
Toward Middle Age:
Western Missions in the Nineteenth Century   81

5.   **Reading the Bible**   83
   Theology and the Interpretation of Prophecy
   in Nineteenth-Century Protestant Missions

6.   **Jerusalem and Antioch**   96
   Western Missions and Non-Western Churches

7.   **"Made of One Blood"**   109
   Race, Culture, and Society in Western Mission Thinking

8.   **How Protestant Missionaries Got into China**   125
   And How China Got into the Missionaries

PART 3
Midlife Crises: Western Missions
in the Late Nineteenth and Early Twentieth Centuries   137

9.   **Protestant Missions Entering Middle Age**   139
   Maturity and Midlife Crisis

10.   **The World Missionary Conference**
    and the First World War   152
    Bright Visions, Dark Clouds, Hidden Happenings

11.   **The Missionary as Specialist**   168
    Healing and the Gospel

12.   **Before the Volcano Erupted**   181
    The Tambaram Meeting and the Eve of the Second World War

Contents

PART 4
*Old Age: The Second World War and
the Western Missionary Movement*   195

13. **The Seventh Chapter of Daniel Continued**   197
    The Legacy of World War II and the Birth of the Indian Nation

14. **Red Sky at Night, Judgment of God?**   212
    Missions and the China Experience

15. **Winds of Change and Latter Rain**   225
    Christianity and the New African Nations

16. **The Theological Challenge of World Christianity**   236
    New Questions and New Possibilities

BIBLIOGRAPHY   249

INDEX   259

Editor's Preface

Professor Andrew F. Walls gave the lectures that formed the raw material for this book at various institutions including the Akrofi-Christaller Institute, Ghana; the City Seminary of New York; and the Overseas Ministries Study Center (OMSC), then located in New Haven, Connecticut, where the lectures were presented in four series of public lectures from 2005 to 2008. The lectures surveyed the history of the Western foreign missionary movement, mainly, though not entirely, in its Protestant form, and with particular attention to missions from Britain and the United States. The first four lectures (the basis of part 1 of this book) were delivered in the fall of 2005; the second series of five lectures (forming the core of part 2 of the book) in November 2006; the third series of five (mostly incorporated in part 3) in November 2007; and the final series of five (broadly corresponding to part 4) concluded the lectures in November 2008.

Whereas most academics move from a formal word-processed text to selections for oral delivery, Professor Walls typically moved in the opposite direction. His lectures were often delivered from handwritten notes, with a good deal of improvisation. That is what made them so delightful, but editors and publishers soon learned that to turn his lecture material into publishable text, recording was advisable. Hence, with this in mind, the New Haven lectures were recorded by the then director of OMSC, Dr. Jonathan J. Bonk, who had invited Professor Walls to give these lectures. As early as December 2007, Dr. Bonk approached editor-in-chief Jon Pott of William B. Eerdmans Publishing Company, who expressed a firm interest in publishing the full series of lectures, three-quarters of which had now been delivered. Members of the OMSC staff, Lois and Dwight Baker, began the transcription of the recordings. On the conclusion of part 4 at the end of 2012, the resulting text was sent to Professor Walls, who added some footnotes.

For a variety of reasons, the book has had a long gestation. In June 2019, David Bratt, then an editor at Eerdmans, suggested that the proposed publication might form a fitting conclusion to the successful series Studies in the History of Christian Missions, launched in 2000. From 2019, therefore, plans were formed to publish Professor Walls's lectures as the final volume in the series, which had by that date issued twenty-seven volumes. Professor Walls commissioned Mark R. Gornik, the director of City Seminary of New York, to begin editorial work on the text. Dr. Gornik was a former student of Professor Walls and had served as editor of his third major collection of essays, *Crossing Cultural Frontiers: Studies in the History of World Christianity*, published by Orbis Books in 2017. In spring 2021, the resulting manuscript passed to me for further editorial work.

The form of this book retains much of the original arrangement of the four series of lectures. It is still in four parts and retains most of the original titles of the individual lectures. Nevertheless, a fair amount of reconstructive surgery was necessary, since there was in parts 2, 3, and 4 a good deal of recapitulation of material included in the previous series; this feature reflected the fact that the four series spanned a period of eight years, and many who attended the later series were not present in the earlier ones. One consequence of the revision is that the first chapter is longer than the others, for it incorporates material that was part of a recapitulation of the ground covered in the first series, yet it expands and supplements what was actually said in the first series of lectures. Another consequence is that three of the original nineteen lectures, one in each of parts 2, 3, and 4, had to be so truncated by the removal of duplicate material that they ceased to be viable as chapters; as a result, the new material that did exist in these lectures has been transferred to one or more of the sixteen chapters that remain. While some integrating themes still recur at various points throughout the text, the finished product is, I hope, a reasonably coherent and largely chronological narrative.

The title originally attached to the whole manuscript was "The Birth of the Missionary Movement," but the integrating motif of the four lecture series was in fact that of a biography of the Western missionary enterprise from its infancy to its old age, and that motif has given rise to the title now selected. For those familiar with Andrew Walls's other writings, notably his three published books of collected essays and addresses,[1] there will be themes in this

---

1. *The Missionary Movement in Christian History: Studies in the Transmission of Faith* (Maryknoll, NY: Orbis Books; Edinburgh: T&T Clark, 1996); *The Cross-Cultural Process in Christian History: Studies in the Transmission and Appropriation of Faith* (Maryknoll, NY: Orbis Books; Edinburgh: T&T Clark, 2002); and *Crossing Cultural Frontiers: Studies in the History of World Christianity* (Maryknoll, NY: Orbis Books, 2017).

book that are familiar. As always in Walls's writings on the modern history of African Christianity, the seminal part played by the freed slave settlement at Sierra Leone, and in particular by the Nova Scotian Black loyalists, is highlighted. Walls insisted that the first overseas missionary movement from North America was a Black Christian phenomenon, and he equally insisted that the first Protestant churches to be planted in modern Africa were the result of Black rather than white missionary initiative, which should be adequate riposte to any accusation that to focus so much on foreign missionaries is to engage in Eurocentric or colonial historiography. There is also much in this volume that is present only in embryo in Walls's existing published works. For example, the current work represents his most fully developed statement of the thesis that the missionary movement was a "semi-detached" part of the great European migration that rose and fell largely in step with the growth and decline of that massive demographic phenomenon.

Professor Walls would have been the first to acknowledge that the lectures, with the exception of what is now chapter 1, say relatively little about Catholic missions, and even less about Eastern Orthodox ones. This book, therefore, is substantially a Protestant narrative. It is also primarily an Anglophone one, with some significant exceptions: early eleventh-century Iceland features in chapter 1, Lutheran Pietist missions from Halle to Tranquebar are given attention in chapters 2 and 3, and chapter 8 includes a case study of a notable Norwegian missionary to China, Ludvig Reichelt. The reader should also bear in mind that the New Haven lectures were written for a general Christian audience. In order to cover the large historical and geographical ground that they do, they necessarily make generalizations, and they make few assumptions about prior scholarly knowledge, though they do tend to assume sympathy with Christian faith. To a greater extent than in many of his existing published papers, Andrew Walls in these public lectures wears his Christian and evangelical heart on his sleeve; he is not afraid to make explicit theological affirmations.

There are inevitably places in the text where scholarship has moved on since the lectures were originally given, qualifying the interpretations Professor Walls gave. In the occasional instances where these qualifications have been significant, I have added a footnote referencing subsequent scholarship, and, where necessary, have made minor changes to the main text. The most significant editorial interventions are signaled by "Ed." In many more cases, I have simply added references or dates where they were lacking, and in some instances have identified individuals who were referred to anonymously in the lectures. Occasionally, I have been defeated in trying to identify a source mentioned in general terms by Professor Walls, and in those cases a footnote records this fact. The text remains relatively lightly footnoted, as befits its origins in spoken discourse. Although I have removed the temporal references in the lectures, such as "yesterday we saw . . . ," I have retained the inimical Walls lecturing style wherever possible. There are sentences that were obviously uttered with a smile or a twinkle in the eye, and I hope that the quintessential "Wallsian" character of the original delivery still survives. Andrew Walls was unsurpassed in his ability to capture a whole mood in a single phrase.

Various colleagues and friends have been of invaluable assistance in addressing the queries that arise from working on an unfinished manuscript. I express my gratitude to them all, mentioning in particular Ian Alexander, David Bebbington, Alex Chow, Jane Dawson, Joan Duffy, Jan Jongeneel, David Onnekink, and Sandy Sneddon. I also wish to give special acknowledgement to Professor Robert E. Frykenberg, my coeditor of the Studies in the History of Christian Missions series. Bob not only answered detailed queries about Indian matters but gave consistent encouragement to this project from the beginning, despite the limitations imposed by his own health and family circumstances. The Overseas Ministries Study Center provided very generous financial support, funding all aspects of Professor Walls's trips across the Atlantic to deliver these four series of lectures. Dr. Jon Bonk, then the director of the Overseas Ministries Study Center, deserves recognition for the crucial role he played in encouraging Professor Walls to turn these lectures into a book, and in commending the idea to Eerdmans. Lois Baker did a fine job in transcribing lectures that were full of asides and obscure names. Dr. Mark Gornik's assured touch on the first stage of editorial work made my task a lot easier. Professor Mark Noll kindly read the manuscript before it reached me, and he offered wise suggestions of the kind of reconstruction of the material that would be needed to make a single coherent chronological narrative.

I am also indebted for their unwavering enthusiasm for this book to David Bratt, long the supervising editor at Eerdmans for the Studies in the History of Christian Missions series, and now to Jon Pott's successor, James Ernest, and his production and editorial staff, notably Laurel Draper. I wish to express special gratitude to Professor Gillian M. Bediako of the Akrofi-Christaller Institute of Theology, Mission and Culture in Ghana for her gracious agreement to write the foreword. Professor Bediako is the widow of another of Professor Walls's Aberdeen PhD students, Dr. Kwame Bediako (1945–2008), who became a lifelong friend and close collaborator of Professor Walls, and whose important works on African theology continue to exercise wide global influence. Finally, all involved in this book wish to acknowledge our immense gratitude to Andrew's widow and literary executor, Dr. Ingrid Walls, for her enthusiastic support of this project.

This book has a long prehistory. Its original conception was in the mind of Canon Max Warren, general secretary of the Church Missionary Society from 1942 to 1963 and editor of some of the writings of his illustrious nineteenth-century predecessor, Henry Venn,[2] who features prominently in chapter 6. Warren had himself published two sets of lectures, given at the University of Cambridge in 1964 and 1965, which surveyed the history of the modern missionary movement,[3] but he never realized his ambition of publishing a major historical work on the subject. In an email message to me on April 8, 2021, Professor Walls made the significant observation: "The lectures [given in New Haven] as they stand represent a failed project. For many years I had planned to write a comprehensive history of the missionary movement from the West. Then Max Warren laid on me a charge to compose the comprehensive history of the British missionary movement which he by then knew he would not live to complete." Warren, who died in 1977, thus passed the baton to Andrew Walls. When, in the final year of his life, Andrew described the New Haven lectures as "a failed project," he was, in his turn, acknowledging that the hoped-for comprehensive monograph would not be forthcoming from his pen. Nevertheless, he was strongly supportive of the plans to turn his lectures into a book that would present the core of his lifelong researches into the history of this much-misunderstood episode in Christian history. Sadly, Andrew's death on August 12, 2021, prevented him from seeing the final text. It has been my privilege and honor to complete the revision of this work for Andrew Walls, the external examiner in 1979 of my PhD at the University of Cambridge, who then became my intellectual inspiration and my friend.

PROFESSOR BRIAN STANLEY
Centre for the Study of World Christianity
School of Divinity
University of Edinburgh
January 2023

2. Max Warren, ed., *To Apply the Gospel: Selections from the Writings of Henry Venn* (Grand Rapids: Eerdmans, 1971).

3. Max Warren, *The Missionary Movement from Britain in Modern History* (London: SCM, 1965); Warren, *Social History and Christian Mission* (London: SCM, 1967).

Foreword

For over twenty years, Andrew Walls's two major publications, comprising material gathered from lectures and articles, themselves originating during the previous decades, have formed basic texts and essential reading for our masters and PhD programs at Akrofi-Christaller Institute (ACI), Ghana. Moreover, we enjoyed his sustained regular presence each year, as he shared in the teaching of some of those courses, well into the second millennium. He was most regular at our daily morning devotions, and we were much blessed spiritually each time he agreed to give the exhortation, when we would be treated to a deep and insightful exposition of a particular passage of Scripture. (We catch a glimpse of his expository gifts in the beginning section of chapter 13 of this book, "The Seventh Chapter of Daniel Continued.")

As his strength declined, he still visited annually and gave us the benefit of seminars on broader topics that revisited old themes, often worked in fresh ways in the light of new insights. On those regular visits he would habitually refer to his two books now in print as the "yellow" book and the "green" book (from the colors of the covers of the Orbis editions). He also kept assuring us that two more books were to follow—the "pink" book and the "blue" book, as he whimsically described them, but it was a good few years before the third one appeared (the "pink" one? the "blue" one?), and with his passing we wondered about the fate of that other volume he had mentioned. So, it was with great delight that I accepted the invitation from Dr. Ingrid Walls to write a foreword to this fourth book, which looks set to join the other three among the staples of ACI course reading material.

I have noted elsewhere that Andrew Walls is a "revered and respected elder in the far-flung corners of the world to which invitations take him."[1] He had such a ready and sustained welcome at ACI, not merely because of the breadth and depth of his scholarship that accompanied his evident and deep Christian piety, but because it was instinctively perceived that here was someone whose exposure to Africa had changed him, had given him original insights into the world Christian story, and whose purpose was not to promote himself or further his career, but rather to persistently encourage those who heard him to pursue a vocation in Christian scholarship and offer counsel in that direction. I believe he devoted so much time and energy to ACI because he saw emerging here one indigenous Christian scholarly and devotional community, an "ashram" rather than an "ivory tower,"[2] whose vision and mission were leading ACI in the direction that he saw was needed.

As I have read through this present volume, I have realized that while the whole is a rendering of seminar series given at the Overseas Ministries Study Center from 2006 to 2012, as Brian Stanley indicates, some of the material had a prehistory in seminars given at ACI or in articles in our own *Journal of African Christian Thought*. This applies, especially, to points he makes in the concluding chapters where he reflects theologically on the trajectory of mission history and exhorts African Christians (and non-Western Christians generally) to take up the mantle of leadership in charting a fresh course for Christian scholarship, for the edification of the world church.[3] I have already noted his 2000 article, based on reflections given in Ghana in 1997. Many such points stressed in this book were aired in this curriculum development workshop, as ACI was launching its masters degree program in African Christianity.

A recurring critique of the Western story in this book, which he would often make in the course of a lecture or seminar at ACI or article in *JACT*, was

1. Gillian Mary Bediako, "Gospel and Culture: Andrew F. Walls in Africa, Africa in Andrew F. Walls," in *Understanding World Christianity: The Vision and Work of Andrew F. Walls*, ed. William R. Burrows, Mark R. Gornik, and Janice A. McLean (Maryknoll, NY: Orbis Books, 2011), 225.

2. See Andrew Walls's guest editorial, "Of Ivory Towers and Ashrams: Some Reflections on Theological Scholarship in Africa," *Journal of African Christian Thought* 3, no. 1 (June 2000): 1–4. This editorial was based on reflections first given at a curriculum development workshop in Ghana in September 1997.

3. Perhaps the best example is the issue of the *Journal of African Christian Thought* 9, no. 2 (December 2006), "Christian Mission and Scholarship (In Appreciation of Professor Emeritus Andrew F. Walls)," in which we included modified versions of two of Walls's articles in *IBMR* (1997 and 1999), as well as two original articles, the first being a transcription of a 2006 lecture, "Scholarship and the Missionary Movement: The China Experience" (pp. 30–33), and the other, "Scholarship, Mission and Globalisation: Some Reflections on the Christian Scholarly Vocation in Africa" (pp. 34–37).

what he saw as the baleful impact of the Enlightenment on mission, when it crosses new cultural frontiers:

> The trouble is that Enlightenment theology, conservative just as much as liberal, is theology for a small-scale universe, and most people in most of the world live in a larger, more populated universe than the Enlightenment allows for, with a permanently open frontier between the empirical world and the world of spirit, constantly being crossed in either direction. In other words, Western theology, Enlightenment theology, is too small for Africa and Asia. . . . It has no answers, because it has no questions. . . .
>
> So the church and the scholarship of the new age have to develop a theology for a bigger universe than the church of the old order has been using in recent centuries. (238)

He could not stress often enough that the task was vast and urgent, given the new responsibility for the gospel laid upon Christians in the new heartlands of the faith in the non-Western world, a task requiring new levels of sacrificial commitment and devotion. Aspects of this point are expounded in the final chapter of this book, "The Theological Challenge of World Christianity," and "The New Agenda for Theology Arising from Non-Western Christian Experience":

> We must hope and expect to see non-Western theologies developing, and many of them will mean breaking new ground, acquiring new skills that few now possess. . . .
>
> There is a huge amount of original research to be carried out in African and Asian Christian history, and it needs the fullest and most rigorous preparation. (239)

> Christianity has always been in principle global. . . . So now in scholarship, as in Christian thinking as a whole, the new theological world of Africa, Asia, and Latin America must redress the balance of the old. (240)

This task would include fresh readings of the Bible deriving from African, Asian, and Latin American religious experiences and a new set of theological questions to be addressed arising from the context, just as the ancient creeds of the church were born out of a process of ask[ing] Greek questions in the Greek language, questions that could not be answered by any single text of Scripture, using indigenous categories of thought, following indigenous methods of debate, making some indigenous mistakes along the way. (242)

The way he presents Christian history and specifically the story of mission thus has a liberating quality about it, further commending the task he now saw awaiting. As I have noted elsewhere:

His insights into Gospel and culture dynamics have the quality of truth that sets people free. For they point to the nonpartial patterns of God's working in history; they encourage Christians of all cultures, and particularly from primal backgrounds, to believe that Jesus wishes to find a home among them; they inspire hope that it is possible to work for the conversion of their cultures and so realize the biblical and eschatological vision. . . . The story of World Christianity constitutes a call to us all to embrace the unprecedented Ephesian moment in which we now live.[4]

As he insists at the end of this book, in relation to "discipling the nations":

Converted diversity will take us nearer the full stature of Christ, and only together, according to Ephesians, do we reach that stature. We cannot get there on our own. (246)

One of Andrew Walls's favorite Twi choruses, which we often sang at devotions, aligns with this vision. It is rendered in English as follows:

> Let every nation praise your name,
> Let every tribe[5] upon you call.
> Let all the universe proclaim
> That Jesus Christ is Lord of all.[6]

This biography of Western mission, from birth to old age, then, narrated meticulously with its strengths and weaknesses, triumphs and failures, is

4. Bediako, "Gospel and Culture," 225.

5. A closer rendering of the Twi word *aman* would be "nations."

6. Hymn no. 3 in *Asempa Hymns*, 2nd ed. (Accra: Asempa Publishers, 1982). In Twi: "Onyankopon, Onyankopon, Aman nyinaa beyi w'aye, Aman nyinaa beda w'ase, Aman nyinaa beyi w'aye, Aman nyinaa beda w'ase." *Onyankopon* is the name of God among the Akan people. A closer translation of "Aman nyinaa beyi w'aye, Aman nyinaa beda w'ase" would be "All nations will praise you, / All nations will give thanks to you," an affirmation of faith.

yet presented as just one episode in the two-thousand-year story of Christian mission, whose future lies predominantly with Christians and churches, scholars, and mission practitioners in the southern continents. The weight of responsibility this entails requires vocational commitment. In a *JACT* article of 2006, he spelled out something of what this means:

> For this [the redemption of scholarship for the edification of the world church] to happen, there is need for scholarship to be perceived and lived as a Christian vocation, and for scholarship to develop in the service of mission and, indeed, as a component of mission. Vocation implies dedication to many years of intense, scrupulous, all-consuming toil in research and teaching. Scholarship as a vocation requires passionate commitment. It is not a hobby or a job but a life-long occupation.[7]

As if to stress the spiritual credentials needed for the scholarship demanded of this new era of mission history, as a final lesson to be learned from this biography of the missionary movement from the West, he makes the following clarion call:

> The church enters God's mission through the Son: the mission to preach and to teach, certainly—a mission also to be and to do . . . so that people may have life more abundantly . . . to seek and serve those who are lost, to call people to judgment, to decision, to make up their minds, to preach good news to the poor and freedom for the prisoners, sight for the blind, release for the oppressed, and the Year of Jubilee where all debts are canceled, and the poor debtors find release. And with that, Jesus breathed on them and said, "Receive the Holy Spirit." (246–47)

May all who read this book have ears to hear!

GILLIAN MARY BEDIAKO
Akrofi-Christaller Institute of Theology,
Mission and Culture,
Akropong-Akuapem, Ghana
May 2022

---

7. Walls, "Scholarship, Mission and Globalisation," 37.

PART 1

Birth and Early Years

The Origins of Western Missions

CHAPTER 1

The Birth of the Western Missionary Movement

Christendom and the Great European Migration

There have been many missionary movements in Christian history. The first was Jewish; we meet it in the early chapters of Acts. The first believers in Jesus, rejoicing in the new assurance of his resurrection from the dead, proclaimed to all who would listen to the joyful news that the Messiah had come. When the persecution over Stephen scattered them, they took that message to their relatives and friends in Damascus and Tyre and such places. Some of them—we do not even know their names—came to Antioch and opened a new chapter in Christian history. They talked about Jesus not just to their own countrymen, not just to the house of Israel, but also to Greeks—that is, to pagans. Cross-cultural mission began in Antioch, bringing new ways of thinking and speaking about Christ. A Greek audience would not be interested by talk about the Messiah, the Savior of Israel, and a message so full of promise for Jews. Cross-cultural mission meant a new vocabulary, fresh ways of thinking, new ways of presenting Jesus, proclaiming him as "Lord" (*kyrios*), the title that Antiochean pagans gave to their cult divinities. So the next missionaries were Greek; and we get pictures of Christian slaves gossiping the gospel to their colleagues and gently introducing it to the children left in their charge, and of Christian intellectuals presenting the gospel in schools as a philosophy, introducing the Christian Scriptures as a textbook.

Before long, there were missionaries from the Syrian church preaching throughout the land we now call Iraq and introducing the gospel within the old civilization of Iran, among the tribes of north Arabia and Yemen, moving across the sea to India, across the steppes of central Asia to the letterless Turkic Mongols and the highly literate civilization of China. This East Syrian missionary movement is one of the most remarkable, but again largely untold,

3

missionary stories of all. There was a Coptic missionary movement associated with a Coptic revival movement in rural Egypt spreading the Christian faith along the Nile valley. A shipwreck brought Christians to Eritrea, leading in due time to an Ethiopian missionary movement, taking the faith into the African interior. My own people in Scotland were evangelized by two missionary movements, one Celtic, one Roman. All of these, and many others, preceded the movement from the West that is the theme of this book. There were thus missionary movements long before the Western one, giving rise to a range of expressions of Christianity in parts of Asia and Africa. But by 1500, when the great European migration got under way, most of these other expressions of Christianity had gone into eclipse or existed under Muslim rule. Some had disappeared; others, like those in Ethiopia and South India, were outside the practical knowledge of European Christians. Western Christians thus came to think of themselves as the representative Christians, and if not absolutely the only Christians, at least representatives of the only authentic form of Christianity. So as Western Christians came out of isolation and met representatives of the old churches of East Africa and Asia, they often regarded them as deviants. By 1500, Christianity wore a more European face than it had ever done before. Europeans had become the world's representative Christians. And these Europeans readily came to believe that their expression of Christianity was, if not the only, at least the sole authentic form of Christian faith.

It is, therefore, important to recall that the Christian faith has always been global in principle, and to a large degree in practice, too. For a thousand years and more, it spread across much of Asia and a substantial part of East Africa. If we are to understand the distinctively Western form of the missionary movement—indeed, if we are to understand our present situation in the Christian faith—we must go back a little. I would like to attempt in this opening chapter a bare schematic outline of some features of the past five centuries. Since it is not possible in this study to separate the history of the church from the history of the wider world, those stories interlock. We will be looking at both; on the last day, after all, the histories of the church, which is God's people, and of the world, which he made and redeemed, will alike be summed up in Christ.

The Great European Migration

During the twentieth century, a great population movement that had been shaping world history for several centuries reached its peak and then came to a halt. We may call it the great European migration. For a long time, the peoples of Europe had been isolated from most of the world, out at the western end of the Eurasian landmass. For centuries, they knew less of India and China than had the Greeks or Romans. They knew next to nothing about Africa except for the Muslim northern and western coasts. They knew nothing of the vast westward landmass of the Americas or of the southern land of Australia and multitudinous islands of the Pacific.

Around the year 1500, this isolation gradually came to an end, and the great European migration began. Over the next four and a half centuries, Europeans, people of European descent, departed from Europe for the world beyond Europe, first in hundreds, then in thousands, until eventually there were many millions of them in the lands beyond Europe. Some went voluntarily, some involuntarily. Some were actuated by greed or lust of conquest; most, probably, were looking for a better life or a fairer society than they could get at home. European Christendom had reached its broadest extent geographically. The last pagan peoples had been brought into it, and Muslim power in Spain had been broken after six hundred years. It had also reached a point of cultural synthesis, with European art, literature, music, and philosophy all dominated by Christian symbols, Christian teaching, and biblical language and idiom, so that it is impossible for twenty-first-century observers to understand any of these without some knowledge of the Christian faith.

It was the Iberian powers, Spain and Portugal, who got their conservative form of Reformation over early, that led the movement that was to take a Europe that knew less of the world beyond Europe than did the Greeks and Romans out of its long isolation. They were the first European nations to develop ocean-going capacity, for this migration was, with one important exception, essentially maritime in character, a migration by sea. The one exception to the maritime expansion of Europe was Russia, which expanded overland, and in the eighteenth and nineteenth centuries spread right across Asia to the Pacific and into Alaska. With that important exception, European expansion was determined to a large extent by who controlled the seas at any given time. Ocean-going ships under the auspices of these powers worked further around the African coast than ever before and found Africa much larger than they had realized. By this means, they found the way to the fabled riches of Asia. Europe's maritime age had begun.

Seeking those same lands and those same riches in the other direction, they reached the great land mass of the Americas, of whose existence they had previously been unaware. In the Caribbean Islands, they found little resistance, small populations with simple technology and no military tradition. In Mexico, an indigenous myth caused them to be taken as returning ancestors, and they soon took charge of the empire that had brought many neighboring peoples into subjection. In Peru, they arrived and found their progress assisted by a civil war, which meant that a very small Spanish force was able to defeat the highly developed empire of the Incas. In all these territories, there was vast mineral wealth, silver especially, and always rumors of more.

In Spain, local society was based on landowners who often held large estates that were worked by peasants who were tied to that particular estate. It thus became an attractive proposal for people who were not themselves landowners in Spain to go to America and to get an estate that would be worked by local people tied to the estate. In Europe, inheritance was usually by primogeniture; that is, the elder son inherited the whole estate. The attraction to America was thus strong for younger sons of landowners, who now had a chance otherwise denied to them of wealth and prestige. So more people came from Spain to America. They often intermarried with indigenous people but kept the Spanish language and the main lines of Spanish culture. So Latin America developed over time a mestizo culture, Spanish in its main lines, Catholic in religion; Spanish in general culture, Spanish in language, but with indigenous elements. This culture was sharply distinguished from that of purely indigenous people, usually called "Indians." These people were treated so harshly in many areas and were so subject to diseases introduced by Europeans that in Central America and some other parts, there was not enough labor to work the estates and the silver mines. So Spain began to bring in labor from Africa, first raiding the African coast and then setting up a transatlantic market in slaves. It was the beginning of the Atlantic slave trade, which over the years was to cause a huge movement of population from Africa to the Americas. In effect, a large piece of Africa was broken off and set down in the Americas.

The Portuguese experience was somewhat different. Their principal journeys took them eastward, down the coast of Africa, around the Cape of Good Hope, up the East African coast, to the Persian Gulf, across to India, then to Southeast Asia, to the Spice Islands in what today we call Indonesia. From there they moved northward to China and then to Japan. This, of course, is a huge area, and Portugal is a very small country. There was no prospect of conquering all this territory or of doing what the Spanish had done in the Americas, setting up an empire. The Portuguese did make some conquests, but for the most part small ones, and their settlements were small, groups of merchants, soldiers, and priests. They were traders, finding rich reward in bringing luxury goods such as spices and silks to Europe, their trading posts made up in the way I have described. It was a male society. Occasionally a ship would come in with orphan girls from Portugal as wives for the colony,

6

but more often the Portuguese united with local women, producing a Eurasian population, Portuguese speaking, Catholic, but merging Portuguese and Indian or Chinese or African or some other Asian culture. For Portugal, a small country with few resources apart from its population, settlement overseas offered a prospect of comfort and comparative wealth.

These developments in southern Europe inaugurated a migration that changed the pattern of world history. Between the last years of the fifteenth century and the middle years of the twentieth, millions of people were to leave Europe for the lands beyond Europe. They were a diverse crowd: adventurers, soldiers, entrepreneurs, desperate characters and destitute ones, indentured servants, convicted criminals, younger sons frustrated by European inheritance laws, and above all, ordinary people looking for a better life or a fairer society than Europe offered. Over the four and a half centuries of this migration, people from Europe and their descendants settled much of the world, especially the Americas and the temperate parts of Africa and the Pacific. Whole new nations came into being: the United States and indeed all the nations of the Americas; Australia; New Zealand; in a very real sense South Africa. Russia, which had so long been bounded by the Urals, grew beyond the Urals until it stretched from the Baltic to the Pacific and for a time into America; it was the only participant in the great European migration that expanded over land rather than by sea.

The new nations that arose as a result of the migration adopted the languages and cultural traditions of Europe. The languages and cultures of the original inhabitants who were unable or unwilling to adopt those traditions were effectively dispossessed or forced to the margins of a society that now lived by European cultural norms.

The great European migration enabled the powers of Europe to redraw the patterns of world trade to their advantage. Frequently the result was baleful, most notable in the case of the Atlantic slave trade, which with the cooperation of some African states generated immense wealth. Another baleful example was the China opium trade. European states moved populations from place to place to meet their needs for labor and production. They broke off a huge piece of Africa and transported it to the Americas in order to meet the migration's labor needs. Smaller-scale operations moved people from India and China to South Africa or the Caribbean. An Indian population was imposed on Fiji in the interests of economic development. Resistance to the desired trade patterns could be met with force. The Western powers literally blasted their way into China and Japan in order to liberalize trade. Economic involvement led imperceptibly to the extension of political control. Some of the earliest and most complex examples of this took place in India and in Indonesia, but by the end of the nineteenth century, almost all of Africa, much of Asia, and all the Pacific had been divided among the European powers. At the beginning of the nineteenth century, the great Muslim ruler was the sultan of Turkey; by the end of the nineteenth century, the great Muslim ruler was Queen Victoria, with more Muslim subjects than the sultan had ever had. During the early twentieth century, the process was extended to the Middle East as the Ottoman Empire, once ruled by the Caliph (or deputy of Muhammad), gave place to territories ruled by Western powers or to newly invented states such as Iraq, with Western-appointed rulers. By the 1920s, it was hard to find an independent Muslim ruler who was not the client of a Western power.

The story of the missionary movement from the West takes place against this background. The missionary movement—first Catholic, then Protestant, then both—makes a single story that arises out of the great European migration and covers the whole period of its existence. The story of the Western missionary movement, then, is inseparable from that of the great European migration. The twists and turns of that story, the rise and decline of the migration, provide the theater in which the missionary movement is played out. The relationship between the two stories is a complex one, and one aim of this book is to try to explore some of the complexities. At the heart of these lies the peculiarity of the European experience of Christianity that for convenience I denominate "the Christendom experience." And that form had been conditioned by the particular way in which Europe had become Christian: by its own pattern of conversion.

European Christendom and Its Patterns of Conversion

When the great European migration began, Europeans described the territory in which they lived as Christendom. The word "Christendom" simply means Christianity. How did it come about that a continent came to be called "Christianity"? The roots of this process lie in the period of European conversion, the centuries that it took—for it did take many centuries—for Europe to turn to the Christian faith. The European peoples accepted the Christian faith as entire communities and essentially in terms of law and custom. It is the nature of law and custom that no one is permitted to opt out. So Europe became Christian territory in which all were to be regarded as Christians, all baptized into the faith, with territorial churches, each family living in a parish with a church that would teach the faith and laws shaped by Christian teaching. Within Christian territory, no idolatry, no blasphemy, and no heresy could be permitted. It was the duty of the state not less than that of the church to ensure that, for all Christian rulers were in principle the servants, the vassals, of Christ.

To understand the European experience of conversion we must go back in time, and to avoid going too far back, let us visit one of the latest parts of Europe to accept the faith, Iceland, on its furthest fringe, in the year 1000. At the Althing, the general assembly of the heads of families in Iceland (there is no king in Iceland; it is a democracy), a heated debate is in process. The issue is whether or not the community should become Christian. Powerful speeches for and against are being made, but there is no sign of agreement. It has been necessary, therefore, to go to arbitration and place the decision in the hands of Thorgeir, one of the most respected elders. He sits, hour after hour, in silence, a cloak over his head, as day passes into night and night into day again. At length he rises, throws aside the cloak, and announces his decision: "We will be Christians," keeping the festivals of Easter and Christmas. There will be a grace period of six months during which those who wish to use the shrines may continue to do so, after which they will be closed. The practice of putting female children out to die is to cease. There is grumbling and manifest disappointment on the part of those who favored maintaining the old customs, but they accept the decision. Iceland has entered Christendom. Here I have followed the account given in the *Saga of Njal*.[1]

It is unlikely that Thorgeir, as he sat under the cloak, was agonizing over the doctrine of the Trinity. It is more likely that he was pondering questions of customary law, of spiritual resources for the community, and of the general well-being of the society. But why was his arbitration necessary? To modern minds, it seems obvious that the solution was for Christian families to follow Christian ways and for traditionalists to follow the old ways. No one in Iceland ever suggested that—it was a recipe for civil war. A single people must have a single code of conduct: "This is our custom." And the code of conduct regulates communal matters, such as festivals. When he emerged from under his cloak, Thorgeir instituted observance of the Lord's Day, Christian fasts, and festivals for Christmas and Easter; these were essential markers of the change to Christian ways. The code of conduct regulates taboos. In Iceland, adopting the Christian code involved a new taboo, a taboo on the traditional population control mechanism of putting female children out to die in a very harsh environment. When the community modifies its code of customs in

---

1. Available in English in various translations and editions; see, for example, George Webbe Dasent, *The Story of Burnt Njal: Or, Life in Iceland at the End of the Tenth Century; From the Icelandic of the Njal Saga*, 2 vols. (Edinburgh: Edmonston & Douglas, 1861–1862), 2:77–80.

this respect by saying that "God has forbidden this thing," it is accepting the corollary, that they must look in faith and prayer to God for feeding of any extra mouths that come.

In earliest Christian times, individuals or family groups entered at baptism the new society of the church. In northern Europe, the existing society is reoriented by means of its code of customs to become the church. Adopting the Christian faith and its resultant code of life enlarged people's views of the universe, creating a new sense of kinship with those of other groups who had adopted the same faith, worship, and code. It was solidified by the use of a single language, Latin, for the Scriptures, the liturgy, and the study and discussion of theology, as well as an attachment to a single apostolic see as a source of authority. Western Christianity was born with territoriality as its outstanding characteristic. Christendom was contiguous Christian territory all the way from the Atlantic to the Carpathians, notionally subject to the law of Christ administered by princes who were themselves vassals of the King of Kings—lands where no idolatry, blasphemy, or heresy could be permitted.

It was a powerful concept, giving a sense of coherence and of identity, conferring a past that went back to the Roman Empire and to the Bible. It provided a kinship that transcended ethnic and linguistic boundaries. Kinship, of course, did not necessarily mean unbroken amity, any more than Christian princes were always ready to heed the voice of Peter speaking through his successors. Indeed, living in central Europe in the eighth century must have been rather like living in eastern Congo during the civil wars that followed the Rwandan genocide of 1994. But many things combined to mark out Christendom over against heathendom. As the *Song of Roland* (line 1015) puts it, "Païens ont tort et Chrétiens ont droit"—pagans are wrong and Christians are right![2]

This sense of identity was strengthened as European Christendom looked south and east to lands once Christian but now ruled by the deputy of the prophet. Beyond Christendom lay Christendom's mirror image: the territory of Dar al-Islam (the land of submission to the word of Allah). Conversely, Muslims regarded the adjacent territory of Christendom, located beyond Dar al-Islam, as Dar al-Harb (the land of war), which had to be called to submit to the teaching of the Prophet. But within Christendom, Christians sought to absorb biblical and Christian traditions, taking them into their inherited traditions and customs. Over the years, they developed a cultural synthesis.

2. *La Chanson de Roland*, trans. Léon Clédat (Paris: Ernest Leroux, 1887), line 1015 (Google Books, https://www.google.com/books/edition/La_Chanson_de_Roland/tZZcAAAAMAA J?hl=en&gbpv=1&dq=La+Chanson+de+Roland+1887+L%C3%A9on+Cl%C3%A9dat&pg=PR3 &printsec=frontcover).

European literature, art, and music burst into flower with a symbolic register drawn from the Bible and Christian history and legend. Theology reigned as queen of the sciences, and its learned practitioners appeared to have canvassed every important question. Such was the situation when Christendom came into contact with the non-Western world, which was also—with some important exceptions—the non-Christian world. This long disquisition on Christendom may seem irrelevant to the general theme of this book. But I am convinced that it is essential to understanding some important aspects of the missionary movement from the West. Western missionaries were children of Christendom, heirs of the idea of a Christian society in which Christian teaching was meant to permeate every aspect of that society, with plurality at best an anomaly.

European Christendom's Encounters with Muslims and Jews

European Christendom's only long-standing contact with non-Christian peoples had been with Muslims and with Jews. As early as the eighth century, Muslim armies had swept into Europe from North Africa. They occupied Spain, and in France were turned back only on the banks of the Loire. Successive waves of invaders from Africa settled in Spain; the Muslim presence there lasted for six hundred years. Gradually Christian princes won back conquered territory, until by the fifteenth century, only the kingdom of Granada, ruling Andalusia in the south, remained as a Muslim kingdom. In the reconquered lands of the north of Spain, a Muslim population remained, peasantry for the most part, living peaceably enough with their Christian neighbors (with occasional outbreaks of friction), intermarrying with them, and sharing a common discourse that included Christian, Muslim, and Jewish elements. The Spanish word for this living together is *convivencia*—and indeed in some respects it was a convivial relationship.

In medieval chivalry, the warrior known as El Cid became the pattern of the ideal Christian knight, and his story caught the later European imagination.[3] But El Cid spent much of his time in the service of a Muslim prince and himself became ruler of Valencia. And "El Cid" itself is a version of the Arabic "Said." In Spain, one could learn Arabic, find Arabic texts. Spain was the place where Western Christendom rediscovered its lost heritage in

---

3. Known variously as El Cantar de Mio Cid or El Poema de Mio Cid, the epic poem El Cid was composed in Spain by the mid-twelfth century. The Spanish text is available at Internet Archive, https://archive.org/, and an English translation at "The Lay of the Cid," Internet Sacred Text Archive, www.sacred-texts.com/neu/cid.htm.

Greek philosophy and science, works originally translated into Syriac by Arab Christian scholars and then into Arabic.

In Spain, the Catalan scholar Ramon Lull (1235–1315), who went on to lay down his life for the gospel in North Africa, developed a Christian-Muslim-Jewish dialogue in Arabic. It should be remembered that there were Jewish communities in the cities and small towns of Christendom. Some Jews were celebrated as physicians and financiers, others scratching a living in humble occupations. Much of the largest community of Jews was in Spain. Jewish communities lived a dangerous life, subject to outbursts of crowd violence excited by lurid stories of their supposedly vile actions, demonized theologically as the murderers of Christ, open to mass expulsion from the countries in which they settled. The Jewish community in Spain was drastically reduced in 1391 after mob violence that induced thousands of Jews to seek Christian baptism. This was but the beginning of troubles. Accusations built up that the conversions were hypocritical, that the converted Jews were still secretly practicing Judaism. Others accused the unconverted Jews of perverting the converted ones. The main business of the Spanish Inquisition in its early period was the investigation of converted Jews or Muslims, the evidence against them perhaps a suspicion of Sabbath keeping, or the lack of avoidance of pork, or the consumption of alcohol, or singing in Arabic. It was not sufficient that Jews or Muslims should convert, not sufficient that they be baptized, acknowledge the faith of the church, or attend mass; they must conform to the cultural norms of their old Christian neighbors, or their conversion would not be accepted.

In principle, Christendom had no place for plurality; in this respect the large Jewish and Muslim communities in Spain were anomalies. In 1492, the logic of Christendom was followed out. That year—the same year that Columbus's expedition (which incidentally was financed by converted Jews) set out to find the new route to Asia—the monarchs of Spain settled on the expulsion of the Jews. The sufferings of those who left were appalling. Many returned, accepting the price of return: baptism. Europe's largest Jewish community was swallowed up in Christendom.

And what of the Muslims? Sometime before this, the monarchs had set about the reconquest of Granada, the last remaining Muslim entity in Spain; and it is in that same year, 1492, that they finally succeeded. Columbus, about to set sail, saw the submission of the Muslim king. From one point of view, this was the culmination of a territorial war that had lasted for centuries, and the first expressions of Spanish rule were not harsh. The archbishop wanted to encourage voluntary conversions and did not force converts to cultural rejection, even allowing use of Arabic at Mass. But government policy overruled, and it was ordained (with some grumbling, though hardly enough, from the theologians) that all Muslims should be baptized, on the ground that "if they don't become Christians, their children and grandchildren will."[4] A grand bonfire was held of Arabic booty. Over the next three decades, the old Muslims of Castile and Aragon, who had lived under Christian rule in *convivencia* with their Christian neighbors over the centuries, met the same fate. Muslim Spain was absorbed into Christendom.

The date of 1492 is significant. Christendom reaches its completion in the years leading up to 1500. In this period, Europe became more Christian than it had ever been before, in two senses. Territorially, those years saw the forced conversion of the last pagan peoples in the Baltic states and Finland, so that only the Saami (or Sámi) of the far north remained outside; and they saw the end of the visible Muslim and Jewish presence in Spain. Culturally, the process of Christian interaction with the languages and thought of Europe reached its height. Intellectually and theologically, a fermentation process was going on that was soon to bubble up in the diverse currents of reform and renewal that marked the sixteenth century.

Supposing the people refused the invitation to submit to Christ, European Christendom had a long-established institution in crusade, the use of force to extend Christendom or to reclaim lost Christian territory. The territorial nature of European Christian experience encouraged Christians to identify the propagation of the faith with the extension of Christian territory, to increase the number and area of localities that were subject to Christian rule. The early crusades had been seen in these terms. The short-lived Crusader States of Jerusalem, Tripoli, Antioch, and Edessa appeared to give substance to the idea; use of the same word "crusade" to describe the Teutonic knights' subjugation of the Baltic States and, most of all, use of the same word to describe the war that brought Muslim power in Spain to an end in 1492 took it still further in that direction. After six centuries of Muslim presence there, Spanish Muslims now had to choose between Christian baptism and leaving the country.

The Crusader and the Missionary as Two Modes of Christian Expansion

The crusading mode and the missionary mode are sharply differing methods of extending the Christian faith. They grew up in the same areas in the

4. Henry Kamen, *The Spanish Inquisition: An Historical Revision*, 4th ed. (New Haven: Yale University Press, 2014), 159.

same period; they coexisted and went on side by side. But they are totally different in concept and in spirit. The crusader may invite, but in the end, he is prepared to compel. The missionary cannot compel; the missionary can only demonstrate, explain, entreat—and leave the rest to God. But if the missionary is to demonstrate, invite, and explain, then the missionary has to gain a hearing. That will probably involve learning a language. The conquistadors in the Americas did not trouble themselves much with languages. The Spanish conquest of the Americas is the last of the crusades. Mexico and Peru are conquered, and conquered remarkably quickly. The gods of their empires were destroyed; Aztec and Inca were themselves great empire builders, and the great national shrines of each contained the images of all the deities of all the peoples they had conquered. The shrines reflected a picture of the heavenly world that reflected the earthly. The Spaniards followed a more radical path: they destroyed all the images and built churches over the shrines. Whole populations were baptized. Mexico became New Spain, with the laws and customs of Old Spain, without idolatry, blasphemy, or heresy. Thus by force and violence, and to the accompaniment of brutality, greed, and extortion on the part of the crusaders, the new lands of America were brought into Christendom to become subject to the law of Christ and the pattern of Christian nations.

In most of Africa, however, and still more in Asia, crusade was out of the question. Portugal, the original representative of Christendom in the east, is a very small country. How could it take on the power of the Mughal Empire in India or the empire of China or of Japan? While never giving up the rhetoric of Christendom, the Portuguese gave up all ambitious ideas of extending it. They settled for survival and profit, for the most part attempting little by way of extending Christendom outside the small enclaves, such as Goa and Malacca, that they controlled. The Dutch, who succeeded the Portuguese in the leadership of the migration, maintained the rhetoric of Christendom, in Protestant instead of Catholic language. The British, their successors, did not even trouble with the rhetoric. Under the British East India Company, it was clear policy that religion must never interfere with business. Colonialism forced the powers of Christendom to choose between their economic and political interests and their religious profession—and we know which they all chose.

Hence, despite the prevalence of the crusading mode of Christian expansion, the first contacts of European Christendom with the non-Western world did include some successful peaceful overtures to states beyond Europe to accept the rule of Christ. One of the earliest was in the state of Mbanza Mbenga, near the mouth of the Congo River, which Portuguese vessels reached in the closing years of the fifteenth century. There followed some years of investigation in which Portuguese and Kongolese exchanged hostages, so that

Portuguese lived in Africa and Kongolese in Lisbon. Then the chief, with the full support of his council of elders, agreed to accept baptism, taking the name John I (the king of Portugal was John II). Many other chiefs were baptized, and many of the people, too. *Nkisi*, traditional cult objects, were collected and a vast bonfire lit; a huge wooden cross was set up in the center of the main town. Mbanza was neither a Portuguese colony nor a Portuguese puppet: it was an independent African state but within Christendom. After a while, indeed, John I and many of his elders decided that the decision to become Christian had not been justified by its results. There had been the great bonfire of *nkisi*, but the Christian teachers insisted on burning other *nkisi* as they appeared. But without them how could the realm be protected from evil influences, from witchcraft, from sorcery?

The Christian answer was, "By the power of Christ." But how was the power of Christ to be made manifest? In the Portuguese model of Christianity, the only one on offer, the answer was, "In the grace of God shown in the sacrament, when Christ's presence is made real and the merits of his sacrifice declared." But the sacrament depended on the presence of priests. In Portugal, there were many of these; in Kongo, very few. King and council appear to have decided that the new way was not offering adequate protection; they renounced the faith and returned to the *nkisi*. But one of the king's sons, Mvemba a Nzinga, who had taken the baptismal name Afonso and who ruled a province under his father, held staunchly to the Christian way; and when John died, after a short war of succession, Afonso succeeded him, reigning as a Christian king and maintaining Kongo as a Christian state for the next thirty-four years. Throughout that time, he sought to maintain the Christian apparatus of rule, though constantly frustrated by his failure to get an indigenous priesthood—the only way, according to the model he was receiving from Europe, in which his land could fully participate in the blessings of the gospel.

Richard Gray, who made an immense contribution to the study of Christian history in Africa, has shown that, despite all the difficulties and contrary to common belief, a genuine African lay Christianity did emerge in the kingdom.[5] In this early African state of Christendom, and one hundred fifty years after Afonso's death, emerged Africa's first known Christian prophet, Beatrice Kimpa Vita, who inspired the first African independent church, the Antonian movement.[6] The final destruction of the Christian kingdom was brought about by Portuguese colonialism.

5. Richard Gray, *Black Christians and White Missionaries* (New Haven: Yale University Press, 1990), chapter 3.
6. Adrian Hastings, *The Church in Africa 1450–1950* (Oxford: Clarendon, 1994), 102–9.

Not all the non-Western world, therefore, was like the Americas. The Portuguese representatives of Christendom found a very different situation from the one the Spanish encountered. The area committed to them was vast; their journeys took them down the western coast of Africa, around the Cape of Good Hope, up the East African coast, across the Persian Gulf, over to the coast of India, right around by Sri Lanka and across the Spice Islands of Southeast Asia, up the China Sea to China, and on to Japan. A revision of the papal map added Brazil to their territories. Portugal is a small country; its tiny armies could never hope to conquer as the Spaniards had done. How could they take on the Mughal Empire in India? Or the vast Chinese Empire? Or the Japanese Empire? Nor did invitations to enter Christendom produce much fruit.

Some depressed and oppressed communities in India accepted baptism in return for protection against Muslim invaders. Some enclaves like Goa could be cleansed, by force, of Hindu temples, with the result that people went to the temples beyond the enclave. The Chinese Empire gave the Portuguese a squalid, uninhabited tidal island at Macao to keep the big-nosed barbarians confined where they could do no harm. In general, neither Hindus nor Buddhists nor Muslims responded to the invitation to enter Christendom, and whatever doctrine of the just war might be invoked, there was no hope of ever compelling them to do so. There would be no more crusades.

In the event, the Portuguese settled down along the coastal fringes of Asia, first to survive and then to profit, and for practical purposes abandoned the idea of bringing the nations into Christendom. They did not abandon the rhetoric, and they jealously guarded their claim to the oversight of the church given by the old papacy, despite the best efforts of later popes and generations of non-Portuguese missionaries. But the concern to extend Christendom remained in the sphere of rhetoric, not of action. Their Protestant successors among the European nations in Asia, the Dutch and the British, did even less. The Dutch maintained the rhetoric, turning it from Catholic to Protestant in expression; the British abandoned even that, proclaiming in India that they were neutral in matters of religion. "England is the first conqueror of India," complained a leading evangelical spokesman in the mid-nineteenth century, "who has not let it be known what his religion is."[7] For years British power in India strictly regulated the admission of missionaries, as of all Europeans from all territories under their control and from all ships sailing to India.[8]

---

7. The spokesman is possibly Lord Shaftesbury, though I have been unable to locate the reference.—Ed.

8. See Penelope Carson, *The East India Company and Religion, 1698–1858* (Woodbridge: Boydell & Brewer, 2012).

The Consequences for Christianity of the Great European Migration

The religious effects of the great European migration were thus mixed. The strangest aspect of all was in the position of Christianity. When the great European migration began in the sixteenth century, Christianity was the religion of Europe and a largely European religion. By the end of the twentieth century, a massive recession in the West, especially in Europe, and a massive accession in the rest of the world, especially in Africa, had transformed the cultural and demographic distribution of Christianity. Christianity had become once more, as in its beginnings, a non-Western religion; and though it was by no means the only cause of the change, the missionary movement, the despised, semidetached appendix to the great European migration, had played a significant part.

I have argued elsewhere that these events are the seeds of the destruction of Christendom and the beginnings of European secularization.[9] Colonialism was the first major solvent of the synthesis that had fused Christianity and European culture as Christendom. A wedge had been driven between the religious profession of the European nations and their political, economic, and strategic interests. The political, economic, and strategic interests would inhibit the European powers from active propagation of Christianity in the lands beyond Europe, and sometimes led them to the active support of other religions. Hinduism as we know it today—as a coherent, confident formulation, unafraid of modernity and the scientific worldview—is a product of the British Raj in India. The Raj also produced the conditions for the emergence of Pakistan as the first modern Islamic state. In both Asia and Africa, colonial rule often deliberately produced a vast increase in the number of Muslims, while at the same time its policy in the Middle East ensured that Muslims felt aggrieved and offended.

If the missionary cannot compel, then entrance is possible only with the consent of those to whom the missionary goes. It is necessary to find a place, a niche, within the society. The fundamental difference between the crusader and the missionary is that the missionary lives and works on someone else's terms. Though the colonial period brought all sorts of modifications, the generalization remains broadly true even today. The fundamental missionary experience is to live on terms set by somebody else.

The missionary mode of Christian expansion from the West began in Catholic southern Europe in the era of the Reformation among those who

---

9. Andrew F. Walls, "From Christendom to World Christianity: Missions and the Demographic Transformation of the Church," in *The Cross-Cultural Process in Christian History: Studies in the Transmission and Appropriation of Faith* (Maryknoll, NY: Orbis Books, 2002), 49–71.

17

remained with the old church but had been revived by the renewing influence that roared through it during that period. The old church had in the mendicant orders, which had been the natural home of radical Christians, and in new and reformed orders and societies, such as the Society of Jesus, an infrastructure for missionary operations. The missionary mode of Christian expansion needed a corps of dedicated people who had the spiritual resilience, the intellectual equipment, and the effective organization to provide the missionary force. In the orders and the new societies that the Catholic Reformation renewed or initiated, Catholic Europe had that corps of workers; Protestant Europe, ironically, slaughtered the goose that laid the missionary egg. It took Protestants another couple of centuries to develop a parallel infrastructure. Accordingly, it was Catholic missionaries who first grappled with the realities of translation and who worked out the details of living on someone else's terms: learning to be a Christian exemplar of the Hindu ascetic, for instance; taking the dress and the diet that go with that of the sanyasi; recognizing that if one was to be accepted as a scholar in China, it was necessary to be a scholar in the Chinese sense and, for the kingdom of God's sake, to know the Chinese classics as a Chinese scholar knew them, and to convey the fruits of Christian scholarship nurtured in a very different civilization at the same time.

The Western missionary movement—first Catholic, then Protestant, then both—drew heavily on radical Christianity, on those seeking utter commitment to the Savior. It went through periods of immense frustration and seemed, especially in its early Protestant days, to invite not just failure but disaster. It operated over the whole period of the great European migration, and it was a product of the conditions of the great European migration. But it was always a semidetached part, for ultimately its spring lay in the Christian gospel. Whatever the missionaries believed they should do, the final reason for their existence was to point to Christ. They were migrants by choice, migrants by force of circumstance. Missionaries, with all their failures, contradictions, and ambiguities that belong to the human condition, were migrants for Christ's sake.

Protestantism and Mission

The Protestant Reformation, at least initially, left the Christendom concept intact, except perhaps as it related to language. The Reformers all wanted to reform the whole church everywhere; unable to effect that, they settled for national reformations in which the whole church in particular political entities would be reformed in a manner befitting each particular nation. Plurality had no more place in Protestant than in Catholic thinking. If there was one area in which Catholics and Protestants could joyfully cooperate, it was in the suppression of Anabaptist movements that attempted to break the link between church and the whole of society.

In 1561, one of the leading figures of the Reformation in England, Bishop John Jewel, affirmed in his *Apology for the Church of England*: "We believe that there is one Church of God, and that the same is not shut up . . . into some one corner or kingdom, but that it is catholic and universal, and dispersed throughout the whole world. So that there is now no nation which may truly complain that they be shut forth, and may not be one of the Church and people of God."[10]

Jewel solemnly insists that at that time, no nation in the world could complain that they were shut out of the universal church of God. But surely, in 1561, most nations of the world could, if they had a mind to, make that complaint. The point is that when this leader of the English church says "world," he really means Europe, and for practical purposes, western Europe. When Bishop Jewel thinks of the world in which the church as he knows it operates, he thinks only of Europe.

The previous year, a national confession had been adopted in Scotland. Its cover page carries this text from Matthew 24:14: "And this glad tydings of the kingdom shalbe preached throught the hole world for a witness to all nations, and then shall the end cum." A grand missionary vision; but what do the framers of the Scots Confession mean by "the whole world"? There is a hint of this in the confession's closing words, which draw on the text of Acts 4:25–29: "Arise, O Lord, and let thine enemies be confounded; . . . Give to thy servants strength to speak thy word in boldnesse; and let all nations cleave to the true knowledge of Thee."[11] The confession is thinking not of the evangelization of the whole inhabited world but of the Reformation struggle going on across Europe. If there is any thought beyond that, it is of what God will do in the last days, not of what his servants are called upon to do in the present. Protestant consciousness in northern Europe in the era of the Reformation does not move far beyond the lands that form the theater of the Reformation itself. Southern Europe, Catholic Europe, had already begun to acquire a wider consciousness.

10. John Jewel, *The Apology of the Church of England*, ed. Henry Morley (London: Cassell & Company, 1888), 32 (Project Gutenberg, www.gutenberg.org/files/17678/17678-h/17678-h.htm).

11. G. D. Henderson and J. Bulloch, eds., *The Scots Confession 1560* (Edinburgh: Saint Andrew, 1960), 28, 80. [The English biblical text used in the confession is, surprisingly, not that of the Geneva Bible but appears to be a composite of existing English Bibles; I owe this point to Professor Jane Dawson.—Ed.]

Christendom was the mode by which Christianity was incorporated into European culture. It created a powerful civilization. It had, however, no equipment for assessing itself, and Western Christians assumed its finality and its normative character. The contact with the non-Western world produced the missionary movement, and it was the missionary movement that proved to be the great learning experience for Western Christianity. This general point leads to consideration of a further aspect of the experience of Christendom, since it is crucial to the missionary movement. In principle, all the communities of Europe were Christian, everyone was baptized, everyone belonged to the church, everyone belonged to a parish with a priest who had the cure of their souls, and everyone received Christian teaching and was subject to Christian discipline. But everyone also could see how far practice fell short of principle, how the very structures of society, with the claims of lord on vassal, perpetuated violence and inhibited consistent Christian living. The sense of sin, of failure—consistent, inevitable failure—steadily built up. The image of the last days was once one of the Lord's vindication and rescue of his saints; now it became the *Dies Irae*, the Day of Wrath, poured out on people who professed Christ's name but broke his laws. Once the image of Christ had been the Savior; increasingly it shifted to that of the Judge. Once the focus of Christian reflection had been on incarnation, on the divine Son's becoming, as Athanasius put it, what we are in order that we may become what he is; in Western Christianity, the theology of atonement is brought into central focus. And the overriding concern of European thought, both in theology and pastoral practice, is coping with guilt.

The Protestant Reformation has to be seen against this background. The leading Reformers had themselves struggled with it; Luther had worked through the whole penitential system of the church and found no relief. At the popular level, there were expedients that were nothing more than moneymaking rackets that traded on the sense of guilt. The central Reformation doctrines, therefore, are about grace, about God taking the initiative in our salvation.

The sense of inevitable, systemic failure had another outcome. At any given time and place, the Christian nature of Christendom was at best a compromise, at worst a mockery. Society manifestly flouted the norms that Christendom proclaimed. But in many a time and place, there were people, men and women, who sought a truer, a more radical discipleship than Christendom usually revealed and than its normal structures sometimes permitted. Such people often had the sense of sin in a very high degree; often they had gone through experiences of spiritual crisis. They tapped into an older Christian tradition that had begun in the Nile valley in the middle years of the third century, when Antony the Copt sought the way to become the disciple that Jesus spoke of in the

Gospels, taking seriously the counsel to sell all and give to the poor, to take no thought for the morrow, to care only for the kingdom and its righteousness.

The monastic movement sought to reestablish the life of the apostolic church and to create a new community in which a consistent Christian life was possible. The communities were not separate from Christendom; they were integral to it. They had meaning only in relation to the wider Christian community. If the model of Christendom itself was Israel, and the model of the Christian prince was Hezekiah or Josiah, the model of the monastery was that of the Righteous Remnant, the true Israel that becomes an earnest of the wider Israel's salvation.

The monasteries, as with all human institutions, suffered from tendencies to corruption, and in Protestant lands were abandoned, for the Protestant Reformers sought the reformation of the whole church, not just a remnant. But in Protestant lands, the same features that had marked pre-Reformation Christendom were soon manifest; Protestant Christendom, like Catholic, veered between compromise and revival. And as in Catholic Christendom, so in Protestant Christendom, men and women sought a truer and more radical discipleship than a nominally Christian society offered or sometimes permitted. Typically, a deep sense of guilt marked the beginning of this quest; typically, an immense, sometimes ecstatic sense of joy and deliverance followed, with the recognition that Christ's atonement brought forgiveness. And this experience of Christ's mercy was typically the entrance to a life of devout striving after the models of life depicted in the New Testament. The monasteries were gone now, and the patterns of experience became more individualized; indeed, wider currents of thought that were stressing the autonomous nature of the self over against the older corporate sense of Christendom perhaps increased this tendency. Those who went this way typically sought others of like mind and like spirit and formed communities more or less formal.

The earliest models of this are to be found in the Anabaptist congregations of the Reformation period. Later versions appeared: the Puritan, particularly in the Anglo-Saxon lands; the Pietists, particularly in Germany and central Europe; the evangelical, begun in the Anglo-Saxon world and merging into European Pietism. These movements are spiritual descendants of the earlier discipleship movements that brought people to the monastic orders and the societies. The Puritan, Pietist, and evangelical conversion movements can be seen as the heirs of these earlier medieval and early modern reformist strands within Christendom. They are equally manifestations of Christian radicalism, and they are crucial to the nature and the history of the missionary movement; at crucial moments, they are the main sources of missionaries. Radical Christians are, generally speaking, converted people, and radical Christians, again generally speaking, are the stuff of which missionaries were made.

Such people could not be satisfied with the compromises effected by nominally Christian governments, or with less than the widest proclamation of the gospel about Christ that they believed to be the vehicle of human salvation. The new position of the powers of Christendom in the non-Western world seemed to lay an added burden, a new responsibility, to proclaim that message. It was necessary to have a new type of Christian proclamation, embodied in people who must offer and demonstrate but could not compel: preachers of the word who would be in a different position from any preacher in Christendom; preachers who must find a way of getting a hearing but could not command, who must learn a language and find a place within a strange society; people who would live on terms dictated by someone else. The fundamental missionary qualification is probably still the readiness to live on terms set by someone else.

So it was in Catholic as opposed to Protestant Europe that the missionary movement began. In due time in Protestant Christendom, Protestant missions arose as Protestants gained a maritime consciousness, the means of recruiting and maintaining an appropriate corps of workers or personnel, and the logistical connection between a Western church and the non-Western. Protestants cannot afford to neglect the Catholic story, for all that the Protestants were later to discover—all the issues about evangelization, inculturation, identification, ethnicity, human relations, and relations with Caesar—were faced by the Catholic missions of the sixteenth century. The missionary movement from the West is a single story in which Catholics and Protestants are inextricably linked.

As this chapter has explained, it is a story that begins in Christendom, in the European experience of Christianity, in the thought of Christian territoriality. Missionaries of Protestant Christendom expected and worked for the reproduction of the Christian society that they knew. In the event, in the providence—maybe the merciful providence—of God, the outcome has been something different: not an extended European Christendom but culturally diverse churches in every continent, in number and significance steadily outgrowing the churches of Europe and North America that even a hundred years ago seemed to provide the representative Christianity of the world.

The End of Christendom

As for poor European Christendom, recent years have seen its obituary notice. The English Romantic poet and essayist Samuel Taylor Coleridge could refer in 1825 to "the standing miracle of a Christendom" that was "commensurate and almost synonymous with the civilized world."[12] For century after century, Europe defined itself by Christianity. However, in 2004, the European Union produced a draft constitution;[13] after much discussion, it decided to make no reference to Christianity, even as a historical episode.

How shall we sum up the position of Christianity at the end of the great European migration? Let's begin with the old Christendom, the old Christian territory, Europe. Over the centuries, old Christendom ideas were relaxed; but even in the nineteenth century, if you asked any informed person what defined Europe, what Europeans had in common, the person would be likely to say it was the experience of Christianity. They might not be Christian believers themselves, they might not even think that the Christian experience had been a positive one for Europe, but they would agree that it had been the defining experience. Europe was old Christendom shaped by the law of Christ: its art, its literature, its missions, its laws all permeated by Christian teaching. But that old Christendom is dead.

Let me take you to my own country. I can show you the William Carey Memorial Church in Leicester in the part of the country from which he came. It is now a Hindu temple—not because of some triumphalist Hindu expansionism but because no one needed it as a church anymore. Come to my own city of Aberdeen in the north of Scotland, and I will take you on a walk of the city center. We will begin with the original building that housed Christ's College, where even in my own time, students were trained for the ministry of the Church of Scotland. You will still see on the front of it the memorial plaques to famous theologians who once taught there, but you will also see the contemporary sign that gives its contemporary name, Babylon, for the ultimate nighttime experience.

Let us go up the street to one of the city's most imposing churches, Langstane Kirk, where a succession of famous Scottish preachers held large congregations spellbound. It is now a luxury bar and night spot called Soul and has been granted a license as a casino. Another church is now a nightclub called Ministry; its original title was the Ministry of Sin. I can take you to church after church that is now a store, an apartment block, a drinking hall, a nightclub, all because no one needed them as churches anymore. The country that once sent out more missionaries than any other has become a desert, desperately in need of the gospel—not a revival, it is too late for that, but primary

12. Henry Nelson Coleridge, ed., *The Literary Remains of Samuel Taylor Coleridge*, 4 vols. (London: William Pickering, 1836–1839), 4:260–61.

13. "European Constitution," European Union, https://europeanconstitution.eu/wp-content/uploads/2019/05/European-Constitution-Full-Text.pdf.

evangelism, cross-cultural evangelism, for our culture is now a non-Christian one. Our God, if we have one, is Mammon, and the altars of Mammon are more gruesome than those of Molech.

The strangest religious development of the great European migration is that the Christian faith declined in what had been its heartland, its center of apparent strength, in the lands whose culture had been permeated and molded by Christian teaching, while it spread to the lands beyond them. It is not the first time in Christian history that a church that seemed to be at the heart of the Christian faith has wilted; it may not be the last. In the twentieth century, Christianity was transformed; the majority of those who professed the Christian faith are now Africans, Asians, Latin Americans, or people from the Pacific islands, and they substantially outnumber the professed Christians of Europe and North America. Further, the trends that have produced this result appear to be continuing. Every year, there are fewer Christians in the West and more in the rest of the world. Even in the United States, if I interpret the figures correctly, the downward trend is clear. And I am struck that the sharpest Christian decline has been in the areas where it was most marked in Europe at the time when that decline began to accelerate: that is, in the cities and among the intellectuals. That the decline is not more marked, again if I interpret the figures correctly, is due to the migration of Christians from Africa and Asia and especially from the Hispanic world.

My work is history, not prophecy. I do not know how long these trends will continue, any more than I know whether we are living in the last days or the days of the early church. But if the trends that I have described were to continue much longer, then within the life and ministry of many readers of this book, it could be that two-thirds of the world's Christians will be African, Asian, or Latin American. One thing is certain: Christianity is now a predominantly non-Western religion and seems set to become progressively more so. How has this happened? As so often with the Lord's dealings, not at all as his children expected.

We have not reached the end of the missionary movement from the West, but it is no longer central to the evangelization of the world, the motive that brought it into being. To that purpose, the Western missionary movement is likely to become marginal, as Christianity is increasingly characteristic of the non-Western world, and leadership is in that perquisite. We have reached the old age of the missionary movement from the West. I am old enough to know and to value the fact that there are still useful functions that the elderly can perform. But it was not my task in the lectures that gave rise to this book. Their function was to exercise another faculty of old age: retrospection, the long look back.

As this narrative unfolds, we will consider the missionary movement in its infancy, the first encounter of Western Christians with the non-Western world, the special position of missionaries as representative Christians and representative Westerners, the early forms of organization, the different patterns in Catholic Italy, Lutheran Germany, Britain, and the United States of America.

By the 1830s, the missionary movement had survived infant mortality, passing to a position of modest success and increasing respectability. Where once it had seemed to be the province of mavericks, cranks, extremists, and lunatics, it was now meeting approval within the Western church and Western society generally. The movement was entering its middle age. Between the 1830s and the 1930s, the movement goes into a period of immensely active life, and that period will be our focus in part 2, comprising chapters 5 to 8. Mission in this period is still the sphere of radical Christians—though that changes a little toward the end, so we will need to look at what was happening to radical Christians as we consider different ways in which radical Christians began to read the Bible. The effect of the missionary movement was to produce a church, and in chapter 6, we will look at the issues that arose as a result. Since the missionary movement took place in the context of the great European migration, in chapter 7, we must consider how missions coped with the issues of race, of culture, and of empire that this provoked. Chapter 8 focuses on three notable Protestant pioneers of mission in China, which since the seventeenth century had been one of the most significant theaters of Catholic, and especially Jesuit, mission activity.

In chapter 9, we introduce the theme of part 3 of the book, namely, how the missionary movement faced a violent middle-age crisis and what happened to it as a result. Chapter 10 is devoted to the great missionary conference held in Edinburgh in 1910, an event marked by confident expectation of future Christian progress, but one that in some ways sowed the seeds of later problems. Chapter 11 examines one of the most attractive aspects of the missionary movement—namely, its contributions to medicine—and yet observes that the escalating investment in medical institutions made its own contribution to the midlife crisis of Western missions. Chapter 12 shifts the scene to Tambaram in India, to the International Missionary Council meeting in 1938 that anticipated at least some of the difficulties that were to beset the movement in its later years. The fourth and final part of the book surveys in turn the respective challenges that the postwar missionary movement faced in the three great fields of India, China, and Africa, before in chapter 16 attempting a reflection on the Western missionary movement as a whole, and the new theological questions raised by world Christianity.

The missionary movement from the West can now be seen as an episode, a crucial chapter, in the history of the church. Frustrated colonialism took Western Christians beyond the crusade, the mode that most readily fitted their past experience, into a new mode that involved, however haltingly and crudely, clumsily or faultily implemented, living on someone else's terms. Even so did the Son of Man live on someone else's terms as the Word became flesh and dwelt among us.

CHAPTER 2

Puritan and Pietist Origins

Jonathan Edwards and the Missionary Significance of Native America

We saw as the narrative began that the propagation of the Christian faith from European Christendom to the non-Western world was expressed in two essentially incompatible forms, which have become confused in later history writing since they sometimes took place at the same time. The first mode of expression was that of crusade, originating out of the long conflict for territory waged with Islam and associated with the idea of extending the territory in which the law of Christ held sway. And we saw that the Spanish conquest of the Americas was the last of the crusades, whereby Mexico and Peru were incorporated into the older Christendom, or appeared to be. The second mode was that of the missionary. This was foreshadowed, perhaps, in the *convivencia* in Spain that for centuries allowed Christians, Muslims, and Jews to live side by side and produced protomissionaries such as Ramon Lull. It was certainly foreshadowed in Francis of Assisi and the early Franciscans, but its matrix lay in the impossibility of enacting the crusade model in Asia, in the realization that there was no way in which what happened in Mexico and Peru could be replicated in India or China.

The Protestant Reformation, we saw, established the principle of Christian plurality in Europe. It did not intend to; the leading Reformers sought to re-form the whole church in the whole state, and the bloody wars that followed in the seventeenth century were part of the outcome. But those same wars proved that in most of Europe, absolute religious uniformity was no longer possible. Religious toleration in Europe was less the fruit of Christian charity than of political necessity. The outcome was that Europe, while not abandoning the principle of Christendom and while retaining established churches, learned to accept, in different degrees, the cohabitation of different churches within Christendom.

We also noted the appearance within the Protestant world of radical Christian movements reflecting disillusion with the Protestant settlement in different countries as not producing that return to the apostolic church that was the spring of the desire for the Reformation. A radical Anabaptist stream within the Reformation opposed Luther's doctrine of faith to his doctrine of the church; if true faith was *fiducia*, saving trust in Christ, rather than *fides*, the acknowledgment of right belief, then surely the church consisted only of those who had *fiducia*; congregations of truly baptized believers *were* the church.

Pietists and Puritans

Within the established Lutheran churches of Germany, there later arose movements that, while not separating from the territorial church as did the Anabaptists, sought to revive its life. The Pietists lamented the concentration that had developed in the Protestant churches on scholastic theology, on bitter controversy; they lamented the lack of attention to personal holiness.

Three figures in particular mark the development in Germany of the Pietist movement. Johann Arndt, who died in 1621, wrote a book called *True Christianity* that influenced many.[1] The title is significant; all these radical movements are concerned with the distinction between true and counterfeit Christianity. Arndt's identification of the roots of true Christianity are characteristic of Pietism: first, recognition of what he calls "the secret and abominable depths of original corruption that cleaves to humanity"; second, Jesus Christ is the sole beginning, medium, and end of our whole conversion to God. In other words, the orthodox Lutheran settlement as it has developed is insufficiently radical in its acknowledgment of original sin and its outcome— insufficiently radical, too, in its recognition of the nature of Christ's salvation. In this latter area, Arndt and his successors drew heavily on old Catholic sources of devotion to the Savior, and to the crucified Savior in particular.

The second figure, Jakob Spener, who died in 1705, takes Arndt's teaching further, proclaiming the apostasy of the spouse of Christ from her first love;

---

1. The four books of Johann Arndt's *True Christianity* were published in German, 1610–1615. They have been translated into English a number of times. See, for example, the American edition of 1868 by Charles F. Schaeffer, which is a revised and corrected version of the English translation by A. W. Böhme (1712). It is available at Project Gutenberg, www.gutenberg.org/files/34736/34736-pdf.pdf.

it is the church of the Reformation that has apostatized. But he also begins to set up an infrastructure for the promotion of true Christianity. Central to this are schools and universities, which must be concerned not only with the studies of their students but also with their lives. There is a wider concern with the teaching and catechizing of children. Spener gained a base when the elector of Brandenburg invited him to the new university he was setting up in Halle, and Halle became the powerhouse of German Pietism for generations to come. Spener also developed a pattern of societies to promote private devotion; in other words, the parish church and its ministry do not yet provide sufficient material for the nurture of true Christianity.

Spener's successor at the heart of German Pietism was A. H. Francke, a professor at Halle who created a storm in the university by combining the study of piety with scriptural research, claiming that the students were being trained for the ministry with no real knowledge of their own souls or acquaintance with the saving work of Christ. Halle became the center from which one expected converted pastors, the center also, as we shall see, of much of the missionary movement.

All this was producing what A. W. Böhme, the historian of Pietism, called a new reformation, but a reformation within the national church; and Böhme was about to introduce that movement to the very different setting of England. Halle graduates began to make a mark beyond Germany, not least in Denmark, where members of the royal house were influenced. The importance of this for the missionary story was that Denmark had substantial overseas territories—in Greenland, islands in the West Indies, and a small colony in India. The influence went further when Prince George of Denmark, much influenced by Pietism and with a Pietist chaplain, married Princess Anne, who was about to become queen of England.

A young nobleman, Count Nicolaus von Zinzendorf, was a student at Halle in the 1710s. Deeply devout, full of this vision of the crucified Savior that lay at the heart of German Pietism, he came into conflict with Francke on some aspects of the nature of true Christian experience. In 1727, Zinzendorf offered to the remnants of the old Moravian Protestants, fleeing from persecution in their own lands, a refuge on his estate at Herrnhut. The Moravian church developed as a Pietist brotherhood, retaining its episcopal structure and still in name a national Protestant church, a national church of the Reformation. A somewhat uneasy relationship developed between Halle and Herrnhut, each accusing the other of misstatements about the true Christian life. Relations broke down completely in 1733–1734 when A. G. Spangenberg, a professor at Halle, was dismissed for favoring Herrnhut views. From now on, Halle and Herrnhut were the twin poles of the Pietist movement, and both became pillars of the missionary movement, a story that we will pursue in the following chapter.

England produced a version of the Reformation that combined a liturgy that preserved Roman features with an episcopal government and a doctrinal statement that was distinctly Calvinist. It had its own radicals who wanted a more thorough revision of the liturgy or an end to episcopacy, or both, and to these the term "Puritan" was attached. The same word was used, often as a term of abuse, about people who practiced, enjoined, or required a stricter form of life and morality than most practiced. Both senses came together in the seventeenth century in a radical movement that in many parts of the country combined the streams of a more thorough reformation of the church and greater strictness of life with a call to personal conversion and a whole pastoral practice designed to lead people through the perils of self-righteousness, false security, despair over sin, to proper trust and assurance of salvation. Puritans sought radical reformation of the national church while remaining within it, but others formed separate "gathered" congregations on the Anabaptist model. Many found England uncomfortable and retreated abroad, some to continental Europe, some to colonies such as Massachusetts and Connecticut.

In the 1640s and 1650s, Puritans effected a revolution in England that removed the bishops and the old liturgy, removed the monarchy, executed the monarch, and eventually set up a rule of the saints until a largely peaceful counterrevolution brought that rule to an end and, in 1660, brought back the monarchy, the bishops, and the liturgy in a form broadly similar to what had obtained before the revolution. From now on, "Puritan" became a term of abuse in England; but its life now centered in North America, and its theological influence began to shape Scottish theology. Pietist and Puritan alike were now to participate in shaping the development of evangelical religion in the New World of North America.

The Enlightenment might have strangled Christianity in Europe, but in fact Christianity adapted to it and survived. In the process, the Puritan, Pietist, and evangelical movements played a vital part. They brought religion into the sphere of personal consciousness and personal decision and thus met the Cartesian threat, while generally retaining the concept of Christendom: recognition by the state and by society at large of Christian norms. The radical movements, all in their different ways, distinguished between nominal, or formal, Christianity and real, or inward, Christianity. Pietist and evangelical religion are protests against a Christendom that is not Christian enough. And evangelical conversion is thus genetically related to that earlier protest against the inadequacies of Christendom, monastic conversion. Both produce radical forms of Christianity; both produce missionaries.

Northern Europeans as Late Entrants in the Imperial Race

The nations of northern Europe were slow to enter the race for colonial settlement overseas, and by the time they did, the Spanish were well established in the Americas. France and Britain both developed interests in North America: the French in Canada, the English further south on the east coast of what was to become the United States. Some of the early English settlements were in fact of religious refugees, radical Christians who thought the Anglican form of liturgy and doctrine insufficiently reformed. The early settlements were small and were interspersed among small settlements of Native American people. Generally speaking, European settlers and Native Americans could coexist as long as there was land and resources for both communities, but hostilities broke out every now and again, and suspicion and mutual fear remained. Gradually the northern European countries developed their sea power and challenged the empires of Spain and Portugal overseas. The English were able to drive the Spanish out of some Caribbean islands, such as Jamaica; the Dutch swept the Portuguese out of their most valuable locations in Southeast Asia and took over the Cape of Good Hope in order to service ships going there. The English, soon to be the British—the turning point is the year 1707 with the union of Scotland and England, so I use "English" deliberately before 1707 and "British" deliberately after 1707, and there is a period obviously when it is difficult to get it right—the English, soon to be the British, took over the trading interests in India, which developed greatly during the eighteenth century, so that Britain actually became the ruler of territory around Calcutta, Madras, and Bombay, and over the nineteenth century extended that rule further and further until it was the effective ruler of India, replacing the Muslim empire of the Mughals that had come in originally from Iran.

Meanwhile, population pressures made North America more and more attractive. British and French colonies were now established in Canada, and further south, as far as Louisiana. These colonies, as they expanded, began to compete seriously with the Native American inhabitants; the latter inevitably lost out, generally moving westward. The new settlers, especially in the southern colonies, found that they needed labor to develop plantation crops like cotton and sugar, and the need was supplied by an expansion of the Atlantic slave trade, which now developed as a sophisticated commercial instrument, with Britain as the main carrier, using the same ships to take British manufactured goods, textiles, and metal goods to be exchanged in West Africa for slaves, who were then taken to the Americas, especially to the Caribbean, the ships then carrying the products of the plantations—sugar, rum, and so on—back to Britain.

The American Version of Christendom

Through this process of settlement, North America became in one sense part of Christendom because its parameters were set by people from Europe with the European experience of Christendom. But there were differences. We have seen that English Puritans set up some of the earliest colonies. These indeed wanted to set up Christendom in the wilderness, as they denominated North America, but not to bring into the land the Christendom of Europe in the way that the Spaniards had sought to do in Mexico and Peru. They wanted to establish a better, a more radical Christendom than Europe had ever known. Other colonies reflected other shapes of Christian society that had never been adopted in Europe, such as the Quaker settlements in Pennsylvania. Others again, especially in the plantation states of the center and south, tried to replicate the parish system of the English church, though with great difficulty and with very meager resources.

North America was an amalgam of European diasporas with no possibility of achieving a common church framework. The pattern arising in Europe of established church and specified tolerated dissenting minorities was impossible. The new republic that emerged in 1776 was a coalition of religious minorities and, rather than face the prospect of a congregational establishment in Connecticut and an episcopal one in the Carolinas, opted to reject establishment altogether. The result was that the United States became a semidetached form of Christendom, with a generalized adherence to Christianity but without a state church. Much of the effort that Europeans had devoted to getting the right form of church was devoted in America to getting the right form of government. The American version of Christendom has, therefore, traditionally sat loose to the idea of church, regarding its form as a matter of private choice, but has been very insistent on the idea of nation and its special form of government. One wonders whether the present emphasis on the export of democracy, with the associated belief that elections are the solution to all human misery, may not represent the secularization of American Christendom.

North America was, however, vital to the early history of the missionary movement. It was the first part of the world where Protestant Christians lived side by side with a non-Christian people. The early colonists, radical Christians of the Puritan tradition, gladly announced that the Redeemer's throne had been set up in America, where once Satan had ruled unchallenged; the early charters of the colonies of Plymouth and Massachusetts give the evangelization of the Native Americans as one of the objects of colonization. But like the old Christendom in Asia, the new Christendom in America was stronger on rhetoric than it was on performance when it came to evangelization. Cotton Mather describes the conversion of Native Americans as one of the peculiar glories of New England, since it represented disinterested service to God; but when he comes to give a history of relations with the Native Americans at length, he speaks of the period as the Wars of the Lord. Evidently the setting up of the Redeemer's throne involved the extension of the kingdom by dispossession rather than by conversion. These protesters against European Christendom were caught up in the structures of Christendom even as they separated themselves from it. The congregational form of church government, on which they insisted, assumed a congregation of covenanted believers calling a pastor. Such a structure had no obvious place into which to fit mission preaching, an intentional approach to those outside the Christian faith.

John Eliot and Mission to Native Americans

The significance of the work of John Eliot in New England from 1646 to his death in 1690 is, therefore, the greater. Through his work, congregations of "Praying Indians," as he called them, emerged, living in their own villages under Christian laws worked out by Eliot in consultation with the elders and members of the villages. The only concept of church available to Eliot is a congregational one, so the Christian villages are "gathered out" (his words) of their tribes. Had not the Massachusetts settlers of his congregation been "gathered out" of corrupt English society? The Indian congregations had the whole Bible in the vernacular—the first Bible, incidentally, printed in America—and an indigenous ministry to teach it. But they were also encouraged to what Eliot called a "civil life": not just reading (which was essential to their Christian nurture) but to settled agriculture, handicrafts, and technology.[2] The Praying Indians are the firstfruits of the Protestant mission enterprise, and it is interesting to find a work published in the Netherlands in the late seventeenth century dedicated to the ministers of the Praying Indians as indicating a new day in the history of redemption.[3] Alas, that day was a brief one. Before long, most of the Praying Indian congregations were wiped out, caught up in the crossfire of King Philip's War.

---

2. John Eliot, *The Light Appearing More and More Towards the Perfect Day: Or, a Farther Discovery of the Present State of the Indians In New-England concerning the Progress of the Gospel amongst Them* (London, 1651), 25, 28, 32, 35.

3. I have been unable to identify this Dutch work.—Ed.

Eliot, however, had come to a remarkable conclusion about the Native Americans. He had started with the conventional Puritan idea that Satan had ruled unchallenged in America until gospel churches had come there within his own lifetime through people like himself. But as he got to know the people and their language better, he came on many ideas that could not possibly have a satanic origin and suggested some traditional knowledge of biblical truth. Their ideas of God and his ways contained much of this truth. Where could these ideas have come from? Whence the contact of the Native Americans with revealed truth? Could it be that they were part of the lost tribes of Israel? If so, the implications were breathtaking. The Scriptures spoke of the "dispersed of Israel"—the lost tribes, that is—returning to God. And that was exactly what was happening as a result of his own work, exactly what he was seeing with the Praying Indians. And on the understanding of biblical prophecy that he and most Puritans had, the return of the dispersed to God would herald the ingathering of the gentiles, and this heralded the consummation of all things.

Eliot had been reading the works about China, too; he saw not a religion of natural reason but fragments of divine revelation. Could it be that the Chinese—perhaps the Indians, too—were descended from the tribes of Israel? Could it be that his humble work with the Praying Indians, which had brought about something that had never been seen before in Christendom as most people knew it—could it be that this was the prelude to a much greater outpouring of God's Spirit upon all the nations?

The tradition of mission to the Native Americans never quite died out, but it was always marginal to the American churches. The Native Americans, after all, were competitors. But in the total story of Protestant missions, the Native American story is vital. For many years, a few hundred Native Americans were all that Protestant Christianity had to indicate that the missionary enterprise was worthwhile. And the Christian presence in North America, the Christian presence among the Native Americans in particular, had stirred thought about prophecy—about where mission preaching stood, or would stand or could stand, in the history of redemption.

The Great Awakening and the passing of Puritan consciousness into an evangelical form brought no great renewal of mission to the Native Americans. Some Indians were brought into white churches, yet there is no sign of any large-scale quickening of Native American mission as a result of the Great Awakening. But one corner of the story of the Great Awakening had an impact on one group of Native Americans, and a much greater impact on the Protestant missionary movement as a whole. The remainder of this chapter will consider the greatest figure in the Great Awakening, Jonathan Edwards

(1703–1758), and the young minister who might, had he lived, have become his son-in-law, David Brainerd.[4]

David Brainerd and Jonathan Edwards

The most direct influence of Jonathan Edwards on the later missionary movement lay in his publishing the journal of David Brainerd (1718–1747), a Yale product, if a somewhat rebellious one, and a missionary of the Society in Scotland for Promoting Christian Knowledge, though he was never in Scotland.[5] Hundreds of missionaries and prospective missionaries in the course of the nineteenth century and the twentieth, too, read that book in one form or another and were stirred by it. By the early nineteenth century, Brainerd had become the ideal type of Protestant missionary just because of the journal. The average missionary candidate of the time was a man in his twenties, as Brainerd was; many now desired to become the sort of person and the sort of missionary that Brainerd appeared to be in the journal. If Brainerd had a rival as a missionary icon, it was the English clergyman and East India Company chaplain Henry Martyn, who was himself deeply influenced by Brainerd's life. They had a great deal in common—young, cultured, articulate, consumptive, depressive, marriage unfulfilled for the gospel's sake, and burning out in the work of God. Martyn was Brainerd come to life again for a new generation.[6]

In the 1890s, Eugene Stock, the historian of the Anglican Church Missionary Society, who knew hundreds of young missionaries and missionary candidates, wrote after describing the great events of Brainerd's preaching among the Native Americans, "But Brainerd did less in his lifetime than his biography, by President Edwards, did after he was gone. In its pages is inscribed the picture of a man of God such as is rarely seen. No book has, directly or indirectly, borne richer fruit."[7]

4. The pages that follow draw on portions of my chapter, "Missions and Historical Memory: Jonathan Edwards and David Brainerd," in Andrew F. Walls, *Crossing Cultural Frontiers: Studies in the History of World Christianity*, ed. Mark R. Gornik (Maryknoll, NY: Orbis Books, 2017), 185–202.

5. Jonathan Edwards, *An Account of the Life of the Reverend Mr. David Brainerd, Minister of the Gospel, Missionary to the Indians* (Boston, 1749). References given below to this work are to Jonathan Edwards, *The Life of David Brainerd*, in *The Works of Jonathan Edwards*, vol. 7, ed. Norman Pettit (New Haven: Yale University Press, 1985).

6. For Martyn's not uncritical admiration for Brainerd, see *The Letters of Henry Martyn*, ed. Scott D. Ayler (Woodbridge: Boydell, 2019), 217, 377.—Ed.

7. Eugene Stock, *The History of the Church Missionary Society: Its Environment, Its Men, and Its Work* (London: Church Missionary Society, 1899–1916), 1:27.

But there was a dash of gall mixed into the spiritual elixir, and every reader could taste it. It is impossible to disguise the depressive strain in Brainerd's journals, and Edwards does not attempt to do so. He reproduces sections where the writer is "filled with sorrow and confusion," "distressed by a sense of spiritual pollution," and so confused by inward anguish that he loses the track of his sermon.[8] Edwards actually warns the reader against this "melancholy," which he did not regard as a necessary ingredient of proper self-examination. He reflected that it might have been contained had Brainerd gone with a companion; after all, the Lord sent his disciples in pairs, and this may be one reason why he did so. Edwards also identified a physical element and thought Brainerd willfully reckless in putting his life into danger.[9] Martyn, with depressive tendencies himself, takes up the hint. He concludes that it was improper for Brainerd to attempt what he did at a time when he should have been in medical care—could it have been from a desire of gaining his own good opinion?[10] The editor of an early short version of the journal advises the reader to discount the melancholy as "purely animal," that is, arising from Brainerd's distressing physical condition.[11] Others found its origin in the theological and pastoral inadequacies of Calvinism. "How much of his sorrow and pain had been prevented," cries Wesley, "if he had understood the doctrine of Christian perfection!"[12]

For the spiritual mentors of the Student Volunteer Movement in the late nineteenth century, deeply influenced by the doctrines and experiences of the Keswick Convention, Brainerd's melancholy was a theological puzzle. "I know nothing more resembling Pentecost than the scenes following [Brainerd's] preaching at Crossweeksung," says A. J. Gordon of Boston,[13] one of the great mentors of the student movement, but how did someone who so manifestly displayed the indwelling of the Holy Spirit miss the exultant spiritual liberty that the evangelical spirituality of Keswick and of Gordon's day associated with the fullness of the Spirit?

For a period at the beginning of the nineteenth century, Edwards's presentation of Brainerd had another place in the historical memory of the

8. *Works of Jonathan Edwards*, 7:272, 278, 284.

9. *Works of Jonathan Edwards*, 7:95.

10. Samuel Wilberforce, ed., *Journals and Letters of the Rev. Henry Martyn* (London: Seeley & Burnside, 1837), 204.

11. Jonathan Edwards, *An Account of the Life of the Rev. David Brainerd* (Newark, NJ: Crane, 1811), preface.

12. John Wesley, *Letters of the Rev. John Wesley, A.M.*, ed. John Telford (London: Epworth, 1931), 5:95.

13. A. J. Gordon, *The Holy Spirit in Missions* (London: Hodder & Stoughton, 1893), 207.

missionary movement. Not only did Brainerd's *Life* provide the icon of the missionary as regards motivation and inner life; it was also one of the very few accessible accounts in English of the day-to-day work of a missionary in contact with people of another language and culture, one of the very few works that reflected on what a preacher so circumstanced should say and how he should communicate it.

When the group of Evangelical Anglican clergymen who formed the Church Missionary Society in 1799 set up their first library, the first of the titles that they selected was Brainerd's *Life*. There were only thirteen titles in all in the library, and five of these were current periodicals. Apart from Edwards's version of Brainerd's journals, the committee could find only a few continental works in translation describing the work of Moravian missions and of the Danish Lutheran missionary Hans Egede in Greenland; these were the only firsthand accounts of Protestant endeavors in modern times to present the gospel across a cultural divide that they could find. Thirteen books, five of them journals. It is something of a shock to realize that this is not how Edwards viewed Brainerd's work. The founders of the missionary society who compiled this library had that maritime consciousness so characteristic of the developing missionary movement: mission lies overseas. Edwards was looking out at the New England that he knew with its diverse layers of population.

The chapter that Edwards appends to the *Life* in which he assesses the significance of Brainerd is instructive here. The first and longest section focuses not on the conversion of the Indians but on the conversion of Brainerd. It analyzes the marks of authenticity in his experience that are missing from the testimony of so many who claim that same experience of conversion to God. The second section distinguishes between the genuine and the spurious in religious affections as displayed in times of revival, rebutting the idea that Brainerd's work at Crossweeksung was of the same kind as some recent revivals among white settlers. Edwards's point, however, is not that the Crossweeksung movement took place in a Native American community as a cross-cultural experience but that, unlike some contemporary movements among the settlers where the response was spectacular but transient, it made a lasting transformation of people's lives. The third section argues that Brainerd's life displays the sharp difference between experimental religion and mere emotional imaginations. The fourth seeks to demonstrate that Brainerd's ministry proves the efficacy of the doctrines of grace, in opposition to Arminian objections. The fifth displays Brainerd as an exemplar for candidates for the ministry, and the sixth as an exemplar for religious practice, notably with regard to fasting.

It is only with the seventh and last section—which is a very short one—that we reach what we would think is the specifically missionary dimension of Brainerd's career: how it encourages God's people to prayer and endeavors for the advancement and enlargement of the kingdom of Christ in this world, and particularly for the conversion of the Indians "on this continent." Edwards pauses to consider how Crossweeksung might be the forerunner of something much more glorious and extensive of this kind, but the visionary pause is brief; he quickly passes to practical matters like sending missionaries in pairs, and to a consideration of the special providences attending Brainerd's last illness and death.

For people building up a library for an infant mission agency, the *Life of Brainerd* was a rare example of Christian preaching among people of another language and culture, or, as they would have said, other manners and customs. For Edwards, who made that life known to the world, it was primarily a demonstration of the true character, authentic experience, and proper doctrine of a Christian minister. An almost contemporary throwaway remark by John Wesley suggests a similar conclusion. Wesley believed that "even so good a man" as Brainerd could overestimate the importance of his own work. And he goes on, "The work among the Indians, great as it was, was not to be compared to that at Cambuslang, Kilsyth [the 1740s revivals in Scotland], or Northampton [Edwards's own work in Massachusetts]."[14] He modestly forbears to mention, "or our own." For Wesley—and Wesley made the first of the many popular abridgments of Brainerd's *Life* that were to appear over the next couple of centuries—for Wesley, it is a "tract for the time," but it is not meant to call people to the mission field. It is meant to teach them devotion and acceptance of harsh conditions in their service in England. For Edwards and for Wesley alike, what we would call the cross-cultural aspect of Brainerd's work is a coincidence. Crossweeksung is the same in kind as Cambuslang and Northampton.

A generation later, in the historical memory of a missionary movement that saw its task as the establishment of the church of Christ among non-Western and hitherto non-Christian peoples, Brainerd, as presented by Edwards, was reconceived as the missionary par excellence. But that is not how he was seen in his own day. The missionary movement, with its requirement to live on terms set by the life of a society other than one's own, marked a breach with the centuries-old idea of Christendom. This latter posited a civil society in nominal allegiance to Christ and a pastoral duty of the church to

---

14. John Wesley, *Journal of the Rev. John Wesley, A.M.*, ed. Nehemiah Curnock, new ed., 8 vols. (London: Epworth, 1938), 3:449.

bring that civil society into true harmony with its Christian profession. There is very little sense of such a breach in Edwards, very little to indicate that he saw any particular significance in the missionary office that was not already there in the ministerial.

Edwards and Brainerd—and, for that matter, Wesley—are transitional figures in the history of the missionary movement. They operate before the movement emerged in the English-speaking world as a distinct element in Protestant consciousness. (It was different among Catholics.) They thought in terms of Christendom and the traditional responsibility of the Christian ministry within it. But they thought as evangelicals, that is, as radical, "totalitarian" Christians. Evangelical consciousness saw all humanity as one in sin, misery, and loss—one in redemption and holiness in Christ. There was thus a single message for the moneymaking merchant in Massachusetts and those whom merchant and minister alike might have described as "rude savages." Brainerd talks about "white heathens" being affected by the movement among the native peoples at Crossweeksung. Heathenism was not a religion; it was a state of mind. It had nothing to do with race.

The Native Americans that Brainerd and Edwards knew lived on the margins of Christendom. These damaged, dislocated, partially demoralized, perennially alcoholic communities had lost the integrity of traditional life. Their whole existence was a marginal one on the fringes of white society. Brainerd calls them "poor pagans," but his own journals reveal that they were not *mere* pagans. A whole spectrum of attitudes toward Christianity can be discerned in what he says about them. His interpreter, Moses Tinda, though at first "a stranger to experimental religion," was nevertheless very desirous that his people should "renounce heathenish notions and practices and conform to the customs of the Christian world."[15] These are very much the principles on which Christendom operated. Among those converted in the movement at Crossweeksung were people whom Brainerd describes as "secure" and "self-righteous," which suggests that they were at least regular churchgoers. Among these was a man who claimed to have been a Christian for ten years.

Brainerd was clearly not working in entirely virgin territory but among people where gradual and uneven accommodation to white society had produced a degree of Christian profession and a degree of absorption of Christian practice. The native community was well aware that there were "white

---

15. Sereno Edwards Dwight, *Memoirs of the Rev. David Brainerd, Missionary to the Indians on the Borders of New York, New Jersey, and Pennsylvania: Chiefly Taken from His Own Journal; Including His Journal, Now for the First Time Incorporated with the Rest of His Diary, in a Regular Chronological Sequence* (New Haven: Converse, 1822), 218.

heathens" who paid little or no heed to the religious norms of white society. Brainerd was working on a frontier district of Christendom, and that district responded to the radical, totalitarian evangelical preaching of Brainerd in a way that contemporary white society in other parts of Protestant Christendom responded to similar preaching (such as Edwards's). Crossweeksung saw the mourning for sin, heard the testimonies to personal experience of the love of Christ, that characterized religions in the nominally Christian areas of all Christendom according to the recognized evangelical paradigm of conversion. Edwards sees Brainerd the missionary as the model of a young minister working under conditions of exceptional hardship.

Not surprisingly, the early Protestant movement, which was principally evangelical in character, initially brought to the non-Western world the same message and the same methods that it brought to the nominally Christian world that produced evangelical radicalism, and it expected the same responses. This had an important and often overlooked outcome. It meant that the early missionary movement was not racist, however "culturist" it might be. Evangelical conviction about the solidarity of humanity in sin and in grace meant that even those viewed as "rude savages" or "poor pagans" were open to the highest operations of divine grace, just as "white heathens," not to mention "secure, self-righteous churchgoers," were open to the same condemnation as "savage heathens."

Brainerd was in general as "culturist" as his contemporaries. He had little sympathy for Native American ways of life and was puzzled that the unregenerate actually preferred these ways as superior to the unremitting busyness of white society. Even the regenerate were not eager to start cultivation and the more laborious lifestyle that would accompany it. When one group refused to abandon a noisy dance despite the presence close by of a very sick man, Brainerd attributed the decision to the callous inhumanity of the heathen heart, but justice immediately forced him to add, "Although they seem somewhat kind in their own way."[16] But it was a different way. No doubt Brainerd took for granted that regeneration would dispose converted Native Americans to adopt "civilized" ways. He was engaged in moving his converted people to conditions where this would be easier when he was overtaken by his last illness, but he was in no danger of identifying regeneration with civilization.

Pastoral experience within Christendom suggested that there was a recognizable pattern of authentic response to the gospel, a paradigm of genuine religious experience. It also recognized common deformations of that ex-

16. Dwight, *Memoirs of the Rev. David Brainerd*, 233.

perience, blind alleys that prevented its attainment. Neither Edwards nor Brainerd had any reason to doubt that the paradigm was universal, and the experiences of Crossweeksung appeared to prove it. If the Native American community there was already reflecting a fair degree of acculturation, the high degree of conformity to the paradigm is not altogether surprising. Brainerd does reflect a degree of puzzlement about the outworking of the paradigm in one instance. We have already seen that his interpreter, Moses Tinda, was, even before he met Brainerd, strongly in favor of "civilized" ways, wanting his people to renounce idolatry. Presumably this was at least part of the reason why Brainerd offered him the job and why Tinda accepted it. Nevertheless, Brainerd believed him to be without experimental knowledge. Already distressed to find that the Native American language had no words for staple terms of evangelical preaching—such as "salvation," "grace," "adoption," or "justification"—and disposed like some later missionaries to blame the language for this, Brainerd was thus further frustrated by an interpreter who showed no fervency.

All this changed a short time before the striking events at Crossweeksung. The interpreter, who had already shown signs of genuine concern for his soul, fell seriously ill. Brainerd recognized the signs of conviction of sin and the signs of the changed life that followed his recovery. His style of interpretation changed; he conveyed Brainerd's fervor as he became fervent himself. He became so committed to spreading the gospel that he hardly knew when to stop. Brainerd found that when he himself had left a place, Tinda would stay behind to explain or reinforce what the missionary had said. The Crossweeksung movement, with its flood of conversions and baptisms and communions, followed Tinda's transformation.

Yet Brainerd was never entirely satisfied about Tinda's personal experience. He had known awakening; he had known conviction of sin. His conduct was exemplary, his fervor was unbounded, his devotion to gospel work beyond question. But Brainerd felt unhappy about the next stage in evangelical conversion, what he calls "distinct views of Christ." Tinda did not exactly conform to the accepted paradigm of conversion, which, says Brainerd, "makes his experience the more doubtful."[17] In the later missionary movement, many another missionary was to be puzzled as people responded to the gospel but not to the missionary's experience of the gospel. Protestant missionaries were beginning to discover what their Catholic predecessors had found two centuries earlier: that a theology, however comprehensive, that had been shaped by the experience of Christendom was not extensive enough or flexible enough

17. Dwight, *Memoirs of the Rev. David Brainerd*, 210–11, 213.

to cover the unprecedented situations that arose from the preaching of Christ in the worlds beyond the West. That David Brainerd himself perhaps had some inkling of this is suggested by one curious incident.

Brainerd had no doubt that Satan ruled in what he called the howling wilderness, with complete sway over the Native Americans in their natural state. He speaks of their religious practices as foolish, puerile, depraved, and their notions of the divine as confused and indistinct. One day, he encountered that religion in its full satanic horror: a shaman advancing toward him in the colored mask, with hideous mien, dancing with calabash rattle in his hand. "Of all the sights I ever saw, none appeared so frightful, so near akin to what is imagined of 'infernal powers.'"[18] Involuntarily he shrank away, even though it was broad daylight and even though he knew who was behind the mask. But sitting down with that same shaman later, he found in him a reforming prophet who believed that he had been called by God, a God whom he claimed he had come to know. He believed he was called to summon his people to repentance. Those people were sinking into alcoholic demoralization because they were forsaking God and the old ways under white influence. Brainerd went through some of the themes of Christian teaching. "Now that I like" or "So God has taught me" were the shaman's responses to many of the things that he said. Their main item of difference was not over the work of redemption but over the existence of the devil. This, said the shaman, was not to be found in the traditional cosmology. He evidently had less difficulty over the work of Christ. "Some of his sentiments," Brainerd notes, "seemed very just," and he adds, "There was something in his temper and disposition which looked more like true religion than anything I have ever discovered among other heathens."[19] One senses a strange fellow feeling between the reforming shaman and the evangelical missionary, both seeking to turn a people to God, both converted men after their respective fashions, both assured of their divine calling, and both outsiders in their own communities. Brainerd puts it that the shaman, like himself, "was looked upon and derided among most of the Indians, as a *precise zealot*, who made a needless noise about religious matters."

Brainerd had lived long enough with the Native Americans to qualify some of the easy assumptions about the nature and results of the devil's role in the wilderness. He knew that the Native Americans had suffered robbery, dispossession, and exploitation at the hands of his own kinsfolk, though his apprehension of the transitoriness of earthly life and the transcendence of the eternal

18. *Works of Jonathan Edwards*, 7:329.
19. *Works of Jonathan Edwards*, 7:330.

may have blinded him to the depths of the consequent trauma. He could see that the experience of maltreatment by whites was a serious obstacle to conversion, and he sought to explain the matter in evangelical terms: these deeds were the work of nominal, not real, Christians. After his initial frustrations at having no words in the Native Americans' language for the standard themes of preaching, and despite his not acquiring competence in the vernacular himself, he began to break down such abstractions as grace and justification into translatable language, a first step beyond Christendom, a first movement toward living intellectually and theologically on terms set by others.

Here again we see Brainerd's and Edwards's transitional status in the Protestant missionary movement. They stand within the bounds of Christendom and work as agents in the revival of Christendom. Brainerd stretched these bounds to their limit as he reached out to the most marginal people in Christendom. Here is a link between the old Christendom and the later maritime-based "overseas" mission for which his image and his work were reinterpreted. He connects revival and Christendom with the evangelization of the non-Western world, showing early traces of the way in which the missionary movement became the learning experience of Western Christianity.

CHAPTER 3

_____

A History and Geography of Christian Obedience

Early Protestant Foreign Mission Initiatives
from Europe and America

Early Protestant Foreign Mission Initiatives
from Europe and America

We began this narrative by considering the birth of Christendom and the influence that this had on the development of Western Christianity; the natural association that developed in the Western mind between Christianity and territory; and the two modes of propagating faith that accordingly developed: the first, crusade; the second, missionary, the latter inevitably associated with going from Christian territory to territory considered not yet Christian, with the hope of making it so.

We continued this exploration by looking at some of the forces by which the Christendom concept became modified. We noticed the effect of the Reformation era, which divided Europe into north and south, Catholic and Protestant, Latin and vernacular, and the increasing difficulty of securing religious uniformity in the various states of Europe—and the ghastly wars of the seventeenth century that resulted from attempting to do so. We observed the general weariness of theological strife; the emergence of radical Christian movements, some of which rejected any idea of a Christian society beyond that of the congregation of true believers; and new currents of thought that stressed reason rather than revelation and the autonomy of the individual rather than the community, thus calling the whole concept of Christendom into question. Beyond these lay the effect of the new involvement of Europe beyond Europe. It had appeared possible at first to establish Christendom by force in Spanish America and by persuasion in a few African states, but any further appearance of Christian states in Asia or Africa seemed a prospect stratospherically distant. And North America was not so close as might have been expected. The very pattern of the European settlements in North America made it at most a semidetached part of Christendom.

Christendom under Pressure, Christendom Renewed, and Christendom Extended

By the late seventeenth century, therefore, signs of the possible disintegration of Christendom are multiplying. In Protestant and Catholic countries alike, there are signs of open challenge to it. The challenge is partly intellectual: movements that reject the idea of revealed religion, which were generally classed by the orthodox as infidelity. It was partly moral: a disregard more blatant than in earlier times in ignoring the moral restraints associated with Christian teaching. It was partly pastoral: the old systems of Christendom depended on the parish and the parish church and steady teaching through that church, and in a changing society these structures were now manifestly inadequate.

The radical movements then present—Anabaptist, Puritan, Pietist—served to renew Christian faith and hinted at the new evangelical form that was to develop in the eighteenth century. But among orthodox churchmen (if we may use the term orthodox for Christians who did not belong to the radical movements and often thought their distinction between true Christianity and nominal or formal was dangerous), there was also disquiet at the growth of infidelity, the growth of vice, the breakdown of the parish system, and the multitudes baptized but without Christian teaching. England was a case in point. The Puritan Revolution had come to an end in 1660, and there was general relief at the end of the rule of the saints. Old church and old monarchy came back together. For those who had been in exile during the Puritan Revolution, it was payback time. The rule of the saints had insisted on strictness of life; now all the saints' restraints must be abandoned. It had been associated with Calvinism; Calvinism must now be held in detestation. It had insisted on psalm singing and long sermons; let those things now be replaced by the joys of wine, women, and song. It had rejected monarchy and church; let monarchy and the Church of England be held together, so long as the church does not interfere with private life.

Against such a background, earnest Anglicans began to fear for the future of their nation. These were not radicals; they hated Puritanism, they loved the established church, they feared anything that created division and might be worried by talk of the necessity of conversion. But they wanted to restore the old Christendom ideal: a Christian nation living under Christian law, with the laws of the realm upholding Christian morality, Christian teaching permeating society through the ministry of the church and producing holy, happy lives. They wanted—in the words of a book title that one of them, William Law, wrote—to send a serious call to a devout and holy life, and they began to get inspiration from Germany.[1]

London had many immigrant churches. Through these German migrant churches, England learned the Pietist model of religious societies: laypeople, usually young men, meeting for prayer, Bible reading, mutual encouragement, and charitable works. A small group of more prominent people went further. Dr. Thomas Bray, a clergyman, was alarmed at the state of the nation but far more, when he went to America, at the religious state of the colonies. The concern must be to bring to the colonies the religious structures of Christendom: to develop parishes and to appoint clergy—good, well-educated clergy, making sure that they had good centers of education and plenty of books. (Clergymen were likely to go to America only if they were very poor and thus would have no books.) Only then could the church in the colonies carry out its evangelistic duty and bring the gospel to the Native Americans and to the Africans in America.

The outcome was the Society for the Propagation of the Gospel in Foreign Parts, founded in the year 1701 by royal charter in order that "a sufficient Mainteynance be provided for an Orthodox Clergy" to live among the king's subjects in his "Plantacons, Colonies, and Factories," and that "such other Provision be made, as may be necessary for the Propagation of the Gospell in those Parts."[2] The greater part of the society's work lay in North America and the Caribbean. The evangelistic aim, to reach the Native Americans and the Africans, remained; but the pastoral aim, to give care to white settlers, discouraging them from vice and Presbyterianism, took precedence. John and Charles Wesley both went to Georgia through this society with the desire to be missionaries to the Native Americans. Each was constantly frustrated in endeavors even to meet Native Americans. The story in the Caribbean with the slave plantations is a little different.

The Society for the Propagation of the Gospel had arisen out of a smaller voluntary society—the Society for Promoting Christian Knowledge—set up in 1698-1699 by a small number of people, mostly laymen of substance. They described their scope as "propagating Christian knowledge" at home and

---

1. William Law, *A Serious Call to a Devout and Holy Life: Adapted to the State and Condition of All Orders of Christians* (London: Innys, 1729).

2. H. P. Thompson, *Into All the World: The History of the Society for the Propagation of the Gospel in Foreign Parts 1701-1950* (London: SPCK, 1951), 17.

"promoting Religion and Leaning in any part of His Majesty's plantations abroad."[3] Note that the Society for the Propagation of the Gospel linked pastoral care of migrants with the hope of the evangelization of Native Americans and Africans; the earlier Society for Promoting Christian Knowledge sought to promote Christian knowledge throughout the world. Both societies think of the first methods of doing good as distributing Bibles and other religious books and then distributing what they call useful books—that is, secular learning—because education is part of developing Christian knowledge. Charity schools, therefore, become an early part of the aim of the Society for Promoting Christian Knowledge, giving an education to people who cannot afford to pay for it. At the back of this idea is Christendom as it should be: the whole of society incorporated into the church, baptized and taught their duty as Christians and as members of society (which is, of course, the same thing). So ignorance is the enemy. There is no idea here of denominations or of the presence of any other church; in principle, these ought not to exist. There was a single national framework for a Christian nation.

The methods, of course, were methods already adopted by the German Pietists, and again the pastors in the immigrant churches in London were the means of the societies' learning what was going on in Germany. There they learned how books were distributed, how children were taught, and how to organize charity schools. They learned of the great orphan house run by Professor Franke in Halle. They learned also of the mission set up in India in the name of the king of Denmark and staffed by Halle graduates. And the Society for Promoting Christian Knowledge came to accept the India mission as part of its own responsibility. And so an alliance was forged between these very orthodox High Church Anglicans in England and Halle Pietists who in Germany were becoming a church within a church, the representatives of "true" over against formal Lutheranism.

A few years later, a Society in Scotland for Promoting Christian Knowledge was set up in recognition of the fact that in Scotland, the Reformation had never really touched the highlands, and with the vast size of highland parishes and the fact that the population insisted on speaking Gaelic when the ministers all spoke English, or at best Scots, the real evangelization of the highlands now began; but the Society in Scotland for Promoting Christian Knowledge had, as did its English counterpart, a clause in its statement of aims that permitted it to work beyond Scotland in promoting Christian knowledge. In accordance with this, it appointed David Brainerd, who featured in the previous chapter, to be its missionary to the Native Americans.

---

3. W. O. B. Allen and Edmund McClure, *Two Hundred Years: The History of the Society for Promoting Christian Knowledge, 1698–1898* (London: SPCK, 1898), 22–23.

By the same means, it introduced Native American converts to Scottish congregations, bringing them around as deputation preachers.

The networks are emerging that the mission story of Germany, England, Scotland (a separate country from England until 1707), and North America shared together. The separate stories are being linked up; the mission story is an international one, with informal networks developing. Equally clear is the connection between mission within Christendom, a Christendom that now seems sick and in danger of disintegration, and the peoples in Africa and America and Asia who had never been part of Christendom.

The Pietists as the Fathers of Modern Protestant Missions

There is a widespread idea in the Anglo-American Protestant world that William Carey (1761-1834) is the father of modern missions. In fact, nearly a century before Carey's enterprise began, organized Protestant missions had begun in India in 1706, based in the Danish colony of Tranquebar, inaugurated by two young graduates of the University of Halle, in Germany: Heinrich Plütschau and Bartolomäus Ziegenbalg. Protestant missions began in Germany and central Europe long before they were taken up in Britain or America, which eventually came to dominate them.

The three hundredth anniversary in 2006 of the beginning of Protestant missions slipped by rather quietly in the West, attracting little notice outside of German Lutheranism. This was not the case in India, where there were huge celebrations. And it was not only Christians that participated in them. Representatives of the government of India, Hindus themselves, were present to acknowledge the contribution that Christian missions had made to the nation. Representatives of the state of Tamil Nadu, in which Tranquebar lies, joined to acknowledge the results of that mission for the Tamil language, results that had flowed from Ziegenbalg sitting on the floor with local school children to learn the language the way they were doing, and from the printing press that the mission established that first enabled Tamil to move in writing beyond what copied palm leaves could bring about. A postage stamp was also issued in India commemorating the anniversary. Halle, recovering from the long sleep of the Communist period in East Germany, also celebrated with a mammoth conference and a massive three-volume history of the mission, which appeared in 2006.[4]

4. Andreas Gross, Y. Vincent Kumaradoss, and Heike Liebau, eds., *Halle and the Beginning of Protestant Christianity in India* (Halle: Verlag der Franckeschen Stiftungen zu Halle, 2006).

It was the German and central European Pietists who first brought Protestant Christians into ongoing mission overseas, and it was the Christendom framework of Denmark that made it possible. The king of Denmark, at whose court there was a degree of Pietist influence, decided to send ministers to the small Danish trading colony in Tranquebar, on the southeast coast of India. His court chaplain identified two former students of Halle, and these arrived in India in 1706, beginning their work in good Pietist fashion, developing education and the teaching of children, translating Scripture and teaching it, developing scholarship. One of the two, Bartolomäus Ziegenbalg (1682–1719), was an extremely fine linguist and an extraordinary scholar, producing a translation of the New Testament in a remarkably short time and instituting a study of local Hindu belief and practice that has stood the test of time. The church that came into being as a result of their teaching was not accepted by the existing European congregation because it consisted of outsiders, another sign of the disjunction between the old Christendom and the new Christianity.

Those earnestly seeking renewal of the old Christendom realized the importance of the India mission, and the Society for Promoting Christian Knowledge in London early came to its aid. It sent a printing press, together with a printer—a German, of course—to India for the printing of the Tamil Scriptures. It went on financing the mission despite grumbles from the ultra-orthodox that Anglicans should not be supporting a Lutheran mission but should be supporting their own. There was a very simple answer: no one could find any Anglican clergy willing to serve in it. Only Pietism at this period could produce the sort of dedication needed for the India service. The India mission continued to be administered by High Church Anglicans of the Society for Promoting Christian Knowledge but staffed by the radical Pietists from Halle right through the eighteenth century and well into the nineteenth. It is the foundational overseas work of the Protestant missionary movement.

We noted previously that Pietism split between camps that we may roughly call Halle and Herrnhut. Herrnhut, the base of the Moravian Brethren after their reconstitution by Zinzendorf on his estate, opens a new chapter in Christian missions. Zinzendorf was a powerful but controversial figure, and the early years of Herrnhut were full of controversy. The Brethren developed their own paradigm of real Christianity and of the nature of the saving faith that brought conversion to it. They lived as a disciplined community; when they went to another location, they went as a community. They developed what they called a choir house system—men's choir living in one house, women's choir living in another, singing and the creation of hymns being an important part of Moravian activity. For important decisions they resorted to the use of the lot, as described in the first chapter of Acts for the election of Matthias. With their devotion to the crucified Jesus, they stressed the spirit of martyrdom and sought to emulate it, so that when a proposal came that they should share the gospel with slaves in the West Indies, two of them, chosen by lot, agreed to be sold into slavery so that they could truly share the life of slaves. Only when it became clear that this was not permitted by law did they desist.

It was again to the Danish colonies that they looked first: in 1732, to the Danish West Indies, the following year to Greenland. Later they went to the Cape of Good Hope and to several Native American locations in North America. It was on an American voyage that John Wesley, one of the subset of orthodox Anglicans seeking a devout and holy life but at the time an unsuccessful missionary of the Society for the Propagation of the Gospel, met the Moravians, was amazed at their serenity in a time of distress, and determined to know the saving faith of which they talked. The Moravians, in fact, became recognized as the missionary pioneers of Protestantism. The account of their Greenland mission, *The History of Greenland*, by David Cranz, translated into English in 1766, was perhaps the first textbook on missions.[5] It was certainly used in this way; everyone knew the story of how the mission was transformed when the Brethren ceased trying to describe the attributes of God and preached about the crucified Savior. It became the theme of many sermons and of discussions about how missions should be conducted and about the relationship of Christianity and civilization. It was the Moravians who put overseas missions thoroughly on the British Protestant agenda. In the late eighteenth century and well into the nineteenth, people considering starting a mission usually sought Moravian advice; they alone had accumulated experience, acquired often in the harshest environments. Following the advice was much more difficult. When the London Missionary Society sent a party of thirty people to the Pacific, they had a Moravian example in mind; but English Calvinistic Dissenters, though used to the idea of a congregation, were not used to the idea of a brotherhood. They came to the work as individuals and as family groups; the disciplined living of the Moravian community was beyond them.

5. David Cranz, *The History of Greenland: Containing a Description of the Country, and Its Inhabitants; And Particularly, a Relation of the Mission, Carried On for above These Thirty Years by the Unitas Fratrum, at New Herrnhuth and Lichtenfels, in That Country*, 2 vols. (London: Dodsley, [1767]).

The Enlightenment Roots of Evangelicalism

There is another influence in the transatlantic background of the missionary movement, which we have not yet considered: the complex of intellectual movements occurring in different parts of Europe, and then reflected in eighteenth-century North America, that have come to be collectively denominated "the Enlightenment." These undermined the concept of Christendom at two points. The Enlightenment magnification of reason could readily be opposed to revelation. In Europe, which lay torn and bleeding after decades of religious war, to people deafened by theological argument, the thought of a universally accessible reason was mightily attractive. The most quoted examples of people living by natural reason, a reason that made religious revelation unnecessary, related to Chinese civilization; but European knowledge of Chinese civilization came principally through the writings of Jesuit missionaries. The object of the missionaries had been to show that China had ideas and knowledge onto which Christian teaching could readily be grafted, but a new thought now arose: if Chinese society operating by natural reason is so attractive, why graft Christian teaching onto it at all? Is not natural reason sufficient for everyone?

The other point of stress with Enlightenment thinking was the autonomy of the individual self, summed up in Descartes's maxim, "I think, therefore I exist." Followed through, this stress on individual autonomy cut to the heart of the corporate allegiance to the Christian faith that lay at the heart of Christendom, the whole mode through which Europe had so far experienced Christianity. It did not necessarily deny the validity of religion, but it moved its adoption to the private sphere. American Protestantism would take this privatization of religion to an extreme that was rarely seen in Europe.

Evangelical religion was a product of Christendom, a civil society that nominally accepted Christian symbols and Christian norms but fell drastically short of those norms in reality. Evangelicalism was thus about "real Christianity" over against the formal and the nominal profession of it—about the inward religion of the heart turned toward God. Evangelicalism was of its nature protest religion, protest against a society that claimed to be Christian but denied that claim in practice. Classical evangelicalism requires nominal Christianity in order to define itself and assumes the presence of a Christian, even if defectively Christian, civil society. It was from these roots that the most influential strand of the Protestant overseas missionary movement sprang.

The Birth of Evangelical Missions in Britain

We have reached the period in which mission consciousness in Britain is beginning to develop. The point has already been made that Protestant missions do not, despite the legends, begin with William Carey. Carey makes that quite clear himself, that he is entering into other people's labors. Carey's famous book, *An Enquiry into the Obligations of Christians, to Use Means for the Conversion of the Heathens* (1792), is only one example of a deep concern manifest among British evangelicals and even beyond the evangelical world at that time.[6] William Carey was no solitary innovator; what he proposed had already been set out and, in some measure, realized by others. The number of emulators and imitators who quickly followed shows how far he represented desires and arguments going on in his time. Nevertheless, there is a certain appropriateness in using Carey's solid figure as a starting point and paradigm. In himself, he represents so many features of the early British missionary movement, and he is one of the few early figures to be both a promoter of missions in the West and an active missionary abroad. He is representative also of the first effective example of what was to become the principal nineteenth-century mission agency, the voluntary society.

So let us consider the influences upon William Carey, born in 1761, the son of a weaver in the village of Paulerspury in Northamptonshire in the East Midlands of England. He was apprenticed to a shoemaker (at this time an industry still carried out at home, not in factories), where a fellow apprentice led him to an evangelical conversion. He joined a Baptist congregation in a period when Baptists were marked by scholastic high Calvinism, and he became an itinerant lay preacher. He acquired enough learning to start a village school, and at the age of twenty-six, he was called and ordained to a village pastorate—still, at first, combining his pastorate with shoemaking and teaching. After two years, he was called to a town pastorate, Harvey Lane Leicester, where the stipend was low enough to receive supplementation from a special central fund. He stayed as minister at Harvey Lane until his departure for India in 1793.

He had no formal education beyond what a village school could provide. He had been a journeyman artisan; he had combined this with his pastoral work. Though he was a minister, he had never attended any sort of theological seminary. His wife, we gather from the fact that she makes a cross on her marriage certificate, was illiterate. His experience was limited to village life

---

6. William Carey, *An Enquiry into the Obligations of Christians, to Use Means for the Conversion of the Heathens* (Leicester: Ireland, 1792).

and a certain sector of the life of a medium-sized town—and this entirely within two Midland counties of England. As far as I can work out, he had never seen the sea before he made his journey for the boat to take him to India. Here we may pause to remember that in these respects, remarkable man as Carey was, he is fairly representative of the first generation of British missionaries. The great majority of them came from the same artisan class as his, journeymen or self-employed tradesmen.

Within his own Baptist setting, Carey's career was not too strange; many Baptist ministers had a similar background. And when, a few years after his departure from England, the London Missionary Society, largely representative of the non-Baptist Dissenters, sent a party of thirty or so missionaries, they were overwhelmingly from the same sort of background. Not only so: the case was not very different in the Church of England. Evangelicals within the Church of England were anxious enough to institute missions but did not expect to find their missionaries where they expected to find their clergy. Melvill[e] Horne, one of the earliest of those to appeal for missions, expresses a doubt whether anyone actually in a church living (that is, holding pastoral charge now) will ever volunteer for missionary service.[7] The Society for the Propagation of the Gospel was never able to get any English clergymen to go to the mission, which was nominally its own, though staffed entirely by Germans.

Thomas Haweis, one of the few Evangelical Anglicans who supported the London Missionary Society, expected to find missionaries in the shop or the forge, not in England's schools and colleges.[8] J. W. Cunningham, vicar of Harrow, addressing the Church Missionary Society, voiced his conviction that "generally speaking, the Missionaries of the Gospel will not be found among the highest orders of society"—not least because indulgence and polite education make men unfit for hardship.[9] And so it proved. Of the first

---

7. Melvill Horne, *A Sermon Preached at the Parish Church of St. Andrew by the Wardrobe and St. Anne, Blackfriars, on Tuesday in Whitsun Week, June 4, 1811, before the Society for Missions to Africa and the East* (Philadelphia: Farrand, Hopkins, Zantzinger, 1811), 22, 24–25. See also Horne, "First Letter," in *Letters on Missions Addressed to the Protestant Ministers of the British Churches* (Bristol: Bulgin & Rosser, 1794), 5: "Would to God that some one among you [the clergy], . . . had stepped forward."

8. Thomas Haweis, *Sermons, Preached in London, at the Formation of the Missionary Society, September 22, 23, 24, 1795* (London: Barrett & March, 1797), 54: "A plain man—with a good natural understanding—well read in the Bible—full of faith, and of the Holy Ghost—though he comes from the forge, or the shop, would, . . . as a missionary to the Heathen, be infinitely preferable to all the learning of the schools; and would possess, in the skill and labour of his hands, advantages, which barren science would never compensate."

9. John William Cunningham, *Sermon by the Rev. John William Cunningham, M.A. Vicar of Harrow, at St. Bride's Church, Fleet Street* (London, n.d.), 25.

twenty-four missionaries of the Church Missionary Society during the first sixteen years of its existence, seventeen were German or Danish. The first two English candidates accepted were sent not as missionaries but as lay settlers to New Zealand. They were both artisans, and they were sent to teach the Maori boat building and twine spinning as preparation for evangelization. Two of the others were trained as elementary schoolmasters; both were later ordained, but not for many, many years. Two were artisans who after some years of preparation were granted ordination to English curacies. One, accepted at the very end of the period, was a Cambridge graduate; his entire missionary service was spent in the Mediterranean. The society did receive one application from a most untypical candidate, Henry Martyn, Fellow of Saint John's College, Cambridge. But as the only field that they had at that time was Sierra Leone, where the expectation of life was very low, the society hesitated about accepting someone so valuable, and eventually the application was withdrawn.

In other words, the early missionaries came largely from a group that, in the established churches of England and Scotland at least, would not have been acceptable on social or educational grounds for the home ministry. We have the curious spectacle of a missionary society, on the one hand, pointing to the dangers and privations of the missionary lot and, on the other, taking steps to see that the mission field does not become a shortcut for social climbers to enter the home ministry. One result of this was that the missionaries, as we have already seen with Carey, often came from a very limited range of experience and with a limited knowledge of the world.

This did not mean that the promoters of missions thought, as happened in a later period, that nothing was needed in a missionary but faith and sanctity. The first party of the London Missionary Society produced a high proportion of casualties, and the Society soon set up arrangements for training. The general desire of missionary societies was to get their candidates as near to the standard of education of the home ministry as could be done with the time and material available, although J. W. Cunningham, in his sermon to the Church Missionary Society already quoted, thought that "the very refinement of polite education" was inclined to "indispose and unfit men for the acknowledged hardships of the Missionary Life."[10] Some in fact attained an impressive degree of intellectual achievement. Carey himself is a good example. Despite his humble schooling, he made prodigious efforts both at ancient and modern languages before he ever thought of becoming a missionary. In India, he took for granted that both the ancient and the modern

10. Cunningham, *Sermon by the Rev. John William Cunningham*, 25.

languages of India, Sanskrit and Bengali and the other vernaculars, should be the subjects of study and translation. And he turned out to be not at all an inappropriate appointment, in due course, as professor in the Government College of Fort William. Carey was certainly exceptional in his capacity for taking pains; but taken as a group, and considering the expectation of their home setting, the first generation of missionaries did not despise learning. Some of them—Robert Morrison, the first Protestant missionary to China, is a good example—introduced new forms of scholarship outside the ken of the rather tired universities of which they had never had the benefit.

As to ecclesiology, Carey was an English Dissenter belonging to that minority of the population that refused to conform to the political and religious settlement of 1662, refusing all attempts to entice them to enter a fully comprehensive national church. This immediately suggested the possibility of political disaffection. The church, after all, was part of the constitution of the nation. Dissenters, or at least Calvinistic Dissenters like Carey, were the descendants of those who had led the revolution that had brought the king and the Archbishop of Canterbury to execution. They had natural links with America; they had supported the American Revolution.

The first missionary societies of the modern type came into existence among the Dissenters, Carey's own group of Particular Baptists (that is, Calvinistic Baptists) being the first. The second was much larger and grander: the Missionary Society (1795), later called the London Missionary Society, which proclaimed its Fundamental Principle to be undenominational but did so in essentially congregational terms. Not surprisingly, Independents or Congregationalists supplied the greater part of the London Missionary Society candidates throughout its existence. Scottish towns—Edinburgh and Glasgow especially—followed the London Missionary Society example. The Kirk looked with a jaundiced eye on voluntary groups subject to neither presbytery nor assembly.

The dissenting interest in missions was for some a matter of alarm. Dissenters were traditionally radical in politics. They had called the crown to account in the past; they had supported the American Revolution recently. They had built-in grievances and disabilities (they were unable, for instance, to enter the English universities). The French Revolution, at least in its early stages, seemed to signal to many of them things that they desired: the overthrow of absolute monarchy, bloated landowners, and a corrupt church. Surely this could only herald the establishment of principles that Dissenters longed to see happening in Britain. There was never much prospect of most Dissenters actually bringing any sort of revolution about, and some—Andrew Fuller is a good example—tried to steer clear from any form of political involvement.

Nevertheless, radical politics was regularly associated with dissent, and the enemies of dissent were always ready to point to Dissenters as actually or potentially dangerous.

Young Carey seems to have been a Republican; he was a member of the Leicester Philosophical Institute, where many people had very advanced opinions. His famous book, *An Enquiry into the Obligations of Christians to Use Means for the Conversion of the Heathens* was published in 1792 by the same publisher as distributed Tom Paine's *Rights of Man*; and the book has what I think is a direct but coded reference to the French Revolution on the recent "spread of civil and religious liberty," which implies perhaps that he thought the French Revolution was an answer to prayer.[11] But sentiments such as these increased the suspicion about early missions. Since they are so often portrayed as the cultural wing of British imperialism, it is well to remember that they began as an assumed or anticipated threat to British interests. Carey could get no passage on a British ship, nor at first was he allowed to work in British-administered territory in India. When a motion to support missions was made before the General Assembly of the Church of Scotland in 1796, great play was made by speakers about the revolutionary sentiments of those who supported missions. How disturbing to church government!

The wonder perhaps is how the more conservative supporters of missions, people devoted to the maintenance of the established church and to the unsurpassed excellence of the unreformed constitution, came to see Carey as an inspiration, and dissenting missionaries as fellow laborers. William Wilberforce (to be considered in the following chapter), who was as far from a social revolutionary as it is possible to be, was a subscriber to the Baptist Missionary Society; so was Charles Grant, a major figure in the East India Company. People whose political and ecclesiastical reflexes were entirely different, and who in Britain stood for interests entirely opposed, were able to recognize in the missionary movement a shared concern.

Carey's theological inheritance as a Baptist was a conservative Calvinism. Calvinism had become a dirty word among conforming churchmen: Baptists gloried in it the more and starkly picked out the implications of the highest doctrine of election. It was called the famous TULIP: T for the total inability of man, U for unconditional election, L for limited atonement, I for irresistible grace, and P for the perseverance of the saints. The limitation of the atonement to the elect was the item that perhaps provoked the strongest cries

11. William Carey, *An Enquiry into the Obligation of Christians to Use Means for the Conversion of the Heathens*, new facsimile ed., ed. E. A. Payne (London: Carey Kingsgate, 1961), v–vi, 79.

of dissent from those beyond the fold. But the average eighteenth-century Baptist believed in it without flinching. But if Christ died for the elect only, then surely only the elect have the power to repent and believe. And if only the elect have the power, then surely only the elect have the duty to believe. Gradually the implications were drawn. Language like "offering Christ" or "offering grace," which even high Calvinists had once used, became intolerable. No preacher could *offer* Christ. No preacher could *offer* grace. Only the elect, who had the power and the duty to believe, could do so.

The effect of this on preaching is predictable. High Calvinists ceased the vigorous evangelistic preaching that had once marked them. The Lord knew them that were his. And even to speak as though anyone in the congregation had the power to turn to repentance and faith was suspect, a mark of "Baxterism."[12] Matthias Maurice, Congregational minister at Rothwell, Northamptonshire, Abraham Taylor, tutor at a London dissenting academy, and above all, Andrew Fuller, pastor first at Soham in Cambridgeshire and then at Kettering in Northamptonshire, each played their part in changing dissenting minds on this issue. Eventually Particular Baptist orthodoxy came to recognize what is reflected in the title of Fuller's book, *The Gospel Worthy of All Acceptation* (1785), in which, while by no means diluting his belief in election, he asserts the duty of all to believe and thus the duty of the preacher to offer, with a demonstration that this is what the apostles did.[13] High Calvinism ceased to be the mark of the Baptist. Carey, no major theologian himself, was a member of Fuller's circle and clearly accepted the argument without demur. It probably accounts for the stress on obligation present throughout his book: "The *obligations* of Christians, to use means for the conversion of the heathens." The great theological battle of his time and place had issued in the conviction, strongly denied hitherto, that the preacher had the obligation to use means for the conversion of anybody.

The high Calvinist conviction about the offer of the gospel obviously had to have standard answers to hard texts. From a high Calvinist point of view, such a hard text is Matthew 28:19, the so-called Great Commission: preach to *every* creature. How does this doctrine square with the doctrine that only the elect have the power and duty to believe? The answer could be traced to a piece of traditional Protestant apologetic that had developed a century earlier

---

12. "Baxterism," used as a term of opprobrium by some, refers to the genius exemplified by the Puritan divine Richard Baxter (1615–1691) for seeking a middle way between extremes, in this case between high Calvinism and Arminianism.

13. Andrew Fuller, *The Gospel Worthy of All Acceptation, or, the Duty of Sinners to Believe in Jesus Christ* (Clipstone: Morris, 1801; orig. 1785).

in response to Catholic missions. It was one thing to say, as Protestants tended to do, that those missions were useless or worse because it was a false faith inspired by the antichrist that was being preached; but how could one say that the *absence* of anything like this in Protestant practice could be defended? The answer came from the nature of the apostolic office. Catholic apologetic claimed to perpetuate the apostolic office through the Petrine office of the papacy and the episcopate. Protestant apologetic held that these powers were usurped: the apostolic office was unique, once for all, concerned with the foundation of the church, and died out with the first holders. So when Catholics pointed to the fruits of preaching the gospel to every creature, it was possible for Protestants to reply, "But the command to preach the gospel to every creature was given to the apostles, and they did it." It ceased with the apostles. Its concern was with the foundation of the church; the church once founded, the command was abrogated. Indeed, to take on oneself the obligation was to make oneself an apostle—the very error of the pope himself.

Carey's book shows that this argument was strong in his circle. Section I of the book is in fact called "An enquiry whether the Commission given by our Lord to his Disciples be not still binding on us," and he argues that it is, on three heads. First, there is no express command to preach the gospel given to anyone but apostles; but the same is true of baptism. Where does that leave us Baptists? Second, if to follow Matthew 28:19 is presumptuous, then all who have ever first preached have presumed; besides how did we receive the gospel? Third, all claim the dominical presence ("lo, I am with you always, even unto the end of the world"); but the promise is coextensive with the commission. If we have no right to claim the commission, we have no right to claim the promise of Christ's presence. He goes on with a list of circumstances in which a divine command may be abrogated or become impossible to carry out; all these tend to the conclusion that Matthew 28:19 is an obligation still.[14]

This has to be seen in the context of what had become known as "Fullerism" and of the opposition of people like John Collett Ryland in his own circle, who is alleged, although the story is probably apocryphal, to have told Carey, "Young man, sit down. If God wants to convert the heathen, he will do it without the help of you or me." Carey is applying Fuller's principles to the wider offer of the gospel. Strong views on election lead to strong views on providence, and the argument was certainly made that one ought to wait for providential openings and not to presume to rush in. But what openings, says Carey, do you expect? Magic carpets or the gift of tongues would not be providential

14. Carey, *Enquiry*, 7–13.

openings but miraculous ones: Look at the discoveries, read Cook's journals, and you will see that we *have* the providential openings all around us.

From providence, it is a short step to *prophecy*. As we saw in chapter 2, a large part of the spring of hope and the stamina of the early missionary movement comes from this. For Carey, the main *reason* for mission is obligation arising from the Great Commission; it is simple obedience to God. And in this doctrine of obedience, he is very much in line with his Calvinist inheritance. But the same heritage gave him a worldview dominated by the history of redemption: that God is working to bring about the rescue of his elect through the historical process, and that the Bible gives a record of that process, past and future. Armed with this consciousness, one could have the same confidence about the future; one knew what it was going to be, even if present appearances were against it. We must not underestimate the importance of the consciousness of the purpose of God for the fathers of the missionary movement.

The Influence of Jonathan Edwards in Britain

We know that Carey's circle had been deeply affected by one work of Jonathan Edwards, *An Humble Attempt to Promote Explicit Agreement and Visible Union of God's People in Extraordinary Prayer* (and it goes on after that; you did not need tables of contents in eighteenth-century books; it was all in the title).[15] It was already an old book, published in Boston in 1747–1748. It might also in some respects be described as out of date, since Edwards had attempted a chronology of the expected course of world events, and it had come unstuck. Nonetheless, the main drift of the argument was powerful.

Edwards's starting point is Zechariah 8:20 and following, with the hope that it gives of a time when "many peoples and strong nations entreat the favour of the Lord." He then goes through Revelation and sees the sixth vial as being poured out about his own time, 1748. The massacre of the witnesses is then to be expected, but then the fall of antichrist, which will be by degrees, through the outpouring of the Spirit of the millennial days, to be expected round about AD 2000. Edwards's detailed scheme was not the point, and the New England ministers who sponsored the pamphlet were noncommittal about it. His English readers did not think it essential to the argument. The point was the *hope* that it provided of a converted world, and the *program*

---

15. Jonathan Edwards, *An Humble Attempt to Promote Explicit Agreement and Visible Union of God's People in Extraordinary Prayer* (Boston: Henchman, 1747).

it proposed of "extraordinary prayer" in which Christians all over the world would join for God to bring about his promised acts of extension of the kingdom. Pray, "Let thy kingdom come," and look for the signs of it.

The idea of a concert of prayer had struck Edwards through what he heard of the meetings for prayer in the Scottish revival in Cambuslang in 1742, where bands of people met by appointment to pray. Edwards's book was read in Scotland and passed by a prominent Scottish minister, John Erskine, to an English Baptist correspondent, John Sutcliff. Sutcliff, pastor at Olney, was one of the pillars of the Northamptonshire Association of Particular Baptists, in which some twenty Baptist churches were joined and the ministers of which met annually for two days or so. In 1784, Sutcliff prepared *Persuasives to a General Union in Extraordinary Prayer for the Revival and Extent of Real Religion*. Andrew Fuller, the dominating figure in the group, read Edwards with enthusiasm, and monthly prayer meetings were called by the association where "the whole world [would] be affectionately remembered, and the spread of the gospel to the most distant parts of the habitable globe [would] be the object of the most fervent requests."[16] Other Baptist associations, such as the Yorkshire Association, and the Western Association based in Bristol, took up the idea, and in 1789, Sutcliff put out a ninepenny paperback edition of Edwards's book.[17] Only at this point does William Carey emerge. When the prayer meetings started, he was a very raw lay preacher who had been baptized only nine months.

The Voluntary Society Model of Mission

The churches of Europe were designed—and this applied also to the extension that came with the migration to North America—for spreading Christian teaching within their own local, regional, or national area. They had no machinery or infrastructure for working outside those areas. Some indeed had constitutional or legal difficulties in doing so. As we have seen, Catholic missions relied very heavily on the religious orders. Among Catholics, the orders were the natural home for radical Christians, people looking for a

16. John Sutcliff's call to prayer can be found appended to Andrew Fuller, *The Nature and Importance of Walking by Faith: And the Importance of a Deep and Intimate Knowledge of Divine Truth; Two Sermons, to Which Is Added Persuasives to a General Union in Extraordinary Prayer for the Revival and Extent of Real Religion, Addressed to the Northamptonshire Association* (Kettering: Fuller, 1815; orig. Northampton: Dicey, [1784]).

17. Michael A. G. Haykin, *One Heart and Soul: John Sutcliff of Olney, His Friends and His Times* (Darlington: Evangelical Press, 1994), 169-71.

closer discipleship of Christ, turning from the world in order to do so. So the Catholic missionary movement revived some of the old religious orders and brought new ones (the Society of Jesus is the obvious example) into being. Protestants had done away with religious orders, so what means could they adopt for bringing the gospel to the non-European world?

We find the answer in the conclusion of Carey's pamphlet, where he outlines his practical steps beyond the persuasives to prayer that his seniors had already advocated. In thematic terms, this is the heart of his book, which is about the use of means.[18] First, his analogies come from the commercial world. Only there was there comparable experience to work on. How do merchants set about getting their trading contacts? And a man whose trading experience is limited to buying leather and selling shoes works out, perhaps a little romantically but essentially correctly, how eighteenth-century venture capitalists worked. Let the gospel messengers take note of the mammon of unrighteousness, and let their operations be built on as solid a fund of steadily assembled information as it was possible to acquire. How little the first generation of missionaries had to go on is evident from the whole of the last section of Carey's book, but Carey is a witness to the way in which they sought to make the best of what they had.

Second, we may be surprised by the slightly tentative note about his next proposal—a company of ministers and laypeople forming a society and appointing a committee. In our day, this seems a natural thing to do: form a society for a purpose, set up a committee to carry out the work. It is hard to remember that it was not always so, that the traditional structure of English society distrusted small groups, that for many, the very name "society" smacked of subversion or terror. Even the great charter societies like the Society for the Propagation of the Gospel and the Society for Promoting Christian Knowledge sought to order themselves on a comprehensive basis, as though they were a corporation of the church; and in Carey's own day, a weary archbishop of Canterbury and a still wearier archbishop of London found to their frustration that this very comprehensiveness stifled their effectiveness as mission agencies. Carey proposes no action to gain the support of all the churches, even of his own denomination; he proposes an immediate start with those prepared to commit themselves. A voluntary society of ministers and laymen was the appropriate means by which to fulfill the recognized obligation.

The thirteen people who assembled on October 2, 1792 in Mrs. Beeby Wallis's house in Kettering to establish the Particular Baptist Society for the

18. Carey, *Enquiry*, 77-87.

Propagation of the Gospel amongst the Heathen, and took their first collection in Fuller's snuffbox, in fact established the means that was used by the greater proportion by far of the missionary movement for the rest of the century. The nineteenth century saw the voluntary society applied for a host of purposes: political, philanthropic, educational, social, and religious; but in no area was its growth as significant as in the missionary society. No major church in England, whether Episcopal, Presbyterian, or Congregational, was structurally able to organize missions. The one church in Scotland whose theoretical structure was so capable took decades of argument over the implications. By 1790, all the arguments about church government were well rehearsed and apparently immutable; but not one had been able to drive the others from the field, and not one of them had provided the means to fulfill the obligations of Christians for the conversion of the heathen.

The voluntary society bypassed them all. Indeed, we may say that it subverted all those venerable forms of church government for which men had shed their blood and been prepared to shed the blood of others. It was adopted by followers of every form of church government. It meant a sort of declericalization of the church for those private persons, that is, laity, who soon made their presence felt on topics on which their knowledge was superior to that of ministers and on which previously only ministers spoke in public. And in course of time, women could contribute to and even direct societies, exercise oversight, without anyone ever raising the question of ordination or even whether a woman might speak in church. It completely altered the power structures of Western Christianity. It opened the way to that Southern Christianity that in the providence of God has emerged over the very time of eclipse of the Western.

Perhaps, after all, the voluntary society was just one of God's theological jokes, by which he ofttimes tenderly mocks his people when they take themselves too seriously.[19] Those anxious about maintaining the sacredness of the church structures as originally given were left to defend them. The Particular Baptist Society for the Propagation of the Gospel amongst the Heathen looked like the concern of a small Midland clique, even to major figures of the denomination. It was a long time before the London Baptists—the wealthiest, the best organized, and the most articulate—caught on to the idea at all. Meanwhile, Carey and Fuller and their companions, having recognized the obligation, found means to fulfill it and set out to convert the world on thirteen pounds, two shillings, and six pence. It does not look so ridiculous now.

19. Andrew F. Walls, "Missionary Societies and the Fortunate Subversion of the Church," *Evangelical Quarterly* 88 (1988): 147.

The True Birth of Protestant Foreign Missions from North America

The year 2006 was not simply the tercentenary of the Halle mission to South India; it also the two-hundredth anniversary of the Haystack Prayer Meeting, which is often seen as the origin of American overseas missions. A handful of students at Williams College in Massachusetts were present at that prayer meeting in a haystack during a thunderstorm. A little while later, when their numbers had grown to a dozen or thereabouts, they challenged the churches of the United States to initiate Christian missions beyond America. They realized that they were not trying to invent missions; they knew that there were established mission agencies in Europe and were prepared to offer their services to them should their seniors so advise. These young people opened a new chapter in American religious history, a new conduit of Christian energy in the world. But I intend to cast no shadow on their memory by saying that they did not in fact initiate missions from America to the rest of the world. There is an older story, largely forgotten, that shows that it was Africans in America who were its first overseas missionaries.

Well before the Haystack Prayer Meeting, it had occurred to many people that Christian Africans in America might be the best evangelists for Africa. Jonathan Edwards's successor as the most eminent of the evangelicals, Samuel Hopkins (1721–1803), was seized with this idea and persuaded Yale to take a couple of African students as future missionaries to Africa. But it was initiatives among Africans themselves that brought the American overseas missionary movement to birth. It came about through the Revolutionary War of 1775–1783, when the British raised Black regiments by promising slaves their liberty and lands that would be taken from their rebel masters; the promise, of course, was predicated on a British victory. When this did not take place, the embarrassed British authorities shipped these demobilized soldiers to less rebellious colonies, such as Jamaica or Nova Scotia (then still largely virgin forest), where they were granted land. Many of these Black loyalists, as they were termed, were devout Christians, mostly Methodists or Baptists, converted during the Evangelical Awakening. A blind Methodist called Moses Wilkinson was prominent among the Methodists in Nova Scotia. A Black preacher in the Countess of Huntingdon's Connexion, John Marrant, who had been a sailor in the British Navy, was sent to Nova Scotia as a preacher from England.

One of the Black loyalists, George Liele, who had been a Baptist preacher in Savannah, Georgia, went to Jamaica and began to preach to the slaves on the sugar plantations as no one had ever done before. Slaves crowded to his meetings and responded to his preaching, first in dozens and then in hundreds. Congregations arose beyond his power to pastor. Hence Liele wrote to the *Baptist Magazine* in London appealing for laborers, who were so few, though the fields were so white. The result was the arrival in Jamaica in 1814 of the Baptist Missionary Society. In Jamaica, as in many other places, missions followed the church, not the other way around. We can trace a similar story from the works of other preachers in Trinidad and in the Bahamas. George Liele's assistant pastor in Savannah, David George, was taken, along with many other demobilized Black loyalists, to the very different terrain of Nova Scotia. Revival broke out in Nova Scotia among Blacks and whites alike, with David George's Baptist congregation one of the centers of revival.

As the years went on, the Nova Scotia land grant process moved desperately slowly. Frustrated, disappointed, disillusioned, the Africans in Nova Scotia decided to send a messenger to London to plead their cause. Thomas Peters made the hazardous journey—hazardous because he might well have been seized as a fugitive slave. In London, he met Ottobah Cugoano, whose memoir of his experiences as a slave had now become a standard account, and who also seems to have become the spokesman for Africans in London.[20] Cugoano introduced Peters to William Wilberforce and his evangelical friends in Clapham, who immediately took up the Nova Scotia land question with the government. But the thought dawned on both parties that the Christian African colonists of Nova Scotia might well be the ideal settlers for the demonstration model of a slavery-free settlement in Sierra Leone.

A lieutenant in the British navy, John Clarkson, brother of Wilberforce's antislavery colleague Thomas, was sent to Nova Scotia as a recruiting officer. He concentrated on the Black churches, and the result was that more than 1,100 people volunteered to move from Nova Scotia to Sierra Leone. Among them was the Baptist congregation of David George. The remarkable story that followed is one that reminds us that the story of the overseas missionary movement from both North America and Britain intertwined with that of Christian endeavors to end slavery. A group of British evangelical Christians had already purchased land in West Africa with a view to securing one place in the continent where the slave trade would never have a foothold, and, looking for Christian settlers to demonstrate that prosperity need not depend on slavery, they found them in the Black congregations in Nova Scotia. In 1792, 1,131 Africans from Nova Scotia marched ashore in Freetown, Sierra Leone, singing, it was said later, a hymn by Isaac Watts, "Awake and Sing the Song of Moses and the Lamb." They had been in the house of bondage; they had crossed the Red Sea; they were now in the promised land, celebrating the victory of Moses, but also of the Lamb.

20. Ottobah Cugoano, *Thoughts and Sentiments on the Evil and Wicked Traffic of the Slavery and Commerce of the Human Species* (London: Becket, 1787).

Sierra Leone was the first continuing Protestant church in tropical Africa. One might see it as the beginning of Protestant missions there, but the missionaries were African and sent from British North America. The Sierra Leone church became a ready-made African church, with its own leaders and preachers. Many frustrations, many disappointments lay ahead for the church of Sierra Leone, but that church was to be the cornerstone of Christian operations across West Africa. In the second half of the nineteenth century, it would produce more missionaries per head of population than any other nation has ever done,[21] and it all began with this now largely forgotten missionary movement from America that in curious ways and with no formal organization anticipated the story of American Protestant missions.

---

21. Professor Walls did not supply statistics in support of this statement.—Ed.

CHAPTER 4

"Honour All Men"

The Humanitarian Strand in Early Protestant Missions

Now, we will stay most of the time (though with an important brief diversion to India), in Britain, where we were for much of the previous chapter—but in a very different sector of it. There, we had examined a British subculture, in the dissenting world of William Carey, a world of artisans and small tradesmen, far from the levers of power and shut out from privilege, a world of radical, even Republican, politics, Calvinist theology, and postmillennial eschatology, a world conscious of America and what was happening there, a world in which people made up for their exclusion from polite learning by unremitting labor at the sources of knowledge open to them. That is indeed part of the story of the making of the nineteenth-century missionary movement, but it is not the whole.

William Wilberforce and the Abolitionist Movement

We can extend the picture of the influences bearing upon the making of the missionary movement by looking first at another William, one who was almost William Carey's exact contemporary but who is in the starkest contrast to him in background, attitudes, and opinions, though sharing with him in evangelical faith and experience and in confirmed concern for missions. Unlike Carey, this man was never himself a missionary, but he represents an important set of influences that went to make up the movement.

William Wilberforce was born in Hull in Yorkshire in the north of England in 1759; he was thus two years older than Carey. His father was a wealthy merchant, and William inherited a considerable fortune when very young.

He was expensively educated, latterly at Cambridge, where he was the center of a bright, hard-drinking, high-spending social circle. He left Cambridge to fight an expensive election and to become a member of Parliament for Hull a few weeks after his twenty-first birthday. Carey was at that time still a lay-preaching shoemaker trying to save enough to get married.

The House of Commons is said to be the best club in England, and Wilberforce was soon the life and soul of noisy parties where practical jokes were played by rising politicians upon each other. Another of this circle, William Pitt, became a close friend, and he and Wilberforce toured the European continent together, discovering to their delight that "Archbishops in England are not like Archbishops in France. These last are jolly fellows, . . . who play at billiards."[1] Soon after their return from playing billiards with archbishops, Pitt surprisingly became prime minister—surprisingly, since he was only twenty-four. His friend Wilberforce was now obviously well placed for high office, but first he went to the continent again. This time his companion was a Cambridge don and clergyman with connections with Hull, Isaac Milner, an evangelical churchman, who was later to become president of Queens' College, Cambridge. Wilberforce returned from that trip a radically changed man. During it, he had gone through a trauma of guilt leading into deep distress. He had come through the experience with a joyful sense of liberation. It was his evangelical conversion. He returned also determined to devote his political life to some great cause. He consulted his friend the prime minister. Pitt suggested that a good cause would be the abolition of the slave trade. At this point in time, Carey was still a young shoemaker and preacher; his seniors, Fuller and Sutcliff, were now planning the concert of prayer and reading Jonathan Edwards.

Wilberforce, save for one short and insignificant period, never did attain the high office he seemed destined for. He stayed on the backbenches of Parliament in order to prosecute the causes for which he had dedicated his life. He became the archetypal evangelical, the person probably people thought of first when the word "evangelical" was mentioned. He wrote a book that became perhaps the most popular exposition of evangelical faith for half a century.[2] Eminent and widely respected, he was far better known than most evangelical clergymen; and it is significant that when the founders of

---

1. James Stephen, "William Wilberforce," in *Essays in Ecclesiastical Biography*, 2 vols., 3rd ed. (London: Longman, Brown, Green & Longmans, 1853), 2:212–13.

2. William Wilberforce, *A Practical View of the Prevailing Religious System of Professed Christians, in the Higher and Middle Classes, Contrasted with Real Christianity* (London: Cadell & Davies, 1797).

the Church Missionary Society wanted to approach the Archbishop of Canterbury to get his approval or at least to ensure that he would not throw a spanner into the works, they had to ask the layman Wilberforce to make the approach. There was no clergyman on their committee whom they could be sure the archbishop would agree to see.

He was not personally austere; he continued to enjoy parties. A lady who was in some trepidation on being placed next to him at dinner said afterward that she had heard that this was the most religious man in London. She had not expected, therefore, to find him the most amusing. Ideas of what constitute worldliness change, and evangelicals of the next generation were slightly embarrassed by the social habits of Wilberforce's day. They certainly do not mention the quantities of opiates that he took (he did suffer from chronic back pain all his life).

Wilberforce became the center of a little group of members of Parliament—writers, researchers, and propagandists—known to some as "the Saints" because of their piety, to others as "the Philanthropists" because of their devotion to humanitarian causes, and later, from 1844, as "the Clapham Sect," a label coined by Sir James Stephen.[3] Many of them had homes in what was then the leafy village of Clapham, where there was an outstanding evangelical rector, John Venn, who was partner in many of their schemes. Chief among these was the campaign against slavery. We may note that Carey talked of the slave trade as accursed and in his book saw the recent attempt by Wilberforce to legislate against the slave trade as an answer to the concert of prayer for the extension of God's kingdom—and perhaps as a sign of the longed-for day of fulfilled prophecy.

Baptists had long opposed slavery, Quakers even longer; and Carey advocated and participated in a trade boycott against slave-produced West Indian goods, additionally suggesting in his *Enquiry* that the money people saved from the boycott on sugar might be devoted to missionary funds.[4] But Baptists in Britain were an eccentric minority, Quakers a more eccentric and even smaller minority; their opinions counted for little with people who thought that they lived in the real world, the world of economic and social reality, where one had to take account of the nation's prosperity and its safety in time of war. Such people might agree that the slave trade had unfortunate aspects, while hoping that some of the tales about it were exaggerated, but slavery seemed essential to national interests. To interfere with it would risk bringing

---

3. For the origin of the label, see Gareth Atkins, *Converting Britannia: Evangelicals and British Public Life, 1770–1840* (Woodbridge: Boydell, 2019), 1.—Ed.

4. William Carey, *An Enquiry into the Obligation of Christians to Use Means for the Conversion of the Heathens*, new facsimile ed., ed. E. A. Payne (London: Carey Kingsgate, 1961), 86.

the British islands in the Caribbean and the port of Liverpool into ruin. And the opposition of others to slavery—Scottish philosophers, assorted radicals—would only confirm many people in the opinion that opponents of the slave trade were either starry-eyed idealists or political troublemakers. This is why Pitt, who personally favored abolition of the trade, did not make it government policy but passed it on to Wilberforce, outside the government but belonging to that central swathe of opinion that would be thought of neither as starry-eyed nor as politically dissident.

Wilberforce took up the campaign following his evangelical conversion, bringing in 1787 a parliamentary bill for the abolition of the slave trade. It was defeated heavily. He vowed to continue the fight and brought it back again next year, and the next, and the next. He got this letter in 1791 from the aged John Wesley, the last letter that Wesley ever wrote.

Dear Sir

Unless the divine power has raised you up to be as Athanasius *contra mundo*, I see not how you can go through with your glorious enterprise in opposing that execrable villainy, which is the scandal of religion, of England, and of human nature. Unless God has raised you up for this very thing, you will be worn out by the opposition of men and devils. But if God be for you, who can be against you? Go on, in the name of God and in the power of His might, till even American slavery (the vilest that ever saw the sun) shall vanish away before it.[5]

It was not until 1807, twenty years after his vow, that Parliament passed a measure for the abolition of the slave trade on the part of British subjects. It was many years after that before the legislation could be made effective. Through all that time, Wilberforce and his colleagues not only kept up constant parliamentary pressure; they collected, sifted, and researched information. They published, they confuted, they screened informants from all over the world, and they developed extraparliamentary pressure on an unprecedented scale, with skillful use of the press, petitions, and public meetings. Indeed, it is likely that the abolition of the slave trade was the first political measure carried through principally by use of the mass media. We have seen that Wilberforce and his group did not invent the abolitionist cause, by a long way, but they so captured public opinion as to make it successful.

5. John Wesley to Wilberforce, February 22, 1791, in John Wesley, *The Letters of the Rev. John Wesley, A.M.*, ed. John Telford (London: Epworth, 1931), 8:265.

For the rest of the nineteenth century, antislavery became part of the British persona, though in the eighteenth century, it had been British ships that had been the principal carriers of slaves. Wilberforce helped to make open hatred of the slave trade one of the badges of the evangelical. As he aged, his mantle fell on another evangelical member of Parliament, more liberally minded than himself, Sir Thomas Fowell Buxton, who battled through bad health to the eventual emancipation of the slaves in the British territories in 1833–1834. Since missionary concern was another badge of the evangelical, the strands of antislavery and missionary endeavor intertwine and interpenetrate. Antislavery is an inevitable part of the missionary movement. The inner connections of the missionary movement and the abolition movement—and of forces in other places that the leaders of those movements never dreamed of—are well seen in a story to which we will turn in a moment.

Wilberforce's opposition to the slave trade reflected a moral radicalism, which we will examine later: the slave trade must be abolished because it is evil. But it is important to remember also that the Clapham men were practicing politicians, who knew that moral arguments alone would be written off as unpractical sermonizing. The slave trade was an economic institution and must be dealt with by economic means. It must be shown that the abolition of the slave trade was in line with enlightened self-interest. The economic argument had to be presented to a British Parliament and public concerned that the end of the slave trade would mean the bankruptcy of the West Indies, the end of cheap sugar and rum, the decline of the Atlantic fleet, and the ruin of the port of Liverpool. It had also to be presented to African coastal peoples who formed the middlemen in the trade and who wanted the British manufactured goods that the slave trade provided. The former might be influenced by demonstrations of the sheer wastefulness and inefficiency of the slave trade, and stimulated by the thought of new sources of plantation crops and new markets for a developing manufacturing industry. The latter would need the assurance that the supply of manufactured goods would be maintained and improved if they gave up the export of slaves.

What the abolitionists needed was an object lesson, conducted at the source of the transatlantic trade in West Africa, something they could point to in order to prove that their theory worked. The first attempt at planting a colony of freed slaves in Sierra Leone was made in 1787 on the initiative of the leading abolitionist Granville Sharp. The intended colonists were impoverished freed slaves from the streets of London, but this first experiment in settlement in a "province of freedom" proved a miserable failure. A Sierra Leone Company was set up in 1791–1792 to develop the colony. But who would come to such a colony? There seemed no answer until the extraordinary news came from Nova Scotia, as described in the previous chapter. The Nova Scotian Black settlers who landed on the shore of Sierra Leone in 1792 appeared to promise a new dawn for the African continent. Wilberforce greeted this development as the Morning Star of Africa. There was much distress and heartbreak ahead for Sierra Leone, but he may well have been right, for, as the next chapter will describe, Sierra Leone was the foundation stone of Christianity in West Africa, fundamental to much that happened later.

The Unity of All Humanity

The close relation of the slavery issue to the missionary cause is reflected in one of the theologians of the missionary movement, one of very few in this earlier period, Richard Watson (1781–1833), secretary of the Wesleyan Methodist Missionary Society and a stalwart of the Antislavery Society. Here is an extract from a sermon of his: "Behold the foundation of the *fraternity* of our race, however coloured and however scattered. . . . There is not . . . a man on earth who has not a Father in heaven, and to whom Christ is not an advocate and patron: nay, more, because of the assumption of our common humanity, to whom he is not a BROTHER."[6] The particular reference here is to slaves in the West Indies. They have a Father in heaven, and Christ is their Brother. And the text for this sermon is 1 Peter 2:17, "Honour all men." In other words, Christians should honor the slaves on the plantations because they are human, children of the heavenly Father, brothers of Christ. And honor, he goes on, does not mean formal courtesy. It means estimating at the proper worth. And the true value of the slaves is reflected in the fact that the Redeemer died for them. It is reflected also in their human potential religiously, intellectually, and morally.

He returns in many sermons to the emerging church of the Caribbean as the firstfruits of Africa's redemption: "In those crowded congregations, in those spacious edifices [this is the big churches in the West Indies, packed with converted slaves], Ethiopia already 'stretches out her hands unto God.' . . . . And the prophetic promise is dawning upon parent Africa also. Hottentots, Caffres, Boschuanas, Namaquas, Corranas, Griquas, in the south, Bulloms, Foulahs, and Mandingos in the west, some of all your tribes are already in the fold, and hear and love the voice of the great Shepherd. We hail

---

6. Richard Watson, *The Religious Instruction of the Slaves in the West India Colonies Advocated and Defended: A Sermon Preached before the Wesleyan Methodist Missionary Society, in the New Chapel, City-Road, London, April 28, 1824* (London: Butterworth & Son, 1824), 3–4.

you as our BRETHREN!"[7] These are the front ranks of the vast millions of the peoples of Africa who will one day be joining in praise to the long-concealed but faithful God of Africa.

Thus, even in the 1820s, this mission theologian had a vision of a Christian Africa and saw the first signs of it in Afro-America. That vision was worked out in some detail with an interpretation of Africa's past glories and present miseries. Watson insisted strongly on a glorious past for Africa, using materials from both biblical and secular learning. He identifies the Africans of the past with the peoples known to the Hebrews as Cush, Mizraim, and Put. He will have nothing to do with interpretations that derive the Africans from Ham and thus subject to the curse of Genesis 9, often used to justify African slavery. With the possible exception of those inhabitants of North Africa of Punic origin, Africans were not the children of Ham. Even if they were, Watson observed, the curse is abrogated in Christ, in whom all nations are blessed.[8]

The achievements of ancient Africa were mighty. Africans produced the great Nilotic civilizations, made Egypt fertile, and gave the world its first writing system. Africa produced heroes, bishops, and martyrs for the early church, and in more recent times, generals, physicians, mathematicians, and merchants. Why then do we not see the same arts of civilization in Africa today? The answer is not in lack of capacity but in the loss of cultivation through the movements of populations. Watson appears to regard Ashanti and Dahomey, along with other African nations generally deemed to be "pagan" and "barbarous," as "semi-civilized," a term most contemporaries reserved for India and China.[9]

At the present time, Watson acknowledged, Africans are "the most unfortunate of the family of man," uniquely harshly treated, as the history of slavery demonstrated.[10] They were consistently traduced and insulted. White savages sneeringly devalued their humanity for the sake of protecting their own profit. Pseudoscientists claimed to be able to demonstrate from skull measurements that they were a lower race. Perverted exegesis burdened them with the curse of Ham. Yet through all this, in spite of all the ill-usage they had suffered from others, Africans had been remarkably patient and unaggressive. They had not employed their overwhelming superiority in numbers against their oppressors in the Caribbean.

7. Watson, *Religious Instruction of the Slaves*, 31–32.
8. Watson, *Religious Instruction of the Slaves*, 8–9.
9. Watson, "God with Us," in his *Sermons and Sketches of Sermons*, 2 vols. (New York: Mason & Lane, 1840), 1:308.
10. Watson, *Religious Instruction of the Slaves*, 6.

Watson's picture of Africa is a triptych: a magnificent past; a brutalized, miserable present; and a rapturous glimpse of a future in the kingdom of God. He believed that he could already see the dawn of that future most clearly in the Caribbean, which was at once the shame of Christendom and the earnest of Africa's redemption. The psalmist's vision of Ethiopia stretching out her hands to God (Ps 68:31) was endlessly echoed through the nineteenth century by missionaries and friends of mission, and above all by Christian Africans. It was clearly articulated early in the century as part of a comprehensive and coherent view of the continent by Richard Watson, who in the days of brutal slavery found the text of 1 Peter 2:17, "Honour all men," to be the fitting text from which to proclaim African dignity.[11]

Evangelicals and India

The Saints in Clapham had other concerns. After slavery, Wilberforce ranked India as his chief preoccupation; and here he had the assistance of his friend Charles Grant, a senior official of the East India Company who had had an evangelical conversion while serving in India and returned to London to hold high rank in the Indian administration. The East India Company, a monopoly company with a charter from Parliament, administered British interests in India and ruled large sections of the subcontinent. Traditionally, the East India Company had proclaimed neutrality in matters of religion. To avoid inflaming religious passions and disturbing trade, it did not usually allow missions; Carey had to begin his work in Danish territory at Serampore. Evangelicals were scandalized at other aspects of the company's government: the tax collected from Hindu temples, for instance—should a Christian government (Christendom again) take revenues from the practice of idolatry?— and the toleration in British-administered territory of practices such as *sati* (the burning of widows on the husband's funeral pyre) and the Bengali rites involving swinging from hooks inserted into the flesh.

In 1813, the charter of the East India Company came up for renewal. Wilberforce and his friends battled to get changes made in it, which would acknowledge Britain's Christian stance as a nation. He believed passionately that Britain had been providentially given power in India and now had responsibilities. Wilberforce and his friends were partly successful: some, but not all, of his "pious clauses" were incorporated in the new charter. A bishop was appointed for Calcutta and, most importantly, a "Pious Clause" was inserted

---

11. Watson, *Religious Instruction of the Slaves*, 3, 31–32.

in the charter committing the company to "providing sufficient facilities" for persons going to India for the purposes of introducing "useful knowledge" and "religious and moral improvement."[12] Missionaries could now apply with confidence for licenses to work in company territory.

The Social Conservatism and Moral Radicalism of William Wilberforce

Although Wilberforce and his colleagues were vigorous campaigners on such issues, they were often conservative on domestic social issues. A Baptist like Carey might welcome the French Revolution, at least in its early stages; Wilberforce trembled at it and supported all the British government's repressive legislation in the wake of it. "I do foresee a gathering storm, and I cannot help fearing that a country which, like this, has so long been blessed beyond all example with every spiritual and temporal good, will incur those judgments of an incensed God, which in the prophets are so often denounced against those who forget the Author of all their mercies."[13]

The political reflexes of Wilberforce were invariably conservative. He had no vision of a new society. He thought, indeed, that the British constitution already embodied all the excellencies. "I might here enlarge with pleasure on the unrivaled excellence . . . of the constitution under which we live in this happy country; and point out how, more perhaps than any which has ever existed upon earth, it is so framed, as to provide at the same time for keeping up a due degree of public spirit, and yet for preserving unimpaired the quietness, and comfort, and charities of private life; . . . In whatever class or order of society Christianity prevails, she sets herself to rectify the particular faults . . . to which that class is liable."[14] Wilberforce believed that Christianity taught affluent people to be generous and not overbearing, and to accept the responsibility of high status as being the condition on which high status is conferred. This makes the inequalities of life less galling to the lower orders of society; and Christianity teaches them to be humble and patient, and that the high prizes sought by the worldly are fleeting and illusory, whereas true peace of mind can be as readily enjoyed by the poor as by the rich, and that

12. Penelope Carson, *The East India Company and Religion, 1698-1858* (Woodbridge: Boydell & Brewer, 2012), 250.

13. Robert Isaac Wilberforce and Samuel Wilberforce, *The Life of William Wilberforce*, 2nd ed. (Philadelphia: Perkins, 1841), 1:145.

14. Wilberforce, *Practical View*, 290-92.

the rich have more and worse temptations than the poor, while in heaven all distinctions would be done away.

This is no social revolutionary. He acknowledges inequality, even that inequality produces evils, but does not expect these to change, does not seem to think of them within the sphere of public policy. Christian activity will not transform society; it will only soften the hardest lines of division, so that the rich act responsibly and liberally. So Christianity helps to *preserve* social order by encouraging the rich to act responsibly and by encouraging the poor to be patient, thus reducing tensions and averting upheavals.

Why then was anyone ever afraid that this man and his companions would subvert established institutions? The answer lies in the moral radicalism of Clapham when persuaded that a particular institution was repugnant to Scripture. Actual cruelty, actual bloodshed was evil and to be renounced. Scripture condemned them. On the slavery issue, therefore, Wilberforce is unshakable: slavery is cruel, it is inhuman, it is corrupting, and it is to be abolished. To take a smaller issue, dueling, the common way of settling points of honor in the upper classes, not least among Wilberforce's parliamentary colleagues, is a matter of pride and vainglory and must be abolished. He is hardly a social thinker at all; he is simply responding to categorical moral imperatives dictated, as he believes, by Scripture.

From another point of view, his social thinking starts from a Christendom axiom, the axiom that Britain is a Christian society, to be guided by Scripture. The state as much as the individual is to respond to the dictates of Scripture. As for the individual, the happiness of the state is bound up with it. So a Christian society whose religious and moral institutions are to be kept in repair must observe the Sabbath, oppose the slave trade, uphold private morality, and open India to missions. All these are of a piece.

Wilberforce devoted much attention to the question of private morality, securing a Royal Proclamation against Vice and Immorality in 1787 and setting up a Proclamation Society and later a Society for the Suppression of Vice to carry it out. It was not a specifically evangelical creation; Wilberforce was keen that it should represent as wide a front as possible. But the underlying thought is that "righteousness exalteth a nation"—though Sydney Smith made the point that in fact it was a society for suppressing the vices of persons whose income does not exceed five hundred pounds per annum.[15]

---

15. Sydney Smith, "Proceedings of the Society for the Suppression of Vice," in *Essays by Sydney Smith (Reprinted from the "EDINBURGH REVIEW") 1802–1818* (London: Routledge & Sons, [1874]), 142.

What Wilberforce and Anglican evangelicals are doing is to recall society to its true and historic basis, the Christendom basis. They are aware that this will run counter to a great deal of contemporary opinion, not because that opinion is explicitly anti-Christian but because *it does not take Christianity seriously*. It does not want its gentlemen's pleasures interfered with; it does not want to give up its conveniences, either nationally or individually. So it will cling to the slave trade; it will oppose missions in India; whereas it is a national duty to oppose the first, as cruel and obscene, and to promote the latter as part of the responsibility that providence has placed upon us.

Wilberforce was already an established politician in 1797 when he wrote the book entitled *A Practical View of the Prevailing Religious System of Professed Christians in the Higher and Middle Classes of This Country Contrasted with Real Christianity*. It became a bestseller, the classic statement of evangelical Christianity. It went on being reprinted for decades, with pocket editions attesting to its use as an extended tract. (I have a battered pocket edition.) Many people, including the great Scottish preacher Thomas Chalmers, ascribed their conversion to reading it. The title conveys the thesis: the upper and middle classes of Britain—the leaders of the nation, that is—profess to be Christian; but their actual religion is not Christianity, because they do not understand what Christianity is. The book is not concerned to address skeptics or infidels or unbelievers, nor is it addressed to the masses but to the leaders of opinion, who mostly go to church.

Wilberforce sees Christianity as having three crucial elements, all three of which are missing in the reconstruction of Christianity by the British upper classes. The first of these is the corruption of human nature; the second, the atonement of Christ; and the third, the sanctifying influence of the Holy Spirit. These in different words run through all the evangelical writers of the period as "the distinguishing doctrines of the gospel." Distinguishing from what? Distinguishing the evangelical understanding of Christian faith from others in what was still essentially a Christian society.

Conversion to "Real" Christianity

These distinguishing doctrines had their analogue in a particular experience, the experience that we have called evangelical conversion, described countless times in the period, an engulfing sense of guilt because of the corruption of human nature, a response in lively piety and quicker effort, a period of hope, a crisis as a result of which comes a sense of deep peace and the assurance of forgiveness because of the atonement of Christ, and perhaps overflowing joy as well. This is described as saving faith, the gateway to a life marked by the sanctifying influence of the Holy Spirit. Wesley indeed had made a paradigm of the experience and regarded it as normal, "the experience of real Christians," as he puts it in the preface to his hymnbook.[16] Others rejected any specific paradigm but still insisted on a necessary transition to personal faith.

This is the hallmark of the evangelical of the period: he passes to "real faith," joins, in Wesley's phrase, "real Christians." Like the distinguishing doctrines, the very phrase implies another sort of Christianity. This experience occurred to people who lived in a society consisting overwhelmingly of believers and to a society that was very much churchgoing. Certainly this applied to the middle classes with which Wilberforce is especially concerned. In the great majority of cases, those who know "evangelical conversion" have, for a greater or lesser time, been sincere followers of religious observance. Hence we come to the distinction between "real" and "formal" or "nominal" religion. Wesley has a section in his hymnbook describing formal religion. It is followed by one describing inward religion. The one describing formal religion includes the lines, "The world, the Christian world convince / Of damning unbelief!"[17] Wilberforce would have understood what that meant. His book is about the contrasts between the Christianity professed by most in his rank of society and real Christianity.

Three Legacies of Evangelical Humanitarianism

I conclude this chapter by considering the historical results of the process of evangelical humanitarianism just described.

First, the Protestant missionary movement grew up with the antislavery movement and was often supported by the same people. So while the missionary message called for those overseas to experience evangelical conversion, it also was addressed to the reform of society, to issues that these days would be called human rights: slavery, infanticide, and war. The reform of society would not come about without education. Education, therefore, was nearly always an accompaniment of missions. The elimination of illegitimate sources of income required the development of legitimate alternatives. Missions, therefore, worked for economic development: Henry Venn, whom we

16. John Wesley, *A Collection of Hymns for the Use of the People Called Methodists* (London: Mason, 1784; orig. 1780), 4; numerous later editions.

17. Wesley, *Collection of Hymns*, 94.

shall meet in chapter 6, introduced cotton growing into Nigeria. All this was in line with the prevailing theology of early nineteenth-century evangelicalism. It was, however, as we shall see in the next chapter, less readily squared with the new premillennial eschatology that became increasingly influential in the second part of the nineteenth century.

A second consequence was the outcome of Wilberforce's combination of political conservatism with moral radicalism, the seriousness of purpose characteristic of the evangelical. There were others to whom this appealed: those High Churchmen of the old-fashioned type, who applauded the moral transformation, the reformation of manners that Wilberforce wanted, who desired the suppression of vice as much as he did. They were probably less excited on matters such as slavery, generally favoring gradualist approaches, but in general, there were many matters in which evangelicals and High Churchmen could make common cause; and in the end, the High Churchmen came in on the slavery issue, too. What alarmed High Churchmen was any fear of subversion of the church or undermining of the social status quo. Evangelicalism was suspect when, as with Wesley, it threatened the one or, as with Carey's sort of Dissenter, both. But Wilberforce and the Evangelical Anglican clergyman Charles Simeon developed an evangelicalism that quiets such fears.

As a result, there is a quiet realignment. As we move into the early Victorian era, most of what Wilberforce argued for becomes accepted at large. Evangelical values become the norm in society, not because evangelicals are in a majority but because those values can be accepted by many who are not evangelicals. The Reformation of Manners takes place. The Clapham Saints become the Fathers of the Victorians.[18] This helps to explain how within the nineteenth century, the missionary movement passes from the fringes of British religious life to its center, from a purely evangelical concern to a thing desired by all serious churchmen. By 1840, the missionary movement is thoroughly respectable. The Saints won at least part of the things that they were seeking for from a nominally Christian government and society. The drawing together of evangelical and other "serious" Christians can be seen on both sides of the border between England and Scotland.

The third consequence arises from the way in which evangelicals understood conversion as an inner spiritual transformation evidenced by a radical outward change in behavior. The missionary movement was the child of the evangelical movement. In its early years, almost every missionary of the groups that we have been looking at came from the evangelical or Pietist

---

18. Ford K. Brown, *Fathers of the Victorians: The Age of Wilberforce* (Cambridge: Cambridge University Press, 1961).

tradition, operated within an evangelical society, stressed the distinguishing doctrines of the gospel, and knew the experience of evangelical conversion or something like it. Now, that experience and those convictions were, as we have seen, related to the experience of a Christian society, a society that professed Christianity; they related to the substance of what most contemporaries recognized in shadow. But the missionary worked and preached the gospel in societies that made no such profession and was seeking fundamental religious change within those societies. The missionaries were calling on people to change their whole frame of life, to give up one religious system and adopt another. And from time to time, this happened. Individuals in India, families in southern Africa, whole villages in Sierra Leone, and whole kingdoms in the Pacific enthusiastically adopted the new way.

If conversion means turning, this was certainly conversion. And yet where were the marks of evangelical conversion that the missionary knew—the conviction of sin, that crisis of forgiveness? And where were the distinguishing doctrines of the gospel? Converts, obviously sincere and enthusiastic, often seemed little impressed with these. They seemed more concerned to set up a body of regulative laws for the Christian community. So the missionary movement abroad, like the evangelical movement at home, becomes centered in the reformation of manners, seen as a normal part of the passage from formal Christianity to real Christianity—in other words, as the fruit of conversion. For them, conversion is something that happens within Christianity rather than from another religious allegiance to the Christian one. They also have certain expectations about the shape of the experience. Evangelical missionaries took these expectations with them to the mission field. They expected those who responded to the gospel to respond as people in Christendom did when they responded to the gospel. So they were sometimes puzzled at their own success when people abandoned traditional worship, enthusiastically adopted Christian worship, but showed no sign of what evangelicals called "conviction of sin." The missionaries sometimes wondered whether these people had been converted at all. They were, in fact, responding to the gospel and not to the missionaries' experience of the gospel.

PART 2

Toward Middle Age

Western Missions in the Nineteenth Century

CHAPTER 5

Reading the Bible

Theology and the Interpretation of Prophecy in Nineteenth-Century Protestant Missions

Chapters 2, 3, and 4 have shown how Protestant missions came into being following movements of spiritual renewal—the Pietist movement in Germany and central Europe, the evangelical movement in North America and the British Isles. These were in a profound sense radical Christian movements, marked by a desire to spread "real" or "scriptural," as opposed to the formal or "nominal" Christianity of European Christendom. The leaders of these movements drew from their reading of the Bible both a set of principles for Christian living and a set of expectations for the future course of history, in which the worldwide progress of the gospel occupied a central place. This chapter examines these themes in more detail and identifies a crucial change in evangelical eschatology that became increasingly influential for the missionary movement as it entered its middle age in the second part of the nineteenth century.

John Wesley on "the General Spread of the Gospel"

John Wesley, an outstanding representative of the early evangelical movement in England, called the Methodist approach to Christian living "scriptural holiness." Initially Wesley's movement emphasized home rather than overseas mission. Wesley believed that the mission of Methodism that he represented was to spread scriptural holiness throughout the land, the land being England or perhaps England plus "North Britain," as he called Scotland. In so far as he gave attention to missions overseas, they were simply an extension, a natural overflow, of this "ordinary" work of the gospel.

John Wesley's sermon "The General Spread of the Gospel" (1783) was included in the fifty-three sermons that were the standard guide for Methodist preachers.[1] This sermon gives an indication of how evangelical preachers saw their work. Wesley's text is Isaiah 11:9, "How does darkness, intellectual darkness, ignorance, with vice and misery attendant upon it, cover the face of the earth!" That is the current state of the world, he says: darkness. In the greater part of the world, there is no trace of the gospel. At that very time, the Pacific islands were being "discovered," and the darkness there appeared to be total. But even in the lands supposed to be Christian, there was little knowledge of the truth. Wesley talks of one of the greatest mysteries under heaven: why this should be; why, after all these centuries, darkness still covered the earth; and why most of the world still had no access to the gospel.

Will it stay that way? he asks. No; Scripture (Psalm 2:8) makes it plain that the Messiah will have the heathen for his inheritance. This was a text that was greatly used by preachers about missions. It is on prophecy, therefore, that the hope for an evangelized world depends. The Messiah will have the heathen for his inheritance. But when? How will it happen? Wesley, a strong Arminian, insists that it will not be by some sledgehammer act of God that destroys human freedom and forces people into the kingdom. It will not be a forced acknowledgment of Christ; that comes at the end. For the general spread of the gospel, God will act in the ways in which he consistently acts. Wesley looks back over fifty years of the evangelical movement as he has seen it, fifty years during which numbers of people have been converted, during which scriptural holiness has been spread throughout England and into Scotland and then into Ireland, and from there to New York, and from there to Pennsylvania, and from there to Nova Scotia. He concludes, "Now in the same manner as God has converted so many to himself without destroying their liberty, he can undoubtedly convert whole nations or the whole world; and it is as easy to him to convert a world, as one individual soul."[2] In other words, the general spread of the gospel is to be an extension of the spread of the gospel that he himself has been part of in the remarkable last fifty years— remarkable, because he quotes Luther (I cannot find this place in Luther, but Wesley says it is there) that no revival lasts longer than a generation, or thirty years.[3] This one has, he says. This has lasted fifty years and is still going. What does this tell us about the general spread of the gospel?

1. John Wesley, "The General Spread of the Gospel," sermon 63 in *The Works of John Wesley* (1872 ed.), Wesleyan-Holiness Digital Library, https://www.whdl.org/en/browse/resources/6881.

2. Wesley, "General Spread of the Gospel," para. 12.

3. Wesley, "General Spread of the Gospel," para. 16.

Wesley is clearly not thinking of a long distant future or a future hidden in the secret counsels of God. Just suppose what we have already seen, he says, what has happened within my lifetime, suppose that it were repeated, the natural spread of the gospel from place to place, just as it moved from England to Scotland to Ireland to America to Nova Scotia. He envisages the gospel crossing the English Channel, as it had done across the Atlantic already, and thus to France, and to Holland. It would be easy to foresee a further spread then to Switzerland and to Germany and then to Scandinavia and Russia.

So far he has been thinking of the expansion of the gospel among nominal Protestants, but when this is done, the spread of the gospel in Catholic Europe will be natural, with Spain and Italy coming last, because the movement of the gospel is always from the least to the highest. This would bring about the turn of the Muslim world, for the greatest obstacle to the conversion of Muslims—the evil lives of professed Christians—would now be taken away. If Christians are transformed by scriptural holiness, then we can look for the conversion of the Muslim world. By the same token, we can look for the conversion of those he calls "the heathen," starting with the Hindus living nearest the British settlements in India, for these lives, too, will have been transformed by the gospel, and again the hindrance to the gospel will have been removed.

As to further regions, Wesley cannot guess how God will bring the gospel to Africa and the Pacific and what he calls the "deepest recesses of America," but God can find a way.[4] By this means (that is, the continuation of the Evangelical Revival that has already lasted fifty years), the evangelization of the world will be complete, and all the promises of prophecy to the church will be complete. And then, the conversion of the Jews will naturally take place.

Notice that Wesley is not setting out a plan for world evangelization or setting up an organization to do it. He foresees it happening as a result of the normal course of revival that has been going on. This is quite consistent with his own policy. He frequently discouraged or vetoed plans for specific missions raised by enthusiastic followers on the ground that the time was not yet ripe for that or there was something more important to do somewhere else. "You have nothing to do in Afric [sic] at present," he told one of his preachers in 1778. "Convert the heathen in Scotland."[5] But notice also the eschatological dimension. We are moving seamlessly from the present day to the last day, with no vast apocalyptic upheaval. Wesley has concluded that he is living, or

---

4. Wesley, "General Spread of the Gospel," para. 23.

5. John Wesley to Duncan McCallum, July 14, 1778, in John Wesley, *The Letters of the Rev. John Wesley, A.M.*, ed. John Telford (London: Epworth, 1931), 6:316.

may be living, in the last times, and the sign of it is the Evangelical Revival and the lasting work of God that appears to have been going on in so many places over so many years. His own work is a proof of it, the first signs of the spread of gospel truth across the world. Home mission, by the grace of God and by means of his wisdom, leads to foreign mission.

We note here that the climax of Wesley's vision, though he does not speak much about it in the sermon itself, is the conversion of the Jews. All contemporary commentators saw Paul's words in Romans 11:25 about the salvation of all Israel in relation to the fullness of the gentiles as prophecies of the end time. Wesley's brother, Charles, has a wonderful hymn, "Head of thy Church, whose Spirit fills," which echoes this theme: "The fulness of the Gentiles call [a reference to that same text in Romans that his brother was using], and take thine ancient people home."[6] Charles Wesley is reflecting here the standard eschatology of his day. The terms "premillennial" and "postmillennial" had not yet been invented, and they are not particularly helpful in describing the view of the last times that most believers held in the eighteenth and early nineteenth century.

Anticipations of the End Time

Most theologians took a broadly historicist interpretation of the book of Revelation, seeing it as charting the course of human history, or human history at least since the incarnation. For Protestants, one point of interpretation at least was fixed: the Reformers had identified the pope as antichrist, the man of sin. This interpretation is enshrined in the Westminster Confession of Faith, the standard accepted by many English-speaking Calvinists and representing the official position of the Church of Scotland. Into this scheme were woven the Old Testament prophecies. There was dispute over how literally these were to be taken. The prophetic Scriptures that leaders of the missionary movement particularly pointed to and delighted in were the ones mentioned by Wesley, that the Messiah would take the nations for his inheritance, and the prophecy that the earth would be filled with the knowledge of God as the waters cover the sea.

What the Evangelical Revival did was to give hope that this time was approaching, when the gospel would spread across the whole world because it was already visibly spreading, not just locally but for the first time on an ob-

6. No. 693 in John Wesley, *A Collection of Hymns for the Use of the People Called Methodists: With a Supplement* (London: Mason, 1779).

viously large scale. Jonathan Edwards as early as the 1740s seized on this idea and became deeply impressed with the thought that we might be approaching that time. His response (as noted in chapter 3) was to issue a call for a concert of prayer for the extension of God's kingdom, that all Christians would join in visible union, as he called it, to pray to that end. Chapter 3 described how the Scottish minister, John Erskine, sent a copy of Edwards's book to the English Baptist minister, John Sutcliff, who introduced it into his ministers' fraternal, and indeed produced a cheap abridged edition. The prayer meetings were called to give visible union to a concert of prayer for the extension of God's kingdom through the world. Beginning from this concert of prayer, William Carey, as a young minister in the same Northamptonshire Baptist ministers' fraternal, received his vision of a converted world.

Carey's whole thinking as revealed in his *Enquiry* is deeply influenced by this view of prophecy. The time of the end is at hand. What marks that time will be a great spread of the gospel. It is time to use means for the conversion of the heathen. This is what God is now calling us to by the signs of the times. Carey sees signs of the fulfillment of prophecy, and he believes that the prayer meetings have had their effect. The signs that he distinguishes are new evangelistic openings, stronger churches, people responding to the gospel, what he calls "clearer statement" of controversies, and, on the wider public scale, the spread of civil and religious liberty, accompanied by a diminution of the spirit of popery. Carey discerned marks of this in the attack on the slave trade launched in Parliament (this is written in 1792, when Wilberforce had his initial motion), and also the spread of civil and religious liberty signified by the 1789 Revolution in France.[7] Carey, as noted in chapter 3, was a Dissenter from the establishment, and like many of his kind, he had radical political views, one of the reasons why the East India Company was alarmed at the thought of Baptist missionaries in India. Carey and his like might rejoice in the French Revolution, but there were other evangelicals who trembled at the thought, and we will need to go back to them and how they read the signs of the times in relation to the prophecies in Scripture.

For the immediate purpose, however, let us stay with the generally accepted scheme of prophecy, the eschatology embraced by Edwards and by Wesley, and note how as a result of the Evangelical Revival, there is coming an apprehension that we are nearing the time of the end, the end inaugurated by a vast expansion of gospel preaching until the earth is full of the knowledge of God as the waters cover the sea. It is the prophetic outlook of the leaders

---

7. William Carey, *An Enquiry into the Obligation of Christians to Use Means for the Conversion of the Heathens*, new facsimile ed., ed. E. A. Payne (London: Carey Kingsgate, 1961), 79.

of the early Protestant missions. The hope of glorious days to come sustained them in the early disasters that befell many, perhaps most, of the earliest Protestant missions. When the missions were established and were showing modest success, this view informed their vision.

Rufus Anderson and the Early Prophetic Vision of the American Board of Commissioners for Foreign Missions

Let us take a representative statement of this vision as articulated by one of the most important American missionary thinkers, Rufus Anderson, and see his reading of the signs of the times, initially in the late 1830s but a vision that he clearly saw no need to revise after twenty years, because the sermon went on being reprinted for two decades. Its title tells out its theme: "The Time for the World's Conversion Come." But who was Rufus Anderson?

Rufus Anderson was born in Yarmouth, Maine, in 1796. His father was a Congregational minister, a disciple of Samuel Hopkins, the leader of the new style of evangelistic Calvinism, which had disinterested benevolence as its constant theme. In principle, disinterested benevolence and indeed the new style of Calvinism was missionary. It spoke of the evangelization of the world. But the way that Hopkins prepared for the evangelization of the world was striking. It would be to teach African Americans, who would be the missionaries to Africa. The vision of a converted world thus extends to Native Americans and to African Americans, though at present there was very little evidence of it in practice. The revival of evangelical religion that Hopkins reflected had led to new colleges and seminaries for the training of an educated ministry: Williams, Middlebury, Bowdoin among the colleges, Andover among the seminaries, especially since Harvard was now theologically hostile to evangelical religion.

The first American overseas mission initiative (apart, of course, from the *very* first, which were the African American mission ventures to the Caribbean and West Africa described in chapter 3), but the first within the terms of the mainstream of the American churches, seems to have arisen in this context: pious students at the new colleges. It was a group of students at Williams College who in 1806 at the famous Haystack Prayer Meeting first resolved to carry the gospel overseas and formed a society to put their intention into practice. They went from Williams to Andover, where their numbers increased, and Samuel J. Mills and his colleagues asked the General Assembly of Massachusetts to send them overseas. This offers quite a contrast with the

British situation, where the last people you would expect to come forward would be university students.

These people were Congregationalists, believers in the independence of the local congregation. Their church structure had no mechanism that could possibly send them overseas. The General Assembly of Massachusetts was sympathetic but had no powers to do anything with them. The result was the constitution in 1810 of the American Board of Commissioners for Foreign Missions. An approach to the English London Missionary Society, which now had fifteen years of experience, did not prove fruitful, and in 1812, the American Board sent out its first five overseas missionaries. It had grown out of the General Assembly of Massachusetts. Connecticut was also involved. Essentially, the American Board had grown out of New England Congregationalism, but a similar movement was stirring among Presbyterians in the central states, and so the number of commissioners was expanded to include Presbyterians from New Jersey, New York, and Pennsylvania. Before long, the board had co-opted a notable Episcopalian and someone from the Associate Reformed Church. The first twenty-six commissioners included five college presidents, two state governors, the director of the mint, a diplomat, and three of the richest merchant princes in the country. The American Board was a national institution, with maritime interests—again, quite a contrast with Britain, where mission interest was marginal and did not come near the heart of the church or church leadership and was not associated with the universities.

This was the position in 1813. Five years later, the young Anderson graduated from Bowdoin College in Brunswick and went to Andover Seminary. After seminary, he offered for mission service but was appointed to assist the secretary of the American Board. In 1826, extraordinarily, he was ordained as assistant secretary of the board, a revolution in congregational polity. The American Board has become, as it were, a church; one can be given pastoral charge within a mission society. Anderson remained at the American Board for the rest of his working life. He became one of the three corresponding secretaries in 1832, the one dealing with missionary correspondence, which was the key appointment; he was soon senior secretary, a position in which he remained until his retirement in 1866. He remained on the committee until 1875, and even after that, he had an office at headquarters where he wrote histories and other works for the board. It is an extraordinarily long reign, starting in the presidency of Andrew Jackson and finishing in that of Andrew Johnson. However, he was never a missionary, though he did on several occasions visit the fields of the American Board.

With this background, let us consider Anderson's tract, originating clearly in a sermon, with the text from Galatians 4:4: "But when the fulness of the time was come, God sent forth his Son." Anderson's point is the fullness of time—*kairos*, the right time, God's time. The great *kairos* in God's plan of redemption was, of course, the incarnation, the right time that Paul is talking of, and a feature of that time was a general sense of expectation. Anderson is probably thinking not only of the expectations evident in the New Testament (with John's preaching and the repeated question, Are you he that should come? Are you the Messiah? Are you Elijah? Are you that prophet?) but also of expectation in pagan sources. There was a poem by the Roman poet Virgil written in the time of Augustus (that is, at the time of the birth of Christ) that was often taken as a glimpse of messianic prophecy in a pagan source, and with the particular chronological reference as being providential. But Anderson sees this *kairos* within the framework of the history of redemption, a history in which there were two preceding *kairoi* and in which there is to be a following one. The first great event that happened only when everything was ready was the exodus from Egypt; the second, the return from exile in Babylon.

Anderson, like most of his contemporaries, sees these as events not in Jewish history but in church history, because up to the time of the incarnation, Israel is the church. So these are things that happened to the church. The church's first *kairos* is the exodus. Its second *kairos* is the return from exile. The third and great *kairos* is the coming of the Lord in his incarnation. And the fourth *kairos* is "yet to come, . . . when the Spirit shall be poured out upon all flesh, with a universal and overpowering influence, and 'the kingdoms of this world' shall become 'the kingdoms of our Lord and of his Christ, and he shall reign forever and ever.'"[8]

Anderson does not say "the time of the Lord's return." The time of the Lord's return is itself just part of this great *kairos* of which the distinguishing marks are the pouring out of the Spirit, the overpowering response to the gospel, and the establishment of the kingdom. What Anderson is expecting is the fulfillment of the prophecies of the messianic age for the church, the filling of the earth with the knowledge of God as the waters cover the sea. Just as when the fullness of time for the incarnation was come we saw signs—from John the Baptist's preaching to the fourth eclogue of Virgil—Anderson believes he can see signs of the time in his day. Indeed, things have happened over the past fifty years (he's doing a Wesley and looking back over a remarkable span of time). It is something more than his own lifetime, but great things

---

8. R. Pierce Beaver, ed., *To Advance the Gospel: Selections from the Writings of Rufus Anderson* (Grand Rapids: Eerdmans, 1967), 59–60.

have happened in that half century. Fifty years ago, America was coming through the birth pangs of the republic, Europe through the horrors of the wars of the Napoleonic era. It had been a dark time. But now a very different age had come, politically, intellectually, and spiritually. The nation has been transformed; the church has been transformed. Here are the signs of the times that tell us that the great *kairos* is at hand.

First, the way is now open for the worldwide spread of the gospel. The apostles did not preach the gospel to the whole world, not literally to all nations. They could not. They did what they could. The early church did fine work in preaching the gospel throughout the civilized world, but it had little or no access to the world beyond the civilized world, for the Roman world was bounded on the one side by India and on the other by the British Isles.

It is interesting that Anderson, who was to direct American missions to the Middle East, seems to know very little about the East Syrian (sometimes and inaccurately termed Nestorian) missions that had in fact brought the gospel to China at almost the same time as it had come to northern England. Anderson follows a conventional Protestant view of the Middle Ages: it is a time of great apostasy in which the true church is represented by a tiny minority over against a vast nominal church in which intellectual activity is dulled (he speaks of the mental imbecility of the time). But in the past fifty years, almost every "heathen" nation has become open. The world is explored; it is accessible. There are exceptions, such as Japan, but India and China are open. Fifty years ago, the governments of Protestant countries (he can only mean Britain) blocked missionary effort; now they protect it. Communications are transformed. There is worldwide commerce. There are technological advances in printing, which means that you can produce two thousand New Testaments in a day. The political situation of the world is transformed. The world is at peace; there are no barbarian invasions, and the two historic enemies of the true faith, the false prophet and the man of sin, are weakened.

To Anderson, the false prophet is, of course, Mohammed, and it was manifest that the political power of Islam was declining. It was centered in the Ottoman Empire, centered in Istanbul, while ruling parts of Europe, Asia, and Africa; but its provinces were one by one rebelling and breaking free. In what some hailed with delight, the Greeks had recently secured their independence; a Christian people had escaped from Muslim rule. The man of sin was the pope, and the power of the Catholic Church had indeed been shaken by the turbulent events in Europe. Catholicism was no longer likely to be a major threat to any Protestant missionary initiatives.

There are other signs of the times in what has happened to Christ's church. It is now for the first time in history possessed of a form of organization that permits world evangelization, the key to the conversion of the world. That form of organization is the voluntary society. Anderson agrees this is not entirely a new institution; monastic orders and religious societies were, in effect, voluntary societies, and he points out how important they were in evangelization in the Dark Ages. But his concern is with the Protestant form of the voluntary society: free, open, responsible, embracing all classes, both sexes, all ages—the masses of the people. Here is, in fact, a new form of church organization, one of the great results of the progress of Christian civilization (his word) in this *kairos*.

Anderson is aware that the voluntary society is a product of particular political conditions that allow free association, and of certain economic conditions; people have disposable income in cash. He is quite prepared to link these with "our" form of government; that is, of course, the American form of government, spreading over an expanding America, moving with the frontier. It is the voluntary society tuned to the service of mission. The American Board of Commissioners for Foreign Missions is the great exemplar that is to be the instrument for the conversion of the world. The process had already begun. How great that beginning! How wide! How many places! It is, he says, the almost fearful progress of the Lord's gracious providence. Liberty of thought, speed of action, a free press, an advancing civilization, and an unshackled universal commerce are marks of that providence. This is the current state of the world and the sign of God's *kairos* that the time for the world's conversion is come.

I suggested earlier in relation to Carey's view of the effects of the French Revolution as answered prayer that other contemporary Christians might have viewed those developments in a different light. The inescapable feature of Anderson is boundless optimism. Political, economic, ecclesiastical, and spiritual developments are being ordered by God's providence for the consummation of the ages. It is, one might say—and I say it without the slightest hint of pejorative reference—a very American view, though the eschatology it employs is that of conventional Protestant orthodoxy on both sides of the Atlantic at the time. But new movements were stirring, especially among those who took a less optimistic view of the signs of the time.

In America, Anderson could look out on a religious development that was buoyant, a church that was advancing with the frontier and busying itself with societies for advancing mission at home or abroad, and in improvement of society, disinterested benevolence, at home and abroad. In Europe, many earnest churchmen looked with dismay on political unrest, social upheaval, riots that burst out or were barely contained, revolutionary movements that overthrew thrones and governments. While Anderson could rejoice in liberty and free press, they could see only too many dangers in liberty, and thought press censorship necessary. Liberty? Surely that had been the watchword of the revolutionaries in France. Anderson might rejoice that the weakness of the Ottoman Empire bound the false prophet, but the weakness of the Ottoman Empire was allowing Russia to expand its power and threaten British interests in India and the Mediterranean. In all these ways, things seemed to be getting worse.

In the sphere of religion over the last fifty years that Anderson was speaking of, certainly there had been improvements. No longer were evangelicals a scorned, derided group dismissed as enthusiasts. By 1830, evangelicalism had become almost the new orthodoxy, not that evangelicals predominated in the population or even in the upper classes, but evangelical values were being acknowledged and respected. It was no longer thought acceptable for people in public life to parade their immorality or their irreligion. But with success had come decline. With power had come the possibility of abusing power. By the 1840s, we reach perhaps the high point of evangelical influence in British public life, with evangelical bishops, even an evangelical archbishop of Canterbury (John Bird Sumner), influencing government. But many radical evangelicals were becoming disillusioned with the church. The church was being corrupted by the world. A reformation was needed.

Primitive Precedent and the Eschatology of Hurry

Reformation took surprising and diverse forms. One was the so-called Oxford movement in the Church of England, seeking to purify the church on the model of the patristic age. One must remember that John Henry Newman, the future cardinal, had begun as an evangelical and was the Oxford secretary of the Church Missionary Society. Most of the leaders of the Oxford movement were disillusioned evangelicals.

Another movement at the same time had led to secession, several movements of that kind indeed; they were attempts to rebuild the church on the model of the New Testament directly. An Irish clergyman, John Nelson Darby, produced a rereading of the Scriptures that he believed to reflect that New Testament model. He and his followers called themselves Brethren; popularly they became known as Plymouth Brethren. Darby insisted that an important feature of the early church was the expectation of the imminent return of the Lord, and he produced a developed scheme to harmonize all the prophecies and replace the accepted eschatology that we have seen in Wesley and Edwards and Carey and Anderson. The historicist interpretation of Revelation was replaced. Revelation is a book not about history but about future events. And hope lies not in the evidence of the approach of a converted world through a renewed church; what Darby saw was an increasingly evil world and an increasingly corrupt church. Hope lay in the return of the Lord. The study of prophecy could help us discern the signs of the times and put the events there foretold in order.

The premillennial interpretation of prophecy took hold among many evangelicals who shared Darby's pessimism about the world, though they did not share necessarily his secessionist instincts. Alexander Keith (1792–1880), for instance, a Scottish Presbyterian minister, began to stress that Old Testament prophecies must be literally fulfilled. This meant giving a significance to the Jews and to the return of the Jews to Palestine that the subject had never had before. This stirred new interest in the Jewish people and in Palestine and prompted, in 1839, the appointment by the Church of Scotland of a Mission of Inquiry to the Jews, which moved through the Middle East and through eastern and central Europe meeting Jewish communities, talking with them, seeking particularly what their messianic interpretations were, meeting universally with the view that since the exile had been literal, the return from exile must be equally literal. Since the dispersion was literal, so must the restoration be literal.

Keith's mission was taken in the company of two young ministers, Andrew A. Bonar and Robert Murray McCheyne. Both were to become influential, though McCheyne died within a few years of the return from the mission. The one concrete outcome of the mission was the establishment in 1841 of a mission to the Jews of Budapest, which is a story in itself.[9] But by this time, many evangelical groups were turning to Jewish mission as the key to all other missions. Jewish missions, they felt, should have priority.

Even the great Anglican evangelical Charles Simeon, who had been one of the founders of the Church Missionary Society, in later years turned away from the society. He came to believe that the most beneficial use of mission time and effort was in the London Society for the Conversion of the Jews. By the middle of the century, about a third of the income donated from Anglican sources for Christian missions in Britain was donated for the purpose of Jewish missions.[10] This seems to have been the case especially among Calvinistic evangelicals in the established churches. The best-known evangelical figure in Britain at the time was Anthony Ashley Cooper, seventh Earl of Shaftesbury and factory reformer, and he was devoted to the cause of Jewish missions.

---

9. Ábrahám Kovács, *The History of the Free Church of Scotland's Mission to the Jews in Budapest and Its Impact on the Reformed Church of Hungary, 1841–1914*, Studies in the Intercultural History of Christianity 140 (Frankfurt am Main: Lang, 2006).

10. Donald M. Lewis, *The Origins of Christian Zionism: Lord Shaftesbury and Evangelical Support for a Jewish Homeland* (Cambridge: Cambridge University Press, 2010), 119.

Anderson's eschatology had led to expectation of an end time of gospel prosperity. The new premillennialists were looking directly for the return of the Lord. This also became a powerful incentive to mission, as the earlier eschatology had been, but its tendency was to a different type of mission. Earlier missions saw themselves in a providential stream of events that would renew the earth. Missions were few, the work hard; converts came slowly. No matter; the foundation was being laid for the future great blessing that the fullness of time would bring.

Henry Brunton (1775-1813), Scottish missionary to Sierra Leone and later the Caucasus, argued that history shows that the revival of religion invariably follows the revival of learning, so that missions should lay a deep foundation of education and Christian teaching.[11] In later generations, this would yield vast fruit. This is how the Reformation had operated across Europe, in Scotland in particular; this is what had happened in recent generations in the Scottish Highlands. Missionaries, in fact, were there for the long haul. The new eschatology introduced an element of hurry, the presentation of the gospel as a matter of urgency—that is, the acceptance of the gospel before the Lord comes.

This new urgency was shortly to find expression in what became known as the Watchword, originally coined by the English Baptist minister Joseph Angus but popularized by the very orthodox Presbyterian Arthur Tappan Pierson, "the evangelization of the world in this generation."[12] Despite being possessed of the same sort of background as Anderson and the people of the American Board, Pierson is the product of new conditions in America and of a premillennial eschatology. Though he cannot be discussed further at this point, he goes on to become one of the formative influences in the missionary movement of the second half of the century.

11. There is a brief article on Brunton by P. E. H. Hair in *The Blackwell Dictionary of Evangelical Biography*, ed. Donald M. Lewis, 2 vols. (Oxford: Blackwell, 1995), 1:157.

12. Dana L. Robert, *Occupy Until I Come: A. T. Pierson and the Evangelization of the World* (Grand Rapids: Eerdmans, 2003), 68, 151.

CHAPTER 6

Jerusalem and Antioch

Western Missions and Non-Western Churches

We are considering how the Protestant missionary movement progressed from infancy toward middle age, and in the previous chapter considered the theme of eschatology and missions, using the occasion to introduce a particularly influential figure in the development of missionary thought in the quintessentially American person of Rufus Anderson. He enabled us incidentally to look at some developments of the movement that were also quintessentially American, and he introduced us to one of the prerequisites of Western mission to the non-Western world, a form of organization that he saw as the key to the world's conversion. It was, of course, the voluntary society. This, we noted, had important implications for the doctrine of the church. So in this chapter, we look to the question of ecclesiology and missions, and, as our leading figure this time, to take a quintessentially English figure as our starting point: Henry Venn.

Henry Venn of the Church Missionary Society

Henry Venn was born in 1796, the same year as Anderson. He had a conventional early career: Queens' College, Cambridge, which was then the college most favored by evangelicals. He became a fellow there, that is, a tutor and member of the governing body. One should remember that Oxford and Cambridge were at this time the only universities in England (my own city of Aberdeen delights in the fact that for several hundred years, we had the same number of universities as the whole of England, because we had two). There were no theological seminaries. The ministry was trained. No, it was not trained; the ministry *went* to the universities. There was no formal ministerial training there, but typically from the universities, bishops recruited their candidates for ordination. What tutor a student was assigned could determine what sort of preparation he would have for ministry. The universities were thus part of the church establishment. This remained so till the later nineteenth century. Part of the secularization of Britain was the removal of the universities from their church structure. One of the odd hangovers from the pre-Reformation period was that fellows of Oxford and Cambridge colleges had to be celibate, so that Henry Venn, like many other fellows, resigned his fellowship when he wanted to get married. As was usual in this position, he became a parish clergyman for some years.

In 1840, Venn's wife died, and the following year, he became one of the secretaries of the Church Missionary Society. He took it as a part-time and temporary position. In addition, it was unsalaried. Venn had a small stipend from a cathedral appointment in London. In the event, the Church Missionary Society post became full-time and so nontemporary that he stayed there for more than thirty years, until 1872, a year before his death. His period of office thus runs closely parallel to Anderson's. Like Anderson, he was the dominant figure in his own society during his incumbency, and again, like Anderson, the most influential figure in the missionary thought of his country at his period. Also like Anderson, he was never a missionary himself. Unlike Anderson, he never even visited any of the mission fields.

Henry Venn was the son of John Venn (1759–1813), who had been one of the founders of the Church Missionary Society for Africa and the East and had been its first chairman. John Venn was at the time of Henry's birth rector of Clapham, and thus the parish minister for Wilberforce and the other members of the group of local evangelicals later called the Clapham Sect, comprising members of Parliament and others who were undertaking the anti–slave trade campaign in Parliament and in the country as a whole. The Venn rectory in Clapham was home to a whole company of African children who had come from Sierra Leone for education in England. Henry Venn thus grew up in the atmosphere of missions and antislavery, and with an awareness of Africa—of Sierra Leone in particular—and with a certain acquaintance with Africans, rather more than most of his kindred would have had at this time. He had grown up with them.

The Church Missionary Society had been founded in 1799 by a group of Anglican evangelicals. There were at least four missionary societies in existence in England already, and two of them were Anglican. Why was it necessary to have another? As recorded in chapter 3, one of the Anglican societies, the Society for the Propagation of the Gospel in Foreign Parts, had been founded a century earlier in 1701 with the American colonies in mind, founded by High Churchmen anxious about the spiritual condition and pastoral care of English settlers in the Americas and the Caribbean. In principle, it was missionary; it was concerned with both Native Americans and Africans in America. In practice, most of its work was directed to people of British origin, with the concern to preserve them from Presbyterianism and vice. It was an official arm of the Church of England, governed by a royal charter and overseen by the archbishop of Canterbury and the bishops. There were no evangelical bishops at this time, and the episcopate, speaking generally, was out of sympathy with evangelicals. The Society for Promoting Christian Knowledge founded in 1698 of High Church origin, had its missionary activities confined to supporting the Tranquebar mission in India, the mission staffed by graduates of the Pietist university at Halle in Germany.

The remaining societies were the Particular (meaning Calvinistic) Baptist Missionary Society, arising principally from Carey's initiative and clearly out of the question for Anglicans, and the London Missionary Society, as it was beginning now to be called. Its proper name was simply "the Missionary Society," founded four years earlier in 1795 as a nondenominational agency, an umbrella for everybody, with the fundamental principle that its purpose was to convey the gospel, and no special form of church government. Church government was to be left to the decision of the churches that would arise from missionary effort. There were some Anglicans who were prepared to work with the London Society on this basis, but for the majority of Anglican evangelicals, it was unacceptable. The reason lay in an earlier phase of the Evangelical Revival.

The outstanding early Anglican leaders of the movement, John Wesley and George Whitefield, sat very lightly to the discipline of the Church of England, of which they were ministers. The Church of England depended on the parish system; the whole country was divided into parishes with strict geographical boundaries, and clergy were appointed with an exclusive privilege to minister in a particular parish. Wesley and Whitefield did not respect this rule, being quite willing to preach in other people's parishes if they believed that the gospel was not otherwise preached there. Wesley in particular constantly breached Anglican discipline, even ordaining clergy, which in Anglican practice is reserved for bishops. In 1784, he appointed Thomas Coke as superintendent for his work in America with a rite that looked suspiciously like that of consecrating a bishop. As a result, although Wesley always claimed to be fully loyal to the Church of England and never wanted anyone to leave it, Methodists were generally, within the church, thought of as troublemakers—and all evangelicals were under suspicion as being Methodists and were frequently called Methodists.

This had political as well as religious significance. The Church of England was established by law. In principle, everyone born in England was a member of it. A threat to the church was thus a threat to the national constitution. Dissenters from the church (like Carey's Baptists, for example, as we have seen) often held radical political views; and Methodists were often, usually wrongly, thought to be of the same tendency. Wesley's Methodists were half in and half out of the Church of England. Evangelical parish clergy, threatened by this, closed ranks and decided to remain firmly within, accepting Anglican discipline fully, scrupulously respecting the parish system, doing nothing contrary to church law. One of the leading figures in the movement had been Venn's grandfather, also called Henry Venn (1725–1797), vicar of Huddersfield.

It was this history that prevented the adherence of most Evangelical Anglicans to a society like the London Society, which would not accept the imposition of Anglican formularies or episcopal government. Anglican evangelicals were in a cleft stick when it came to missions. They could not work in the Society for the Propagation of the Gospel in Foreign Parts, because it was not committed to the gospel as evangelicals understood the gospel. Nor could they support the London Missionary Society, because it was not committed to the church as Anglicans understood the church. Their only recourse was to start their own society.

The Ambiguities of Being an Anglican Voluntary Society

Henry Venn inherited the dual allegiance to the evangelical gospel and the Anglican formularies and structure. But the Church Missionary Society was a voluntary society, not supervised by bishops, directed by its own elected committee, a church society that was absolutely independent of the church. Venn vigorously guarded the independence of his society, which led to all sorts of ambiguities in his position. For instance, in Anglican theory, clergy are under the pastoral care and superintendence of a bishop. They are unable to function without that bishop's license. But there were areas in India and New Zealand, for instance, where the bishop claimed the right to move missionaries in the best interests of his diocese, that is, the best interests of the church. Venn objected to this abuse, as he believed it, of episcopal authority, and he justified his resistance to bishops on a rather strange legal ground. In the Church of England, a system obtains whereby the appointment of clergy to a parish is the responsibility of a patron. The patron at this time was usually lay, often the local landowner. Venn argued that the Church Missionary

Society was in the position of a lay patron. The bishop could not, therefore, move its clergy without the patron's consent. From the bishop's point of view, this was a most un-Anglican proceeding.

This all reflects the ecclesiological inconvenience of the voluntary society. A missionary society of its nature sought to bring a church into being, and yet there was no place for it in any of the classical doctrines of the church or in the working theology of any denomination.

Venn wrote no systematic exposition of these views. Most of his writings were produced as in-house memoranda for the Church Missionary Society or for the society's periodicals. This was a mode that more than any other he developed to a high degree. When missionaries went to the field, whether as new recruits or after leave, there was a public valedictory service. Venn or some other official of the society would give a charge to the departing missionaries, technically called "instructions." A small part of this would be directed to each missionary individually. The greater part was a sort of missiological essay directed to the group as a whole and clearly aimed also at a wider audience, a sort of policy-setting document. The document "On Nationality," dating from 1868, is such instructions.[1]

The Idea of a National Church

These instructions begin with a reference to the Great Commission of Matthew 28, but the well-known words are given a direction that one suspects would have surprised some of its hearers. In the King James Version, the words of the Lord read, "Go ye, therefore, and teach all nations." But "teach all nations," Venn points out, is actually "disciple all nations." The missionary task is not to take some disciples from each nation, to take disciples out of the nations; the missionary task is to disciple the nations. It is to move a whole nation gradually toward the point where it adopts Christianity as its national profession of faith. That was, of course, the position in Britain, from which Venn was writing as a minister of the established church. Christianity was the national profession of faith; the Church of England was, and still is, by law established in England. There is, let me insist, no established church of Britain. There are established churches of England and of Scotland, the latter, of course, being Presbyterian rather than Anglican. The implications of this in colonial times are immense, the assumption that there is an established

1. Henry Venn, "On Nationality," in William Knight, *Memoir of Henry Venn: The Missionary Secretariat of Henry Venn, B.D.* (London: Longmans, Green, & Company, 1880), 282–92.

church of Britain—until somebody in the Church of Scotland notices that it has happened and a question is raised in Parliament. That need not, however, trouble us now.

The purpose of mission is to produce the same situation that you have in Britain: a national profession of Christianity—which, of course, does not mean that every single person is converted but that the nation professes the Christian faith and would be guided by it. There were established Protestant churches at the time in most north European countries. Venn expects the same development as a result of mission activity. At least this should be the goal of mission activity: gradually move the whole nation to a profession of Christian faith.

Notice the "gradually"; he uses that word (Venn, "Nationality," 282). Venn belongs to the older school that expects missions to be slow, laborious, and is prepared to wait for generations for results, not of the later "let's race to do it quickly" outlook that we saw in the previous chapter emerging from trends coming up later in the century. Venn belongs to this time before the "hurry to complete the task," before the motivation of completing evangelization before the coming of Christ, and without the rhetoric of numberless souls passing into a Christless eternity—which is something you do not hear among early nineteenth-century writers, coming from this providentialist view of God as having taken a long time to bring us to this point, and looking out on a world in which missions are few and often struggling and in which most people have not yet heard the gospel.

Venn's framework, like Anderson's, is this long, providential course of history. But in his case, unlike Anderson's, it issues in national churches. Anderson is a Congregationalist who is thinking of churches called out from the society; Venn is an establishment Anglican thinking of nations that make a profession. It may strike us as fanciful: a national church of India, a national church of Yorubaland. Perhaps we should notice in passing that today the term "national church" is used in a sense that Venn would not have recognized. When we talk about "the national church" now, it is usually over against the foreign mission society. Venn's language for that was "native church," and in his instructions, you will see the term "native" church meaning what nowadays people usually mean by national. I suspect our current usage came in in the post–Second World War era as what had once been colonies became nations and the word "native" became pejorative.

The national church? The whole of Europe was organized, we have seen, with national churches. The United States was different, but that was outside Venn's immediate consciousness. Even in the United States in certain parts of the country, especially New England, there was something like a national church in his sense. In other parts of the world, national churches had certainly appeared by this date. Samoa, Tahiti, and Tonga—small states but states nonetheless—had declared themselves Christian. Congregational missionaries serving the London Missionary Society in the Pacific Islands had by this time stopped adding names to the church membership roll on the ground that Christianity was now the national profession. Everybody wanted to be on. These good Congregationalists, used to defining their identity as Dissenters from the Church of England, had no way of coping with this.

Methodist missionaries in Tonga had been embarrassed when called upon to advise the king on a written constitution for the nation. Tonga was now to be a Christian nation, and it wanted a Christian constitution. In other parts of the world, though there was no thought yet of a nation, the whole community could be described as broadly Christian: Jamaica, some other Caribbean islands, and, above all, Sierra Leone, that child of the antislavery movement, where for decades people had been taken off intercepted slave ships and brought under Christian teaching, where the literacy rate and proportion of people at school was higher than in most European countries, where church attendance was far higher than it was in England, and where the colonial government had occasion to step in to prevent the mosques of the Muslim minority from being burned by overzealous Christians.

When in 1868 Venn wrote "On Nationality," there were missionaries from Sierra Leone with a Sierra Leonean bishop (Samuel Adjai Crowther) at their head working in what is now Nigeria on the staff of his own society. And then, Sierra Leone had its own national Anglican church, self-governing. The colony of Lagos had another self-governing Anglican church. National churches, something that Venn can reasonably view as being the missionary norm, had already begun to happen.

Venn's vision of national churches was a reflection of that vision of a converted world that was inspiring Anderson and arose from the providentialist eschatology of the time. A converted world, of course, does not mean that every individual in it is regenerate in the evangelical sense, but that Christian influence in society is dominant; the knowledge of God is covering the land as the waters cover the sea. It is not to be expected that all these national churches will appear at once. Venn points to the differing rates of response in different fields of the one society, and even within the same field. In India, more Hindus are converted than are Muslims, and far more tribal people than of either. Note that Venn thinks of these groups—Hindu, Muslim, and tribal—as different nations, where national churches will appear at different times.

The nineteenth-century mission secretary who receives the correspondence and who goes about the country hearing what people say at missionary meetings indicates that people in the pew are often disappointed at the slow progress of mission statistically. Why are so few communicant members noted in the statistics? They have been expecting a much quicker response than they are seeing in so many fields, but the secretary points out that something else is being noticed in Europe. Few things have been more striking than the surprise that has been excited by the changes taking place in the public mind of India and the undercurrents of thought that are continually arising in native publications. The Indian press is being quoted in *The Times*; it is being noticed in England. People are reading in the heavy quarterlies about what Indian intellectuals are saying. What the mission secretary presumably has in mind are the reform movements in India, especially the Brahmo Samaj, led by important intellectuals deeply influenced by Christian teaching. The great exemplar of this movement, Ram Mohan Roy, had by this time been dead for many years, but his followers were maintaining his campaign against idolatry, against abuses of caste, in favor of women's rights. It was this sort of change in Indian opinion rather than clamor in Britain or missionary intervention that had made the abolition of sati possible.

Furthermore, there were now Indian Christian intellectuals, such as Krishna Mohan Banerjea (also spelled Banerji and Banerjee), who were publicly arguing the Christian case from the Vedas, saying that the Vedas foretold the incarnation and atonement of Christ, that no Brahmin should feel ashamed of becoming a Christian when his own Scriptures pointed to Christ. There were what Venn called "intelligent observers" of the progress of missions who were fixing their hopes upon the approach to Christian truth by the educated natives rather than simply on the accession of individual converts.

Venn's paper "On Nationality" was a strong evangelical piece of writing. It sets out the case that the work of mission is not simply the gathering of individual converts. In this long-haul providential view of the missionary task, the effect of missions is not to be measured only statistically; part of the work of mission is to alter the climate of thinking of nations. It is to plant ideas that will take root and grow and affect national life over the course of generations.

Will India ever make Christianity its national profession? Estimating from the trend of his arguments, Venn's answer might well be, give it time, and work not just to pick up individual converts but to change the climate of thought in a Christian direction.

The rest of Venn's memorandum is a meditation on the Christian significance of nationality. He turns to the missionaries in front of him and begs them to "study the national character of the people among whom you labour, and show the utmost respect for national peculiarities" (Venn, "National-ity," 283). The language seems odd to us now. Venn is, of course, talking about what we would call culture. In 1868, that word was not yet used in the sense that we take for granted today. Were Venn writing today, I suspect he would have used a phrase like "cultural identity," whereas in 1868, the natural word to use was "nationality."

Venn points to the fact that the British in his day were seen in continental Europe as notoriously culturally insensitive (Venn, "Nationality," 284). Their refusal to use anyone else's language, their insistence on having things just as they were at home, made them a byword as tourists in Europe. If that is the way we behave when on holiday, how much more mischief is this attitude going to do in a missionary setting, especially among people who are in any case downtrodden and bullied, as so many missionized groups were. He is probably thinking of those we now term the Dalit peoples in India. Cultural sensitivity, cultural study: these are to become second nature to the mission-ary. It will not come easily; it has to be built up as a habit. Practice it, and your assessment of the local church will alter. We should not make judgments on the basis of what church life is like at home. Venn makes an interesting point here; throughout the ages, Christian reformers have sought to go back to the model of the New Testament church. Venn says the standard of Christian life in the apostolic church was in fact far lower than what we have come to expect in our churches today. We have had in Britain a thousand years in a favored vineyard under the hand of the great Vinedresser and his shears. But when all the errors, all the imperfections, have dropped away, Venn still expects cultural differences between national churches to remain, and far from these being a blemish, they will be to the churches' perfection and glory.

The next warning to missionaries is about factors that affect the relation between the missionary and the local church and the part that national, in-deed racial, identity plays in this. First, it is necessary to acknowledge that these differences are there, and here he quotes the Roman poet Horace: "You may expel nature for a time by force, but it will surely return" (Venn, "Nation-ality," 284–85; citing Horace, *Epistles* 1.10.24). The differences may be hidden for a time by the warmth of Christian fellowship, but then they will burst out embarrassingly at some conference or other when you least expect them. What is more, the intensity of conflict will rise as the mission progresses. You will notice it less in the early days than later on. It will rise as converts become more assured, more capable of expressing themselves; it will become more intense when they can rival the missionary in the power of argument, rival the missionary in the pulpit or on the platform. The temptation for the mis-sionary will be to complain of presumption and ingratitude, or, as Venn puts it, to stand on his British prestige. There are New Testament models of the proper behavior in these instances. But expect this to happen, and develop a church policy that reduces the number of occasions where it can interfere.

Venn's next point is about congregational structure. The Church Missionary Society was bound, as we have seen, by Anglican formularies. This stout Anglican argues that national (or as we would say, cultural) factors should be taken into account in forming a congregation. Let a native church be organized as a national institution using local patterns of consultation. He gives an Indian example, the *panchayat*, or village council of elders. Let every congregation have a *panchayat*, a consultative mechanism, where people can develop their own means of organizing and supporting the church. Now, this is interesting, because there was no *panchayat* or anything like it in most of the congregations of the Church of England. Anderson as a Congregationalist was used to a congregation electing its leaders, the elders and deacons, and calling its pastor, but it would be very hard to find a parallel to anything like this in most English parishes. Venn is stretching Anglican structures and mental horizons to the limit. Train up the native church to self-dependence, to self-government, from the very first stage of the Christian movement, he says (Venn, "Nationality," 285).

The Three-Self Principle

By this time, the principle of the three selves—that the aim of a mission should be to produce self-governing, self-supporting, and self-propagating churches—was well established in Venn's thinking and in the official policy of the Church Missionary Society. It had originated in Venn's mind from his meeting with a Sierra Leonean Anglican in London. The man was a wealthy Freetown merchant, part of the new Freetown middle class, traveling to Britain on holiday. Venn was astonished that such a thing was possible. "If you can spend so much money on your travels," he said, "you ought surely to be able to do more towards the support of your own clergymen in Sierra Leone." The merchant's answer was, "Of course we could, Mr. Venn; but so long as you treat us like children we shall behave like children. Treat us like men and we will behave like men."[2] From that point, Venn sought to produce national self-governing, self-supporting churches on the mission field.

He had to do this, of course, within Anglican structures. With a little ingenuity, he devised these two national church structures that I have mentioned

---

2. Knight, *Memoir of Henry Venn*, 546.

for Sierra Leone and for Lagos, but he recognized their incompleteness. Anglican structures depended on episcopacy. For forty years, the society's African missions had no bishop, which meant no African clergy could be ordained unless they were sent to England. From the early 1840s, provision was made for a bishop in Sierra Leone, but the bishop was a missionary. Venn was determined on the indigenization of the episcopacy. He knew whom he wanted as the first African bishop. Samuel Crowther, born Adjai in Yorubaland, had been captured as a slave as a boy of thirteen. The ship taking him to America had been intercepted, and he had been taken to Freetown, where he had been converted and baptized, had become a teacher/catechist for the Church Missionary Society, and had become an outstanding preacher, not least in his native language, Yoruba. He had received the highest education that the colony could give and had taken part in the exploratory mission to the Niger commissioned by the British government in 1841. His contribution to the expedition itself and to the development of subsequent mission policy had been such that he had been brought to England for further education and for ordination. He returned to become a missionary in his own homeland and was a significant presence there, playing a crucial part in the translation of the Bible into Yoruba and opening up new missionary opportunities. He was a person of great ability, great experience, and solid character. There was one fatal objection: several European missionaries operating in the field were senior to him, and none was willing to serve *under* him.

Venn was forced to follow another expedient: the creation of a new Diocese of the Niger Territories Outside the Queen's Dominions (wonderful title!) and secured Crowther's appointment to that. Here he had an entirely African missionary staff, mostly from Sierra Leone, some from Yorubaland. This was as far as Venn ever got in indigenizing of the episcopate. When Crowther died in 1891, nearly twenty years after Venn, he was succeeded by a European, J. S. Hill. While there were various assistant bishops, there was no African diocesan bishop until after the Second World War.

To return to the document, Venn makes a point that he had made many times before in arguing for the three-self formula. A missionary should never become a pastor; he does not have the knowledge, he does not have the capacity, and he will stifle initiatives and produce dependence in the congregation. The missionary—and here comes the most controversial part of Venn's argument—is external to the church. The most important duty of the missionary is the training of pastors and evangelists, especially in the Bible. Missionaries may also be evangelists where there is no organized church. In that case, however, the missionary and the missionary's African colleagues are not part of the church; they are part of the society.

Venn was a mission theorist, but his theories had to be enunciated within what was practicable in his own particular situation, not in the theologically ideal situation. Venn's goal is the national church rooted in the soil; the missionary task is the euthanasia of the mission, all this with the object of enabling the emergence of national churches. National churches, he goes on to say, will have another feature: they will supersede denominational distinctions. These distinctions have been introduced from abroad. Respect cultural identity, and denominational differences will be subsumed. Churches of different denominations will grow more like each other, because they will be sharing the common features that come from their nationality. Therefore, be open to other denominations and even, as he puts it, to the irregular efforts of unattached evangelists. They are all moving in the same direction.

But what about the Church Missionary Society commitment to Anglican structures and formularies? Is not what Venn is arguing a very un-Anglican position? Not at all, he replies. It is the Reformation position, enshrined in the English Book of Common Prayer and in the Thirty-Nine Articles of the Church of England. The Reformers recognized that different styles of church order were appropriate to different nations. It was for the nation to determine what style of church order was appropriate for it. Lutheran in much of Germany and Scandinavia, Calvinist in Switzerland and part of Germany and Scotland, Anglican in England—these were all national reformed churches, sisters in the faith. That is why an Anglican society like the Church Missionary Society, like the Society for Promoting Christian Knowledge before it, had been able to recruit Lutheran missionaries from Germany in their dozens. They belonged to a sister national church. The national postdenominational churches of India and Africa and China would, like them, be sisters, daughters of the Reformation.

This, then, is Henry Venn's vision. His contemporary, Rufus Anderson, uses the same language of the three-self churches, but there is a note in Anderson that I do not detect in Venn. Anderson favors removing institutional works as far as possible, as encumbrances to the native church. Anderson, like the London Missionary Society in Britain, sought to settle the ecumenical question in another way, by passing the issue of church government to the church that would in the future arise from missionary preaching. Venn's approach is different; he is thinking of church and nation together, as an establishment Anglican does. He has that phrase in the document, "Let every member feel himself doubly bound to his country by his social as well as his religious society."[3] Your church membership is going to increase your sense of nationality, or at least confirm it.

---

3. Venn, "Nationality," 285.

Mission societies did what churches had formerly done: they appointed missionaries, who were usually ministers, provided their salaries and allowances, exercised oversight and discipline over them, and to a large extent directed their work. But these societies were outside the church, and they were not subject to the authorities of the church. Missions became an anomaly as regards traditional church order in the West. But equally they created other anomalies in church order as new churches came into being on the mission field. On the field, mission societies were acting, often, as an upper tier of management for a native church, though they themselves were neither a church nor part of a church structure.

A self-governing church needs principles of church order. A self-supporting church needs an economic basis. It needs an educated leadership. Thus we find Venn active in pioneering the growing of cotton in what is now Nigeria. The first purpose of this was to provide an alternative source of income to the slave trade for the Yoruba state of Abeokuta, where the society was working. But this involved ensuring that the cotton could be exported, so Venn made arrangements with a Manchester merchant that he met at a missionary meeting to take Nigerian cotton. It had to be processed, so Venn persuaded one of his major donors to invest in a cotton processing plant for Africa. The machinery needed servicing, so two young men were recruited in Sierra Leone and trained in Wales, and then went to Abeokuta as missionary technicians. Abeokuta cotton had a mini boom when the American Civil War closed down Southern cotton for Manchester. The time was to come when evangelicals would question whether missions had anything to do with growing and selling cotton or cleaning machinery. The questions that Venn posed are still with us.

CHAPTER 7

"Made of One Blood"

Race, Culture, and Society in Western Mission Thinking

In the previous chapter, we considered some developments in the ecclesiology of the missionary movement during the period that it was reaching middle age. We noted that the encounter with the newer churches of the non-Western world were causing missionary thought to burst the old bounds of Western theology and church order. We also noted a new factor being considered, what in the 1860s Henry Venn was calling "nationality" but which we would probably call "culture." And we saw the growth of the assumption that the new churches would be self-governing, self-supporting, self-propagating, and different.

Race, Culture, and Civilization

Here, we approach the issue of culture in a different form and in the context of race. The early Protestant missionary movement had a very simple theology of race; it was based on the declaration in Acts that God has made of one blood all nations of the earth. All humanity was one in terms of its sin and in terms of God's grace toward it. Evangelical preaching was the same everywhere. The spiritual position of an unconverted Englishman, though he be a peer of the realm, was the same as that of a Hindu or an African idolater. Only with liberal theology late in the nineteenth century does race become an issue for theology, as ideas of supposedly "scientific" racism enter into Christian thinking.

Culture is a different matter. In the period we have been considering, the word was not used in the sense that we use it today. As we have seen, Venn used the word "nationality." But the word that people earlier in the nineteenth century used most readily in this area was "civilization," a word

TOWARD MIDDLE AGE

that for them had several layers of meaning. At the back of it lies the European experience of the Roman Empire. In many ways, the old division of the world to which the apostle Paul bears witness, the division between Greeks and barbarians (that is, between "civilized" people who share a common discourse, and people outside that discourse who do not know the language, whose language is "barbar" and who are, therefore, "barbarians"), continued to underlie European thought. The old Roman division was adopted by my ancestors in northern and western Europe whom the Romans had thought of as barbarians. There is thus a historical element in the idea of civilization.

It is a compound of ideas and practices, a body of literature, a heritage of Greek philosophy, of Roman law, and—this is important—of Christian teaching. Europeans, and for that matter, Americans, too, saw themselves as the heirs of the Roman Empire but of the Roman Empire converted. Civilization was thus a heritage of art, of literature, of philosophy, of law, all suffused by Christian faith. Civilization was not a static acquisition; it needed cultivation, a sort of intellectual digging and manuring. So we find Thomas Fowell Buxton, the central figure in this chapter, denouncing the white planters of Jamaica as barbarians and insisting that the former slaves in Jamaica are the civilized inhabitants of that country.

There was also a technological element to civilization. It included anything that improved life, as at this time life was being improved by better drainage, better water supply, improved agriculture, and the manufactured goods that saved labor.

In the text that we are looking at in this chapter, Thomas Fowell Buxton's *The African Slave Trade and Its Remedy*,[1] civilization sometimes means something close to what today we would call development. It was a commonplace of Western Christian thought that civilization was closely associated with Christianity. Many, indeed, in Europe would use the terms interchangeably. Evangelicals, the backbone of the missionary movement, could not do that, but most of them did believe that the two were associated and that preaching the gospel would produce civilization. They also believed that since God has made all of one blood, and all humanity are alike in sin and covered by the same redemption, all humanity had the capacity for civilization. Just as people of all races might fully display all the gifts of the Spirit and all the graces of Christian character, so all humanity had the capacity to display the full height of human attainment—that is, the full range of civilization.

1. Thomas Fowell Buxton, *The African Slave Trade and Its Remedy*, 2nd ed. (London: Murray, 1840). The first edition was two separate pamphlets, the second of which, *The Remedy: Being a Sequel to the African Slave Trade*, was republished by Cambridge University Press in 2010, with a digital version available from 2012 (https://doi.org/10.1017/CBO9780511783920).—Ed.

In the first half of the nineteenth century, there was a degree of confusion and heated debate about the status of the ancient civilizations of China and Japan and India. The most immediate issue related to civilization, however, was with regard to Africans. So in this chapter, we turn to mission developments in Africa, but first we need to return to the theme of the great European migration, which wielded so much influence on the early years of the Western missionary movement.

The Khoi of the Cape Colony

The great migration that began in the last years of the sixteenth century reached southern Africa in a significant form in 1652, when the Dutch took over from the Portuguese the Cape of Good Hope in order to service their ships going further east. The people living in the Cape were a hunter-gatherer people known as the Khoi.[2] Under the Dutch East India Company, surplus population from Holland and other parts of Europe was brought in to populate the land. They settled on land that the Khoi had formerly ranged over, farming it with the aid of slaves brought in from Southeast Asia, from India, and from Madagascar; they took many of the Khoi to work for them also. The Khoi moved to the fringes of European life, where they were frequently exploited and generally despised. They were denominated as "the heathen," over against the children of Christendom, the European settlers.

The first mission to the Khoi was instituted by the Moravian Brethren in 1737. George Schmidt worked for six years in what the settlers took to be a useless enterprise, believing as they did that the Khoi were beyond reach of civilization or the gospel. He set up a school, and Khoi learned to read. He planted a garden, and the hunter-gatherer Khoi began to grow crops. He started a church, and Khoi began to attend worship. That is, the Khoi began to cross the barrier into things that whites did, things that no one could despise them for doing. This uprooted, downtrodden people began to acquire a certain dignity.

It was in the interests of the settler community, however, to keep them degraded, and Schmidt's work became more and more difficult. By 1743, he judged it was intolerable, and he left. His congregation lingered on, and when the mission resumed fifty years later, they found one old woman still conducting Bible readings under the pear tree that Schmidt had planted in his garden. The Khoi now entered on a time of misery. They were decimated by smallpox and other diseases from Europe. They were more and more squeezed off the

2. Now more often referred to as the Khoikhoi.—Ed.

land, and when they sought to move back onto it, they were treated as vermin and hunted down.

During the Napoleonic War, the British seized the Cape for its strategic value, and from 1806, the arrangement was made permanent. The British thus inherited the problem that the Cape settlers were facing. As their settlement spread, they came into more and more contact, and more and more conflict, with the Black Xhosa people to the east. They were competitors with them for the same land, and both Black and white were subsistence farmers and cattle raisers. The British sought to stabilize the frontier, but the Xhosa never accepted a frontier across what they saw as their land and their cattle grounds that the white settlers had invaded. Nor did the settlers respect these boundaries. They moved steadily beyond the frontiers that the British thought they had established and moved into Xhosa territory.

It is against this background that a new chapter of Christian missions opens. The Moravians reopened their work in 1792, the very same year that the Black settlers from Nova Scotia established the renewed colony in Sierra Leone as a Christian settlement. They went to Schmidt's old center, found the old lady under the pear tree, and started other work, too, with the Khoi. All the settlements were highly organized, communities of the Moravian style with rigorous discipline and with marked emphasis on agricultural development.

Johannes van der Kemp and the London Missionary Society at the Cape

Some years later, in 1799, the London Missionary Society, the first sign of British Christian interest, started its own work. Its first missionary was a Dutchman, Johannes van der Kemp, who was in every respect a most unusual missionary. For one thing, he was already fifty years old when he started. For another, he was both a learned man and a published author of scholarly distinction, and he had been a professional soldier as well. For yet another, he had been a sinner on a quite spectacular scale. If you look at the papers of the London Missionary Society where people give account of their conversion and of their period of mourning, the most common sin of which they are convicted is misimproving their talents—in other words, wasting time in youthful trifling pursuits. Van der Kemp had been doing other things.

His recruitment was the fruit of cooperation with the Netherlands Missionary Society (established in 1797) and seemed very appropriate for a Dutch settlement, and van der Kemp certainly did seek good relations with the

Reformed church in the settlement. He also sought support there for what he really wanted to do: to reach the Xhosa people to the east, people whom he and everyone else called "the heathen." But a shadow soon fell across this relationship. Van der Kemp was shocked by slavery and by its obvious harshness, particularly shocked that church members should keep slaves. His white congregation was angry when they found him beginning to collect a congregation of slaves and Khoi and allowing them in consecrated premises. They wanted not only to have the heathen cleared out of the church but also the seats washed and a wall built around "their" graveyard to keep them out.

Van der Kemp's aim had never been to settle with the colonists but to reach the non-Christian population beyond. His two colleagues went westward to the desert land hunter-gatherers; he went eastward to the troubled frontier and established relations with the Xhosa. He soon realized, however, that in this time of conflict, there was no hope of establishing a consistent mission. Furthermore, the colony and the local settlers were calling on him. He soon found that what they wanted was to use him for their own purposes, and he realized that these purposes, in the eyes of government, were to put a buffer across the frontier. If he could induce the Khoi to settle there, that would create one more difficult area for the Xhosa to cross before they could reach the colony. From the point of view of the settlers, such a settlement would be useful as well in enabling them to exploit the Khoi and acquire them for forced labor.

For the present, van der Kemp laid aside the evangelization of the Xhosa, though he never ceased to have it on his heart, and concentrated on the original inhabitants, the Khoi. He soon found that this task was not just an evangelistic one; he had to secure their very survival in the colony. The abolition of the British slave trade in 1807 meant that South Africa as crown territory was cut off from its labor supply from outside. The colonists responded by still harsher impositions on the Khoi, who now had to replace the slaves. Abuses multiplied; the situation of the Khoi became worse than ever. Van der Kemp and his colleagues found themselves first being expected to be party to what nowadays would be called human rights abuses, and when he refused, he turned to documenting and attempting to get justice through the courts for the Khoi people. This brought him not only overwhelming unpopularity but also prosecution and, indeed, a short period in prison. When he married a young Malagasy girl of slave origin, all fears were confirmed.

His last years (he died in 1811) were both stormy and miserable. He wanted to build a refuge for the Khoi where they could be free of all settler impositions. Government gave him one, which was optimistically called Bethelsdorp, the village of the house of God. It was situated on an area of barren hillside where farming could never be productive, and there are word pictures of van der Kemp in his last days wearing a threadbare jacket and Khoi sandals, moving about between its miserable buildings. It gave the settlers satisfaction because it looked as if it could never succeed. In terms of government policy, its main purpose, as noted, was to put a Khoi buffer between the colony and the Xhosa, and, of course, the Xhosa regarded the land as theirs anyway and wanted to retake it.

John Philip and Thomas Fowell Buxton

These clashes intensified, and in 1818, the London Missionary Society sent a delegation to inspect the South African mission. One of its members was a Scottish weaver turned Congregational minister, John Philip (1777–1851), a man marked by many of the radical traditions of Scottish weavers. Philip began with public denunciation of what he saw of Cape slavery and Cape abuse of the Khoi. Still worse, he published it widely in Britain, where it was taken up by the humanitarian evangelical pressure groups, and notably by Thomas Fowell Buxton.

When Philip returned not just as a visitor but as superintendent of South African missions for the London Missionary Society, the feeling against the missions intensified. Philip's political activity was too much for some of his colleagues, but his propaganda was very effective, and he had a grip on practicalities that van der Kemp had never had. He transformed Bethelsdorp, for instance, by one simple addition: persuading someone to invest in a store. The presence of obtainable consumer goods gave the Khoi new incentives, and the community developed, even though its farming activities were stretched across a wide area. It became the seat of small-scale industries, processing other community goods, and it became a community of refuge for Khoi from outside. Philip saw this as being infinitely reproducible.

On the legislative side, Philip, through Buxton, was able to get a parliamentary declaration that all Khoi and all free Blacks in the colony had equal status in law with whites. Equality before the law was established on grounds of theological principle. Indeed, Buxton's speech in Parliament had been so theological that many members seem to have thought he was just using pious phraseology and there would not be much harm in saying "Yes, of course, we all believe that." Only later did they realize what they had passed. It was the high point of evangelical influence a few years later when, again by Philip's persuasion and Buxton's agency in Parliament, the British government handed back to the Xhosa a substantial piece of land that the settlers had taken. The colonial frontier went into reverse.

In the Cape, the early missionaries going out with the simple intention of preaching the gospel had found themselves, by the process of doing the Christian thing, deeply involved in humanitarian activity, defending the humanity of the Khoi, building a Christian society parallel to but outside the corrupted Christendom structure. In Britain in particular, the missionary movement had grown up in close alliance with the antislavery movement. Evangelicals had led the fight in the campaign to get the slave trade, of which Britain was the leading carrier, legally abolished, which was achieved in 1807. They continued to lead the campaign for the abolition of slavery itself. The apologists for slavery habitually argued that Africans were naturally fitted for manual labor but naturally unfitted for the arts of civilization. This evangelicals disputed on grounds of theological principle, insisting Africans given opportunity were capable of all the attainments under nature and grace. It gave evangelicals an incentive to prove that Africans were indeed capable of civilization, to point to every evidence of it: the African children in Clapham rectory, who did as well at school as their English agemates or better; Sierra Leone, where an African population was maintaining an orderly, literate worshiping community on British lines; and Jamaica, where the Africans were more civilized than the whites.

The African Slave Trade and Its Remedy

All of this ensured that the evangelical missionary tradition was also a humanitarian one. And the figure who embodied the evangelical humanitarian tradition by the 1840s was Sir Thomas Fowell Buxton, whose thinking had a great effect on mission thinking right over the middle period of the nineteenth century. Buxton wrote the first work in English to expound a comprehensive and coherent view of Africa, the first study of Africa's place in world history and in the history of redemption, and, incidentally, the first serious essay, I think, in development theory. All of these titles can be applied to his book, *The African Slave Trade and Its Remedy*, originally produced for private circulation in British government circles in 1839, and published in an expanded form the following year.

Buxton, born in 1786 (so he is ten years older than Venn and Anderson), was a member of Parliament for Weymouth from 1818 until he lost his seat at the election of 1837. When he entered Parliament, he already had a reputation as a champion of Spitalfields, the area of London where the brewery that he managed was situated. It is interesting to note that all the great brewers in England at this period were evangelical: Guinness, Whitbread, Hoare (though most members of that family were bankers), Charrington, and Buxton. Spitalfields had been an area of distress, and indeed starvation, under postwar conditions. Buxton had organized schemes of relief, promoted a campaign for relief funds, and attempted measures for long-term recovery, reestablishing the salt fish trade in the area, setting up savings banks, and developing the local schools. As a parliamentarian, his first concerns were in the area of penal reform, in which he worked to reduce the number of capital offenses. His increasing interest in missionary matters led him to Indian questions and then to Aborigines' rights, of which he became the prime exponent in Parliament, chairing the parliamentary committee that concluded that European settlement was always (they found no exceptions) to the detriment of the original inhabitants of the land.

In 1821, the aging and ailing William Wilberforce asked Buxton to take over leadership of the parliamentary campaign against slavery. Every aspect of the campaign as conducted by Buxton was based on carefully documented research. Its culmination was the Emancipation Act of 1833, which liberated all slaves in the British dominions, marred perhaps by a tactical concession, which Buxton eventually decided had been a mistake, to allow a transitional period of apprenticeship on the part of the slaves to their former owners. The apprenticeship system was abandoned in 1838 before it was due to finish; by that time, Buxton was no longer a member of Parliament and was in poor health but still active in the antislavery movement, and his increased leisure enabled increased reflection and research, leading to the book.

A survey of the official figures convinced him that by 1837, the transatlantic slave trade, far from being abolished, was not even reduced. Indeed, it had doubled its volume since the parliamentary campaign forty-five years earlier. More slaves were going across the Atlantic to the Americas than in the days when it was legal. Africa was being depopulated at the rate of half a million people a year.

The African Slave Trade and Its Remedy is an attempt to survey the contemporary condition of Africa on the basis of all the available sources. Its double aim is encapsulated in the two biblical texts on the title page of the second edition. The first is "This is a people robbed and spoiled; they are all of them snared in holes, and they are hid in prison houses: they are for a prey, and none delivereth; for a spoil, and none saith, Restore" (Isaiah 42:22 KJV). The other is, "The desert shall rejoice, and blossom as the rose" (Isaiah 35:1 KJV).[3] The book is about the then current condition of Africa and its potential fu-

---

3. Buxton, *African Slave Trade*, title page. The title page is not reproduced in the digital edition of 2012.

ture. The current condition is that of a people robbed and spoiled, marked by depopulation, endemic warfare, oppressive regimes, and cruel institutions. The continent does not share in the technological advances that have eased the lot of other sectors of humanity.

All of these things have a common origin: the systematic exploitation of Africa by the West over several centuries through the slave trade. The violence observed in African societies can often be traced to this source. The literature suggests that before the slave came, where the slave trade was not a factor, African societies were traditionally peaceful. The West is thus morally responsible for the present misery of Africa.

The second stream of argument is the rich potential of Africa. Africa's miseries are unnecessary. Its deliverance can be accomplished by calling forth her own resources. It is the argument of the book that these resources are not just economic but also human. The human resources are evident when one looks at the African Christian communities, not just the small one in Sierra Leone but also the substantial one in the Caribbean. In the latter, as we have seen, it is the Africans who are civilized, literate, orderly, self-determining, and missionary. It is the white planters who are the barbarians. The evidence that the African desert can blossom like the rose is already to hand in Jamaica and Sierra Leone. Africa's own resources, which include the multitude of African Christians in the New World, can deliver Africa. Then Africa will be a free and equal partner within the world trading system instead of a passive, exploited one.

The interests of Christianity, commerce, and civilization, all now inhibited by the slave trade, lie together. All three can be stimulated together. The blight of Africa, the slave trade, can be removed. The real remedy, the true ransom for Africa, will be found, he says, in her fertile soil. Here was the germ of the new Africa policy, which is the theme of Buxton's book.

In one sense, there was little new in this. It was the thinking that had founded the Sierra Leone Company and maintained it in its early days when its object had been to set up a demonstration model in West Africa of a slave-free economy, a state of free farmers prospering through agriculture, practicing all the arts of civilization. In fact, while all these arts were manifest in Sierra Leone by 1840, they had little to do with agriculture, but evangelical humanitarian thought as represented in Buxton had by this time moved beyond demonstration models and good examples toward a comprehensive, multidimensional plan for African development. The stimulation of agricultural production was one component. The economic argument against slavery and the slave trade had long been that they were not only unjust and cruel; they were wasteful institutions. In what other trade, asked Buxton, do half the goats perish in order that the other half will reach the market?—which was what was happening, he calculated, with the slave trade. Free labor would be far more efficient, particularly if the best scientific knowledge were applied to African agriculture and animal husbandry. Buxton's assumption was that investment in experimentation and research would be necessary to identify the most appropriate materials and methods.

The second component must be the guarantee of regular trade. Western countries must be prepared to buy African produce; and since Western countries control communications, they must also arrange for the collection of produce. Regular traffic must be set up between Britain and Africa. Britain must also supply the manufactured goods, which the slave trade had provided and which were attractive in Africa. Given a regular alternative and one that would soon be seen as more profitable than the slave trade, African states would lose any incentive to participate in the trade, which would be strangled at its source. Treaties between Britain and African nations could put the guarantee of regular trade in exchange for nonparticipation in the slave trade on a formal basis and thus exclude the slave trade's operations.

In the meantime, the spread of the Christian gospel alongside the healing of the earth would bring not only its own blessings but also those that inevitably accompanied it, that is, civilization. "Let missionaries and schoolmasters, the plough and the spade, go together, and agriculture will flourish; the avenues to legitimate commerce will be opened; confidence between man and man will be inspired; whilst civilization will advance as the natural effect, and Christianity operate as the proximate cause of this happy change."[4] Africa would move into the same comity of nations as the West. The institutions that were most improving the quality of life in Britain—good drainage, better water—would bless Africa, too. Building standards would rise. Printing would be among the first African industries, giving a further edge to the forces of civilization. Indeed, in due course, steam power, which was now revolutionizing British industry, could be equally a part of the African scene.

The paths of Christianity, commerce, and civilization thus intersected. Christian teaching was essential, and it would be the surest, perhaps indeed the only, source of civilization. The development of a viable alternative to the slave trade was needed in order to clear the way to both.

It may be worth pausing to consider some of the things that were *not* part of this vision. First, it was not a plan for extensive settlement or for the acquisition of territory. Buxton did assume that some white settlement would be necessary to initiate experiment and production, but he had no idea of

---

4. Buxton, *Remedy* (2012 digital version), 229.

another Cape colony. His long interest in colonial problems had already led him to believe that white settlement had a harmful effect on the original inhabitants, who invariably lost out in land deals. As we have seen, not so long before this, acting on information supplied by John Philip, he had raised in the House of Commons the matter of the expansion of the Cape frontier and of land seizures from the Xhosa in the War of 1835. In a departure from convention, the government actually pulled the frontier back and restored to the Xhosa what Buxton called "the territory we lately stole."[5] In a letter of this period, he adds this: "The hand of the proud oppressor in Africa has been, under Providence, arrested"—the hand, that is, of the British government. "Only think how delighted must our savage friends be and with what feelings must they have received our retreating army."[6] "Our savage friends"—here is the language of civilization again. There are Greeks and there are barbarians, but the savage friends have their rights to be protected from the proud oppressor.

Nor is this a scheme to maximize profit. Buxton did indeed believe that Britain would benefit financially from his new Africa policy and that enlightened self-interest lay in that direction. In general, he supported free-trade principles. When the government of the day applied them to breweries like his own, he agreed that their profits had in fact been too high anyway. But the African proposals have no hidden agenda. They reflect no desire to control trade. Nor is it a matter of bringing Africa into the world trade system. It was there already, and that was the source of its misery. The whole point is that Africa should become a free partner, an equal partner, in trade as in civilization. At present, she is held captive in her trade and imprisoned in barbarism as a result. The West owed reparation to Africa for the centuries of injustice and exploitation. When compensation for the slave owners was under discussion in 1832, Buxton had said, "I am a friend to compensation, but it is compensation on the broadest scale. . . . Do you ask compensation for him who has wielded the whip? Then I ask compensation for him who has smarted under the lash."[7]

In *The African Slave Trade and Its Remedy*, he argues this: "Without doubt it is the duty of Great Britain to employ the influence and the strength which God has given her, in raising Africa from the dust, and enabling her, out of

---

5. Charles Buxton, ed., *Memoirs of Sir Thomas Fowell Buxton, Baronet: With Selections from His Correspondence* (Cambridge: Cambridge University Press, 2011 [orig. 1848]), 368, https://doi.org/10.1017/CBO9780511751042.035.

6. Buxton, *Memoirs*, 369.

7. Buxton, *Memoirs*, 204.

her own resources, to beat down Slavery and the Slave Trade."[8] The book is above all a manifesto for action.

The Niger Expedition

In 1841, the British government gave a trial to the new African policy by setting up an exploratory mission to the Niger. It would survey the possibilities of agricultural development and pledge regular commercial traffic in exchange for a guarantee not to sell slaves. Three purpose-built ships were commissioned with state-of-the-art ventilation; the assumption at this time was that malaria was caused by *mal air*—that is, bad air—and so ventilation systems were going to be the key to safe travel. The ships had handpicked crews of the highest character. Scientists and agriculturalists were recruited as advisors and experimental workers. A stack of Arabic Bibles were taken to present wherever Arabic literacy might be found. The chief rabbi sent a letter in Hebrew in case the expedition found any Jews up the Niger. They had found Jews in China; they had found Jews in India. Why should they not be up the Niger?

The expedition called in Sierra Leone, where it took on board numbers of the liberated Africans, the people from the intercepted slave ships, who would act as interpreters, for in Freetown there were people from all the Niger territories. It also took on two mission-society representatives, the Reverend J. F. Schön, a German missionary of the Church Missionary Society who had been interested in African languages and had made some study of Hausa and of Ibo in Sierra Leone by talking to recaptives of Hausa and Ibo background. The other was Venn's eventual designated person for indigenizing the episcopate in Africa, Samuel Adjai Crowther, then still a lay teacher and catechist in Freetown.

In August 1841, the three ships crossed the bar of the Niger Delta. By the beginning of October, the last of them was limping back. Death had claimed many of its officers, crew, and scientists. Its cabins were crammed with the sick and the dying. The captain was dead; the medical officer was in command of the ship. Down below, the expedition's geologist was trying to work the engines with the aid of a manual. They had the best people with the best equipment—but the expedition had been a disaster. Forty-one people had died.

It was the end of the new African policy. Conventional wisdom drew from the expedition the conclusion that Europeans could not survive in inland

---

8. Buxton, *Remedy* (2012 digital version), 247.

Africa. Charles Dickens, who reviewed the account of the expedition for *The Examiner* magazine in 1848,[9] had great fun with the idea of schemes of African development, and a decade afterward, he was still laughing at the Niger expedition with his portrait in *Bleak House* of Mrs. Jellyby and her scheme for cultivating coffee and settling colonists at Borrioboola-Gha on the left bank of the Niger.[10] Buxton was discredited, blamed for causing the deaths of forty people, and died a broken man.

Journals of the Rev. James Frederick Schön and Mr. Samuel Crowther: Who, with the Sanction of Her Majesty's Government, Accompanied the Expedition up the Niger, in 1841, in Behalf of the Church Missionary Society, the report from Schön and Crowther, the two mission-society representatives, is in sharp contrast with the other accounts of the expedition.[11] The expedition had called in at Cape Coast, in what is now Ghana, on its way, and there Crowther had seen a memorial inscription to the Reverend Philip Quaque, who had been chaplain of the Royal Africa Company in the previous century. He was amazed to think that there had been an ordained Anglican African clergyman as long ago as that. Why should there not be nowadays? In Sierra Leone, missionaries always preached in English; he himself had begun the innovation of preaching in Yoruba, and even the imam of the mosque was calling his people to hear such good Yoruba being spoken.

Schön begins his appendix to the two men's report with a sort of language map of the Niger—Benin, Ibo, Igara (Igala), Fulani, Nupe, and Hausa—and Schön identifies the last as the most important language of all. Schön, you might say, is the real discoverer of the importance of Hausa.[12]

While the mission society committee regularly stressed language study for all its missionaries, its injunctions had had little effect in Sierra Leone, partly because missions were too busy, partly because of erroneous ideas. One of these was that Sierra Leone proved that English could replace all the languages of Africa; so language study was really a waste of time. And since all the riches of English literature would be open to Africans, there was no

9. Review of *A Narrative of the Expedition Sent by Her Majesty's Government to the River Niger in 1841 under the Command of Captain H. D. Trotter*, by William Allen and T. R. H. Thomson, *Examiner* (August 19, 1848): 531–33.

10. Charles Dickens, *Bleak House* (London: Bradbury & Evans, 1853), chapter 4, "Telescopic Philanthropy."

11. James Frederick Schön and Samuel Crowther, *Journals of the Rev. James Frederick Schön and Mr. Samuel Crowther: Who, with the Sanction of Her Majesty's Government, Accompanied the Expedition up the Niger, in 1841, in Behalf of the Church Missionary Society* (London: Hatchard & Son, 1842).

12. Schön and Crowther, *Journals*, 355–57.

need for an African literature. African languages would die out, and it would be no particular loss.

In fact, Schön argued, Sierra Leone proves the opposite. At least thirty-six African languages were in use, and none of these was in any danger of dying out. The children of liberated Africans, as recaptives were called, spoke fluently and accurately the language of the countries from which their parents came. It was, therefore, essential to invest heavily in language study and translation. Not much good could be expected to result from missionary labors unless the various nations were addressed in their own languages and portions of the sacred volume were put into their hands.

But language study must be a specialized work of missions, with two or three qualified people set apart for it. "It is not a business that may be taken up at any leisure hour, like the study of a language already cultivated. You have no books at your command which you may consult, except those that you [write yourself]. You must collect all information from the lips of Natives. Things that you take for settled and fixed, you find to be wrong by the next inquiry. Frequently I have spent hours before I was satisfied about the signification of a single word. . . . I have often observed persons commencing a language with great zeal—take down a few hundred substantives, and commit them to memory—also a great number of verbs—but who have, after all, never obtained a full knowledge of the character of the language."[13] He goes on to characterize the travelers' word lists, with no regard to grammatical structure, as useless. Next, the place to carry out language study was Sierra Leone. It was a natural language laboratory where speakers of all West African languages could already be found.

The second theme of the report was that the evangelization of inland Africa must be carried out by Africans. Schön accepted broadly the conventional wisdom that the expedition proved that Europeans could not survive in inland Africa. But not one of the African members of the expedition had died; very few had been ill. And Crowther had shown himself invaluable on the expedition. There were others like him in Sierra Leone, people who already spoke the languages of the Niger basin. What is more, liberated Africans in Sierra Leone were now keen to return to their homelands, a thing that had never been known in earlier years. Sierra Leone was the obvious place to look for missionaries and the place to train them, for in Sierra Leone, the Fourah Bay Institution, of which Crowther had been the first student, had been set up to educate Africans beyond the normal standards of schools. At that time, the college was languishing, very short of funds and in danger of

13. Schön and Crowther, *Journals*, 360.

closure. It should be built up, said Schön, and built up for theological education, which, like translation, should be a special branch of missions. Those teaching should not be assigned to other duties, nor should students be taken out of college for mission purposes before they had finished their course.

The recommendations made by Schön and Crowther were adopted, at least in part. Crowther was brought for study in England and ordained there, setting the precedent for an ordained African ministry. The Fourah Bay Institution was rescued and put on a new basis, and an African American Episcopal clergyman was brought in from New York as its principal.

It took a few years more to get the specialist branch of linguistics established, but it was effectively done with the appointment to the Fourah Bay Institution, or College, as it was now called, of Sigismund Wilhelm Koelle. This extremely learned, extremely eccentric, and rather cantankerous German missionary singlehandedly invented the science of comparative African linguistics. Schön calculated that thirty-six languages were spoken in Freetown; Koelle identified over a hundred, and in his vast *Polyglotta Africana* (1854) began their comparative grammatical analysis.[14] Koelle learned from his African informants that English was a comparatively poor language with a very limited vocabulary; a language like Kanouri had a much wider range of expression and would be much more suitable for translating the Scriptures. The other work for which Koelle was appointed was to teach Arabic in the college for students preparing to work with Muslims. At least one of these went on for further study of Arabic at Cambridge.

The 1850s, then, showed a flowering of vernacular language study. And the missionaries flowed from Sierra Leone. Only a minority were ordained, like Crowther; still fewer had the academic training that Henry Johnson, the Arabist, had received at Cambridge. The evangelization of the Niger basin depended to a great extent on laypeople from Sierra Leone. The nineteenth-century population of Sierra Leone colony probably never exceeded fifty thousand people, and yet that tiny country produced a hundred ordained men in forty years and hundreds of lay missionaries. It seems likely that in the second half of the nineteenth century, Sierra Leone produced more missionaries per head of population than any other country has ever done.

It has rarely been noted how deeply Buxton's ideas affected missionary thinking. They were a key influence on Henry Venn, who took office in the Church Missionary Society just about the time of the Niger expedition. They

---

14. Sigismund Koelle, *Polyglotta Africana: Or a Comparative Vocabulary of Nearly Three Hundred Words and Phrases in More Than One Hundred Distinct African Languages* (London: Church Missionary Society, 1854).

were put into action by David Livingstone, who as a young accepted missionary candidate attended the valedictory meeting in London of the Niger expedition. Both saw Africans as the key to the evangelization of Africa. Both were concerned for the economic basis of the African church. Both looked to legitimate trade as an ally. And both saw economic, social, and intellectual development as an outcome of Christian mission.

Livingstone and Venn both died in 1873. The following years clouded these ideas. The alliance with trade looked doubtful when a high proportion of trade goods consisted of European gin. The new acceleration of missionary recruitment seemed to reduce the need for self-governing, self-supporting, and self-propagating churches, as well as for a vast native African missionary force. The African leadership was replaced by Europeans with at least a touch of the new racial theories, which had the same effect as the crude old slave trade arguments about African inferiority. In the new form, the theory was that Africans were not fitted for leadership. The new influences in evangelicalism and the new eschatology with its stress on the urgency of the verbal communication of the gospel before the Lord's return reduced the attention to gospel-induced social change.

Moreover, the dawn of the colonial period reduced the interaction with independent African rulers. Missionaries were now less dependent on African rulers than on colonial district officers. Before 1870, the European colonial presence in Africa was not large; by the end of the century, only Liberia and Ethiopia had not been parceled out between European powers. Such had also been the fate of the entire Pacific and large areas of Asia. As the missionary movement reached middle age, the great European migration was reaching its climax, and one manifestation of it was an empire on which, supposedly, the sun would never set. Subsequent chapters will recount the implications for the Western missionary movement of the discovery that the sun, after all, was indeed sinking below the horizon.

CHAPTER 8

How Protestant Missionaries Got into China

And How China Got into the Missionaries

We have thus far studied three representative figures whose ideas were formative for the development of Protestant missions—Rufus Anderson, Henry Venn, and Thomas Fowell Buxton. We now focus on three further figures, all associated with missions to China, who between them cover 150 years of the Protestant missionary movement. Perhaps the stories of these figures, their impact on China, and the greater impact that China made on them will between them indicate something of the transformation of the missionary movement over that time, a transformation that occurred without any alteration of the original missionary motive to pass on the good news about Christ.

Robert Morrison

We begin with Robert Morrison, the first and for a long time the only Protestant missionary in China. Born in a Scottish family in the north of England in 1782, like many, perhaps most, British missionaries of his generation, he came from the artisan class. His father was a maker of the wooden frames used to give shape to boots and shoes, and Robert was his father's apprentice. He started work early, with little opportunity for formal education; but after his evangelical conversion in teenage years, he devoted himself to intense study. The experience of the early nineteenth century was that evangelical religion stimulated the intellect and gave a thirst for knowledge generally. Missionary candidates might come from the sections of society that did not receive much formal education, but the missionary calling itself often stimulated them to immense efforts of intellectual endeavor and search for learning.

A glance at the candidates' papers of the early missionary societies shows that among the sins young aspiring missionaries most lamented was mis-improving their talents—that is, wasting time. The young Robert Morrison does not seem to have wasted much time. He taught himself to read while walking so as not to waste time when walking to and from his work. Then he decided he could waste still less time if he took his bed to the workshop and slept there. He kept a book propped up on the workbench so that he could read while at work; remember that the work involved looking down at a lathe, but by concentration one could learn to take in one line of print as one's head came up from the lathe and bring it up for the next line. He learned shorthand so as to be able to take notes when it might otherwise be socially inconvenient. He attended classes in Latin for an hour a day and got to work an hour earlier in the morning to make up for the time. In after years, he had two regrets: first, that he had not had access to more books in his early years, and second, that missionaries in general did not have enough books to enable them to be as efficient as they should be.

When about twenty, Morrison offered for the Presbyterian ministry, and while studying for this, offered to the London Missionary Society. He talked of going with Mungo Park to Timbuktu. But when in 1807 the London Missionary Society directors made their decision, they ordained that he should go to China as soon as possible and translate the Scriptures there. The direction is an example of the magnificent ebullience of the early missionary movement. A later, wiser, more experienced missionary directorate would probably have concluded that such an appointment was out of the question. For one, how could it possibly be carried out? China, by long and strictly enforced policy, did not allow foreigners on her soil with the sole exception of licensed traders who themselves had to keep strictly to their factories. British trading interests in China were in the hands of the East India Company, whose attitude to missionaries verged on the paranoiac. The company had done everything it could to impede dissenting missions in India; the presence of a nonconformist mission in the still more sensitive setting of China was hardly something they would forward.

Suppose these difficulties overcome, how could anyone translate the Scriptures? There were no facilities in Britain for learning Chinese—no courses, no books, and no way of starting. As far as anyone knew, only one British person knew the language at any depth at all, and he was the East India Company official in charge of trade operations in China. The reason for this was that the Chinese government prevented foreigners from learning the language; it also prohibited the sale of Chinese books or their export from China.

Under these circumstances, Morrison began the study of Chinese. He went to the British Museum. It had two Chinese manuscripts, a harmony of the Gospels and a translation of the book of Acts and the Pauline Epistles, both evidently made by Jesuit missionaries in the seventeenth century. Morrison set to work to copy them, character by character, without, of course, having the faintest idea of the sounds. He then learned that the Royal Society, the chief scientific body in the country, had another manuscript, a Chinese-Latin dictionary six hundred pages long. He settled down to copy this out, too.

At this time, he was also undertaking other studies. He attended a London hospital to learn medicine; and, in view of the well-known Chinese interest in astronomy, he studied at Greenwich Observatory, which gave him plenty of opportunity to read while walking.

Eventually Morrison did get to China. The mission tried to send him in an East India Company vessel, but the company refused. So he took ship for New York. Someone in the missionary network there had access to Secretary of State Madison, and by this means, Morrison got at last to Canton, where he took up residence in the American factory. The Americans were not much more pleased to have a missionary in their midst than the British would have been. Morrison's way was strewn with pitfalls. On the principle of being a Greek to the Greeks, he decided to wear Chinese dress, grew his hair into a queue, and grew his nails long. He was denounced as a spy. He shaved his hair, pared his nails, put on the black suit of a Presbyterian minister, and was denounced as a missionary. There was only one way left: to don the white jacket and straw hat of a Western trader—how galling for the earnest missionary to appear to disguise his status as a minister of the gospel! He was assumed to be very wealthy, since he never seemed to buy or sell anything.

Morrison tried to find a reason for existence in the American factory. Could he be the chaplain? Could he conduct their services? Everyone was too busy for services. Out of pure kindness of heart, one trader sat still while Morrison read the Scriptures and prayed; no one else came. He was soon conscious that he was outstaying his welcome, and he moved into a disused building that had once belonged to the French company. His letters at this time are doleful. He was never of a sunny disposition, and his immense endowments do not seem to have included a sense of humor. He agonized over his proper role. Surely as a missionary, he was bound to preach the gospel, but if he did, he would undoubtedly be ejected. He must stay quiet, or was this only the carnal nature, a fear of man?

The one thing he knew was that he must try to learn the language—and this itself was perilous. If he were caught in the attempt, he would certainly be deported, if nothing else. As he had no proper status with any company, no one would protect him. Every time anyone came in, he had to hide his books and papers; for he did get some books and papers. It was, of course, illegal to sell them, but by hook and by crook, by gifts and by sanctified bootlegging, he managed within two years to acquire a library of 1,229 volumes in medicine, law, religion, and other topics. He had valuable help from a Chinese Catholic who acted as a teacher. By all these means, he began to piece together a knowledge of Chinese. He learned to speak Mandarin; he learned to speak Cantonese. He learned that country speech was different from town speech, and something of the south China dialects. Using his transcription of the old Jesuit manuscript, he pressed on at the translation of the New Testament. Day after day, dawn to dusk, the plodding work went on, with Morrison always frustrated at not being able to do more.

In a couple of years or so, he had made such progress by careful use of the concentration built up by reading while walking, and note-taking while talking, that the East India Company, which did not want to know about him, offered him a post as their official translator. After some hesitation, he accepted. There were advantages, chief of which was that he had a legal status for being there; and he had a salary, generous by missionary standards, which relieved the mission of his support. He also had opportunities he would never have had any other way, accompanying an ambassador from England, for instance, to Peking [Beijing] and making a long interior trip by riverboat that he carefully recorded in detail.

Plodding doggedly through the shadows, he produced a Chinese grammar, then a New Testament (the signal to start on the Old Testament), a series of tracts, and then more ambitious things. He persuaded the London Missionary Society to establish in 1818 an Anglo-Chinese college at Malacca in what is now Malaysia. Here, with Chinese and European students, the Chinese and English languages would be studied together. It would be a China mission in waiting, preparing for the time when China would be open to missions; and it would raise up a mission force among the overseas Chinese right from the start.

Morrison turned his mind to Chinese language of every kind, but he soon realized that Chinese people had an immense reverence for the words of Confucius. "In reading with me his 'four books,' they seem quite enraptured."[1] Morrison struggled to find out why they were, and he found the ancient books almost impossible to read. "The very particles, moreover, which, in

1. London Missionary Society, *Transactions of the Missionary Society* (London: Bye & Law, 1807–1810), 3:339.

other books, are mere expletives, are here full of meaning; and there is in the reasoning of the philosopher, they affirm, a depth which requires the utmost sagacity to fathom, and a fullness that requires a long paraphrase to unfold."[2] As he got further into the old texts, he could readily agree to the excellence of their moral teaching and sought to expand on the barrenness of a Christless moral system but came up against a brick wall. He pressed on.

As for other attainments, there was above all the pioneer translation of the New Testament, which he finished in 1813. Then in 1819, with his first colleague, William Milne, had come the complete Bible. There had been a pioneer Chinese grammar to reduce the labor for his successors. There were many tracts, service books, and statements of Christian teaching. There was a review of China for philological purposes. And there was a dictionary—and what a dictionary! It was not just a dictionary; it was a multivolume encyclopedia.[3]

In 1824, he took his first and only leave. He had a period of fame and acclaim. The man who had never been to university received various honorary doctorates; the student who had identified the Chinese manuscripts in the Royal Society became a fellow of the society. But Morrison used his leave to seek to establish in the West the new understanding of China that he had begun. More, he wanted all the languages of Asia to be studied, and he campaigned for the establishment of a language institution, which would undertake them all. The prime object would be the spread of the gospel, but all useful purposes would be served and encouraged. Missionaries would study at the institution prior to departure for the field.

There was an enthusiastic response. A constitution was devised, a committee appointed, carefully balanced between the various sectors of the Christian church. A series of eminent vice presidents took office, including William Wilberforce, who was vice president of every society under heaven. Morrison himself agreed to teach Chinese until he should return to China. A Baptist missionary taught Bengali. A well-disposed East India Company official taught Sanskrit. And Morrison presented the institution with his Chinese library, those thousands of volumes collected in the way we have noticed. All went thunderously well for the institution for the two years of Morrison's leave. But with his return to China in 1826, enthusiasm waned. The institute

---

2. London Missionary Society, *Transactions*, 3:339.

3. Robert Morrison, *A Dictionary of the Chinese Language, in Three Parts: Part the First, Containing Chinese and English Arranged according to the Radicals; Part the Second, Chinese and English Arranged Alphabetically; and Part the Third, English and Chinese* (Macao: Honourable East India Company, 1815).

languished, and not even the array of its eminent vice presidents could maintain it. It was quietly wound up, and Morrison received the sad report that there was no one to use that library.

Morrison had arrived in China in 1807; he died at his post in 1834. In that time, he could point to very few Chinese led to Christ. The first, Liang Fa (1789–1855), was carrying on Morrison's sort of work, particularly with tracts. Morrison probably never knew how important Liang would become or how widespread the effect of his work as the first ordained Protestant evangelist in China. Morrison died before China was open to missionary activity. He had seen nothing but disappointment all his life, but he had completed the task for which he had come. He had begun the modern Christian encounter with China. He had sought to introduce Christ to China. In the process, he had introduced China to the West, brought the Chinese language into Western learned discourse, and laid the groundwork for the Chinese appropriation of Christianity.

James Legge

We now pass to another generation and meet a countryman of my own, James Legge, born in the little Aberdeenshire town of Huntly in 1815 while Morrison was in his early years as a translator and, unlike Morrison, having an excellent classical education at the University of Aberdeen. He, too, felt the missionary call at an early age. He, too, was accepted by the London Missionary Society. He was able to study Chinese at University College, London, as a result of Morrison's earlier work. In 1839, he was appointed to the Anglo-Chinese College in Malacca and, as we have seen, the China mission in waiting. He did not have to wait long. Within three years, China was opened to the West by the first Anglo-Chinese or Opium War, and Hong Kong was annexed by Britain. Legge moved the College to Hong Kong, where he stayed for the next thirty-three years. In 1876, he returned to Britain to occupy the new chair of Chinese at Oxford, where he continued, a very active professor, until his death in 1897. This sounds an uneventful if busy life. In fact, James Legge was responsible for the transformation of the Western Protestant approach to China.

We have seen that Morrison saw his first function as the translation of the Scriptures for China (no serious Christian would be likely to challenge this as a first object), and we have seen the immense and complex labors that it involved. We have also seen that he found the ancient texts particularly difficult, partly because he could not see why the Chinese were so enraptured by them. One feels that when he was talking of Confucius and trying to lead Confucians to Christ, he was aware that he was missing something. There was something that spoke to the Chinese heart.

It is the immense achievement of Legge that perhaps more than any other Westerner before him he saw what that something was. He realized that translation was a two-way process. Yes, of course, the Scriptures must be translated into Chinese. Yes, of course, missionaries must learn to speak good idiomatic Chinese, pronounce it properly, not mix the dialects if they are to communicate the gospel in China. But not only must the missionary get into China and Chinese; China and Chinese must get into the missionary. This involves penetration to the heart of the central traditions of China, the consciousness at the core of the nation formed by centuries of reflection, influencing millions of people who are never aware of the source of that influence.

In 1841, while still a novice missionary at Malacca, Legge began to translate the Chinese classics. He continued the task for the rest of his life, finishing the last text a few months before his death. The labor was enormous. These were translations with the utmost rigor, and they were annotated deeply with references to the whole tradition of Chinese learning. Legge describes his method thus, speaking of an ancient text, which had been translated by two others: "I undertook the labour of translating afresh for myself, transcribing at the same time the original and happiest portions of Chinese commentary upon it, because I have learned by experience that such a process gives one most readily a mastery of the old books of China. Their meaning and spirit sink gradually into the mind. My long dealing with them has not yet enabled me to make them throw open their gates at the first summons."[4]

What was the purpose of all this labor? It was, he said, that the rest of the world should really know this great empire, and especially that missionaries should understand it with sufficient intelligence to secure permanent results. After more than a hundred years, the translations are still in use, still circulating in China.

To describe Confucius as other than a religious teacher, he says, is absurdly unfair—and thus we have already moved beyond Morrison. Legge made a pilgrimage to the place where the master died in order to tread the very ground where Confucius's dust was mingled. His reverence for Mencius was profound, and of the ancient ruler T'ang, he can burst out lyrically, "let it be borne in mind that he ascended the throne of China two hundred years before Moses was born according to our common chronology. . . . How

---

4. James Legge, *The Religions of China: Confucianism and Tàoism Described and Compared with Christianity* (London: Hodder & Stoughton, 1880), 215-16.

grandly he speaks of our nature as given by God! How nobly he conceived of the work of the sovereign!"[5]

Legge's deepest emotion—and it is clear that this rather dry Scottish scholar is on occasion deeply moved—comes from his contemplation of what he believed to be the historic heart of Chinese religion. Confucius may be the key to Chinese religion, but he is not its climax. Confucius and Mencius recognized and safeguarded a tradition much older than themselves, the communal sacrifice by the emperor on behalf of his people in the temple of heaven. This act is the witness to what is left of the oldest, truest religion of China, a true monotheism, the worship of the God of heaven. Legge writes,

> It is indeed a wonderful fact to think of, that a worship of the one God has been maintained in the vicinity of their capitals by the sovereigns of China almost continuously for more than four thousand years. I felt this fact profoundly when I stood early one morning by the altar of Heaven, in the southern suburb of Peking. It was without my shoes that I went up to the top of it; and there around the central slab of the marble with which it was paved, free of flaw as the coerulean vault above, hand in hand with the friends who accompanied me, I joined in singing the doxology, beginning—"Praise God from whom all blessings flow."[6]

Legge's verdict was that "K'ung [Confucius] was a great and wonderful man; but I think the religion which he found, and did so much to transmit to posterity, was still greater and more remarkable than he."[7]

Karl Ludvig Reichelt

We move to my last figure, who takes us into the twentieth century: Karl Ludvig Reichelt (1877–1952), who entered the seminary of the Norwegian Missionary Society in 1897, the year of Legge's death. Legge says very little about Buddhism in China, I suspect because he did not really regard it as Chinese. With Reichelt, we meet a new type of study, a study that works not only from texts but also in interpersonal relations. In educational background, Reichelt belongs to the more modest end of the spectrum. He did not go to university but trained as a teacher. In theology, his education was solidly conservative.

5. Legge, *Religions of China*, 99.
6. Legge, *Religions of China*, 251.
7. Legge, *Religions of China*, 149.

He belonged to the Pietists in a mission tradition in Norway. He had had an evangelical conversion in his teens. There is not a sniff of liberalism in his theological formation.

Reichelt came to China in the era of the Boxer Rising at a time when the missionary movement was suffused with the thought that the modernization of China was at hand. The hope for the gospel lay in a readiness of China to adopt the ways of the West. The period when Reichelt began his work seemed to offer less missionary incentive for the study of China than there had been in the days of Morrison or Legge, and the young missionary entered the usual routine of open-air preaching and Scripture and tract distribution.

One fateful day in 1905, he went to a Buddhist monastery. The experience was shattering. The evident genuineness of the monks' faith and his own inability to communicate his own beset him. Let me quote his own words: "Pained and distraught, I walked about and wrestled with the question: 'Are we permitted to believe that the Spirit of God and the Spirit of Jesus Christ may also be at work within these melancholy walls, where superstition and idolatry walk side by side with the loftiest longings for truth, purity and liberty?" Reichelt sat down with a pious monk and worked through the great Buddhist text, the *Heart Sutra*, and reflected on how he longed to be able to communicate the "unsearchable riches of Christ" to the monks but found to his distress that none of them would listen. He continues, "There was no question of my sleeping: the inward struggle and pain was too great. I was therefore thankful when I heard the bell ring at 3 a.m. for the monks' first worship. . . . Like grey shadows the monks slipped silently into the sanctuary. . . . There was a soft stroke on a gong, and the long monotonous act of worship began."[8]

He gives an account, written many years later, of what he remembered as happening next.

> When the dawn came, I crept out through the back gate and followed a path among the bamboos. Soon I was at the top of the hill. Just at that moment the first rays of the sun were spreading across the breathtaking mountain landscape. Everything breathed the freshness of the morning and the power of resurrection. The birds began to sing. . . . I sat down in quiet meditation. . . . It was as though I heard the Lord's voice. It came to me in the form of Paul's words in the Acts of the Apostles: "God is not far from each one of us. For in him we live and move and have our being."

8. Eric J. Sharpe, *Karl Ludvig Reichelt: Missionary, Scholar and Pilgrim* (Hong Kong: Tao Fong Shan Ecumenical Centre, 1984), 39–40.

"God has never left himself without witness." Long before the missionaries came to China, God was in China. What you find of glimpses of truth and points of contact, he has placed there. And how has he done it?

For the first time I began to understand what the Gospel of John states in its prologue: God has been active from eternity through his word, that is, his only-begotten Son. . . . What has to be done is to gather all the rays of light that there are . . . so that these may help the individual to go deeper and reach further . . . to . . . an understanding of "the Word that became flesh and dwelt among us." . . .

I need not say that it was a quite different missionary who walked down Weishan hill an hour or so later. It was a missionary whose heart was full of holy power and joy.[9]

This conversion experience led Reichelt to unrelenting study of Chinese religious tradition. Not in Legge's sense; he concentrates on Buddhism, and it is his meeting with Buddhists that is so striking. He tells us that he spent days and weeks in monasteries, not only in worship in the temple halls but also in the meditation sessions. He concluded there were plenty of charlatans, plenty of perversions in monastic life, but so much sincere piety, wholehearted and holy devotion, beauty of character and spirit. If only they met Christ, what spiritual heights might they not attain, a blessing to the church and to China!

When Reichelt tried to talk to monks about Christ, he found first that they readily accepted that Jesus was the merciful Savior from the West and readily agreed that the teachings of the Bible were true. He also universally found that it was said that followers of Jesus, whether Western or Chinese, were deficient in gentleness, and thus in the first characteristic of the religious life. In particular, followers of Jesus spoke harshly about Buddha and about Buddhism and said things that were not true. The trouble with this indictment, Reichelt concluded, was that it was justified, and most of it was based on ignorance. He promised to try to follow his Master in doing justice to Buddhists and in demonstrating what they had of truth, because it comes from the Father and the Logos.

I would we had time in this brief chapter to meet his brotherhood, formed first with a converted monk, a brotherhood seeking to produce a sort of halfway house where Buddhists and Christians could live together, where they could study together, where the setting would fit the religious culture of the

9. Sharpe, *Karl Ludvig Reichelt*, 40–41.

seekers—what he came to call the Chinese garment: Buddhist architecture, the distinctive symbol of the cruciform lotus (the lotus cross), and an atmosphere in chapel reminiscent of the temple, with bells and incense, meditation, and reading of the Scriptures—the Christian Scriptures but also those parts of the Tripitaka that were in harmony with Christian teaching. He met remarkable encouragement from time to time, and his book *A Transformed Abbot* records the testimony of a converted Buddhist abbot.[10]

As we have seen, this is a Lutheran Pietist with no liberal influences in his upbringing. Any movement has come from China, not from the West. He remains entirely orthodox in theology, seeking no creedal revision. His brotherhood acknowledged the Apostles' and Nicene Creed, as well as the canonical Scriptures, and "salvation lies in Christ alone" is the whole thrust of his work to introduce Buddhists to Christ. But his own mission dropped him. He used bells and incense as in the Buddhist temples, and for conservative Lutherans, this savored of Rome. He used the symbol of the cross growing out of a lotus, and there were howls about syncretism. But, said Reichelt, what we are showing is that the cross of Christ is central to all we do and that the Christian faith, centered in the cross, can grow out of Buddhist soil.[11] His own evangelical Lutherans turned away from him as liberal. Liberals supported him but usually for the wrong reason. He was not preaching a universal religion; he was not proclaiming the unity of Christianity and Buddhism. He was calling Buddhists to Christ, with the assurance that Christ had been in China and among Chinese Buddhists before him, preparing the way that thousands of years of Chinese Buddhist tradition could be turned toward Christ.

There we must leave him and our other paradigmatic figures marking different stages in the missionary encounter with China. We know better than China watchers did in 1952, when Reichelt died, that the most important period of Chinese Christianity was just beginning.

Perhaps the proper conclusion is one that was pointed out to us by Origen long ago. Think, he says, of the gold cherubim that surrounded the tabernacle. Think of the gold vessels. Where did the gold come from to make the tabernacle in the wilderness? The answer, of course, was that the Israelites had spoiled the Egyptians. It is Egyptian gold that decorates the tabernacle; it is Egyptian gold from which the signs of God's presence are made. The taber-

---

10. Karl Ludvig Reichelt, G. M. Rose, and A. P. Rose, *The Transformed Abbot* (London: Lutterworth, 1954).

11. See Notto R. Thelle, "Karl Ludvig Reichelt 1877–1952: Christian Pilgrim of Tao Fong Shan," in *Mission Legacies: Biographical Studies of the Leaders of the Modern Missionary Movement*, ed. Gerald H. Anderson et al. (Maryknoll, NY: Orbis Books, 1994), 216–24, at 220.

nacle is hung with curtains of Egyptian cloth. It is the business of the people of God, Origen goes on, to take the things that are misused in the heathen world and to furnish from them things for the worship and glorification of God.[12] That was Ludvig Reichelt's philosophy of mission.

12. It is unclear which passage in Origen's *Homilies on Exodus* Professor Walls had in mind. Origen's thirteenth homily, in *Homilies on Genesis and Exodus*, trans. Ronald E. Heine (Washington, DC: Catholic University of America Press, 2002), 337, asserts that it is clear that the Israelites were expected to find the gold, silver, and other precious materials needed for the construction of the tabernacle from their own "boxes and storerooms," but it makes no explicit reference to the gold having been taken from the Egyptians.—Ed.

PART 3

Midlife Crises

*Western Missions in the Late Nineteenth
and Early Twentieth Centuries*

CHAPTER 9

Protestant Missions Entering Middle Age

Maturity and Midlife Crisis

In 1842, the famous Baptist preacher Edward Steane preached a sermon in Kettering, Northamptonshire, on the occasion of the fiftieth anniversary of the formation of the Baptist Missionary Society. It is a review of what he calls the first fifty years of the progress of the missionary enterprise, which can be said to mark "a new era in the history of the Christian Church."[1] He points out the change in climate for missions since Carey's time. Then, in the 1790s, the East India Company kept missionaries out; now they would not dare to. Then, politicians and journalists scoffed at missions; now they heap praise on them. What Steane is reflecting is in fact the general acceptance of missions in British society at this time. It does not mean enthusiasm for missions. It does not mean people pushing to become missionaries; in fact, very few did. But it means that missions are accepted as honorable and beneficent in tendency, whereas once they had been freakish or dangerous. What Steane does not—and could not—say is that this period in which he is writing, the early 1840s, is probably the high-water mark of evangelical influence in British public life. Fifty years earlier, it had been marginal; in the 1840s, it had become mainstream. Not that most people were evangelical, but that evangelical values had penetrated and become conventional, and with them went approval for missions.

---

1. Benjamin Godwin and Edward Steane, *Two Sermons Preached at Kettering on the 31st of May, and the 1st of June, 1842, before the Baptist Missionary Society, at a Special General Meeting Held in Celebration of Its Fiftieth Year: With an Account of the Meeting* (London: Houlston & Stoneman, 1842), 39–83, quotation at 40.

Protestant Missions Reaching Maturity in the 1840s

In the 1840s, the missionary movement was still quite a small affair. Nevertheless, it was in this decade that Christian missions became accepted, on the whole approved, recognized as being there to stay. At earlier times, one could see missions as heading for disaster; now they are part of the national life. The results have not been spectacular, but they have been sufficient to justify the enterprise. In the 1840s, the missionary movement reached maturity. In this decade in Britain, Protestant missions seem to take off, and missions become an accepted part of the wider story of British influence in the world.

The 1840s are significant for different reasons in different parts of the world. India was the heart of the Protestant missionary enterprise, the region that drew most missionary effort, and here there was just enough encouragement to convince even some skeptics that the endeavor was worthwhile. In Africa, where the missionary presence hitherto had been almost entirely coastal and confined essentially to the west coast (the old slave coast, in fact) and to the Cape of Good Hope, the 1840s saw in both the west and the south the beginnings of a crucial movement into the interior. It is in the 1840s also that the first endeavors are established on the east coast of Africa, though as yet the entire interior remained untouched. In China, the same decade saw missions move from their staging post in Malacca to establish a series of coastal footholds in the Qing Empire, in the wake of the Western gunboats that battered these Chinese ports into submission to bring about trade relations. The Protestant entry into China was a major development that in time would alter the whole shape and mood of the missionary movement. The decade is also significant for what happens in New Zealand, which was perhaps the first field to raise in pointed form the recurring question of how missions should relate to the invasive power of white settlement.

By the 1840s, there were also two apparent success stories to which the missionary movement could point. One of these was the Caribbean, where there were strong churches in many of the old sugar islands based on the recently emancipated slaves. There were, in fact, more African Christians in the Americas at this point than there were in Africa, and there was an expectation, soon to be partly fulfilled, of a Caribbean mission force evangelizing Africa. Indeed, surprisingly large numbers of missionaries from the Caribbean did go to various parts of Africa in the second half of the nineteenth century. Incidentally, this remains a story that has never been told in full; it is always told in terms of particular regions or particular denominations. No one has ever looked at the impact as a whole.

The other success story of Protestant missions by this time was in the Pacific, where, as we noted in passing in chapter 6, there were now Christian island kingdoms in Tonga, Samoa, Fiji, and Hawaii, where something close to the European idea of Christendom had actually developed. The Methodist Kingdom of Tonga, for instance, was its official title. The missionary record in the new Australian colonies was less encouraging, owing to the power of white settlers and the shocking treatment of the Aboriginal population. New Zealand was at first less attractive than the South Sea islands on account of the famed fierceness of the warrior traditions of its peoples. When by 1840 that objection was over, it followed a similar path to the Australian colonies. Unlike the Native Americans or the Australian Aboriginals, the New Zealand Maori were too numerous to be completely marginalized; but they lost much of their land, much of their pride, and what had once been a Maori church now became an extension of British models.

In the Middle East, the middle of the century witnessed a consolidation of American missionary efforts in the Ottoman Empire, the Sultan's dominions. Some of the Boston merchants who were developing trade with the empire were supporters of the American Board of Commissioners for Foreign Missions, and so the Middle East became the first epicenter of American missions and raised a whole new set of mission issues. Within the Sultan's dominions, it was not permitted to attempt directly to convert Muslims. The missions, therefore, had to be directed to the old Christian communities in the Ottoman Empire. That empire extended into Europe, so that what is now Bulgaria was one of the early American mission fields. The Ottoman Empire covered most of the Middle East, so that Syria and Palestine were very much part of it, too. The hope was that these ancient Christian communities of the Orthodox and Oriental Orthodox, so long under Muslim rule, once revived and renewed with Scripture teaching, would be in time the evangelists of the Islamic world.

The 1840s also witnessed the emergence of new nations whose languages and cultures were formed by Europe, arising throughout the Americas, in the Pacific, and in southern Africa. In the same decade, British influence was extended in India, while the Dutch consolidated their hold of Java. The French already controlled the majority of Algeria. China, Japan, and Korea resisted the European advance for a long time. The mid-nineteenth century saw the European powers blasting their way into the China ports, and the Americans into Japan from 1853, in each case in the interest of the doctrine of globalizing free trade. China took a long time to overcome the humiliation of that process, and though, Hong Kong apart, it was never a colony, no other nation has resented colonialism more strongly.

The mid-nineteenth century, then, is a crucial era in missions, which introduces a period, we might say, of mission maturity. Well, maturity marks the onset of middle age, and middle age can last quite a long time. So I suggest that what we have over the second half of the nineteenth century is the middle age of the missionary movement, which transitions into final years of the century, the onset of the great imperial age, when missionaries move from being at the disposal, for instance, of African rulers—and if the African ruler will not let them in, they cannot go—to being at the disposal of the colonial district officer. This further new era for missions begins in the 1880s.

Theological Diversification

One sign of the maturity of the mid-nineteenth-century missionary movement was its diversification in theological and denominational character. Hitherto it had been very much the preserve of evangelicals or Pietists on both sides of the Atlantic. From the 1840s, though, increasing interest in missions appears among Anglicans who were not evangelicals. Again the interest is strongest among the radicals, those affected by the Oxford movement, the new Anglo-Catholic version of High Churchmanship, many of them people who had had an evangelical background. They originally included the future Cardinal John Henry Newman, until his conversion to Rome in 1845. As noted in chapter 5, Newman had been brought up as an evangelical and had been the local secretary for the Church Missionary Society in Oxford. These are the new High Church radicals, and they become interested in missions.

A new mission was founded directly on these new Anglo-Catholic principles in 1858–1859 in response to David Livingstone's reports about central Africa when he came back from his first great journey across the African continent. Livingstone, himself a Scottish Congregationalist, took the Anglican bishop, Charles F. Mackenzie, and his High Church clergy to set up their mission in what is now Malawi. This was the Universities' Mission to Central Africa,[2] and it was based on Anglo-Catholic principles because it was to bring the church in its fullness; in other words, there should be a bishop from the beginning heading the mission, whereas in other parts of the world, you built the church first and then appointed the bishop. No, the church would come in its fullness with its bishop.

The fact that this was a universities' mission was itself significant. Hitherto the English universities had had little to do with missions, and there had been comparatively few university graduates from England in any missions. From this time on, this begins to change, and the universities become one of the re-

---

2. The Universities' Mission to Central Africa was founded as the Oxford, Cambridge, and Durham Mission to Central Africa and also drew some support subsequently from Trinity College, Dublin.

cruiting grounds for missionaries, where once there had been virtually none from that source (a very different picture from the United States, where from the beginning, the missionary movement operates among college students). We are seeing, then, from the 1840s a widening of the missionary constituency; both denominationally and socially, it is touching areas of society that it did not do before. The movement is no longer simply an evangelical preserve, nor is its staple necessarily the artisan class, the shopkeeper class that had produced the majority of the early missionaries.

We have suggested that over the period that followed, missions experienced a sort of midlife crisis. There were many sources of this crisis. From within the movement itself came theological tensions as new streams of thought and devotion took hold in the Western church. One of these, as noted in chapter 5, was the steady growth among evangelicals, still the heart of the missionary constituency, of premillennial eschatology. Earlier missions had been prepared for their activity to be long in bearing fruit. Alexander Duff and his successors in the Scots colleges in India hoped to alter the whole climate of Indian thought by higher education in order to enable the conditions to arise for evangelical conversion. We have noted that the Church Missionary Society grew cotton in Nigeria to prove that this could be more profitable than the slave trade and to ensure an economic basis for a self-supporting church. But if there was no hope for human society except in the Lord's return, were not such operations a waste of time? Should not all effort be concentrated on enabling as many people as possible to hear the word before the day of the Lord? This seemed the more important in view of the vast areas of the world completely untouched by the gospel. The obvious blanks on the missionary map were the interior of China and the interior of Africa. In each case, only the coasts had been touched; for though following the First Opium War of 1839–1842 foreigners could live in China, and missions had gone there in droves, it was only in a few designated ports within the Chinese Empire that they were allowed to reside. The vast interior was completely untouched.

Holiness and "Living by Faith"

Another current of teaching affecting evangelicals in particular related to holiness and the Christian life. Some of these ideas emerged in the same radical evangelical circles as were embracing premillennial eschatology. A man of German Pietist origin, George Müller (1805–1898), was struck by the simplicity of the words of Jesus about faith. He was trying to build an orphanage, and he concluded that the methods that Christians commonly used for fundraising were in fact those of the world. He would not beg for funds. He would pray that the needs of the orphanage would be supplied. And his experience was that, time after time, he had enough to feed his orphans. Müller's written account had a powerful effect on many evangelicals.[3] At the same time, new teachings on holiness were emerging that argued that there was a higher plane of Christian living that could be reached, where the believer knew inward peace instead of struggle.

We saw in chapter 6 that the practice of missions raised all sorts of issues about the relation of missions to the church, and we analyzed some of the reasons why this was the case. All these strains—the premillennial, the prayer of faith, the higher plane of Christian living, and a rethinking of the church—meet in the figure that I would like to consider now: James Hudson Taylor (1832–1905), who is a seminal figure in the development of nineteenth-century missions. Taylor has left his own account of his early life and thought.[4] It is interesting that Taylor thought that the best way of explaining the principles on which he was working and the principles on which the mission he founded would operate was by telling his life story.

Taylor's premillennial expectations heightened his desire for the rapid spread of the gospel, particularly in the untouched interior of China. What were all those missionaries doing, crowded together, treading on each other's toes in the treaty ports like Shanghai? Why were they not out in the interior? He was interested in the Müller principles. In his own life, he had tested them and believed that they worked. Surely there was immense waste and bureaucracy in the way that missions currently operated, with their London offices, often burdened with debt. Surely debt was itself dishonoring to God. Surely the patterns of funding that missions were using were unscriptural. Why these endless appeals for money at these monster meetings and in every missionary magazine? Why these missionary bazaars and missionary teas? Why that missionary basket going the rounds of middle-class homes, full of useless articles to be sold to people who did not want them, in order to support missions? Should not God's people simply pray, and would not God then provide, according to his promise? But what were the funds for, in any case? Why should missionaries expect a salary? When Jesus sent his missionaries out, he told them not to take a second coat with them; again, such self-denial was part of the new holiness teaching of sanctification, where you laid everything on the altar. Surely missionaries, like mission societies, should look to God to supply their every need.

---

3. George Müller, *Brief Narrative of Facts Relative to the New Orphan Houses, on Ashley Down, Bristol, and Other Objects of the Scriptural Knowledge Institution for Home and Abroad* (London: Scriptural Knowledge Institution for Home and Abroad, 1846).

4. James Hudson Taylor, *A Retrospect* (London: China Inland Mission, 1894).

And why this denominationalization of missions? Why do you have these Anglican, these Congregational, and these Baptist missions? Why should missions be divided along those lines? Should not a mission accept any true believer, whatever his or her views on baptism or church government, if he was truly and manifestly called to a mission service? Yes, his *or her* views—for why should not the call of God come to women as well as to men? And what does the call to God have to do with either ordination or education?

The China Inland Mission

These were the questions that the young Hudson Taylor faced and that he wrestled with in his early years of missionary service in China. He himself had a basic medical qualification, but he saw his task not as a doctor but as a missionary, an evangelist. He first went to China in 1853 as an independent missionary and began to penetrate into the interior behind the treaty ports, wearing Chinese dress, and eventually, in 1865, launched a new type of mission: the China Inland Mission. Among its principles were, first, that faith and prayer are the basis. There would be no fixed salaries, no solicitation for funds, and the mission would never go into debt. Second, the direction of the mission would take place not from London but in the field. Third, missionaries would be accepted from any Christian denomination. Fourth, those who were seen to have a true calling as missionaries could be accepted whatever their degree of education. And finally, women could be accepted as full missionaries on the same terms as men.

The China Inland Mission was the first of what became known as the faith missions and was the model for many others, though very few copied it exactly. I have not found any who followed the original China Inland Mission model in its entirety, though many other missions that were founded later had the word "interior" in their name. Going into the interior—up to now Christianity has been a thing of the coasts. It is into the interior that the new missions go: this is a new wave of missions. The missions reflected the new evangelical spirituality, and in China it did lead to Christian advance far beyond the treaty ports.

Social and Intellectual Aspects of the Midlife Crisis

There were other aspects of the midlife crisis that came from changes in the religious structure of Britain, and indeed in much of Europe. Two features were announcing the decline of Christianity in Europe, though their significance was not fully realized at the time. One was acceptance that a large part of the population of the great cities and of the industrial areas had no connection with the church. Soon after H. M. Stanley wrote a famous book about his African travels called *In Darkest Africa*, William Booth, the founder of the Salvation Army, wrote a book called *In Darkest England and the Way Out*.[5] In other words, dire need was not just something to be found overseas. It was there in the heart of the British urban areas.

Throughout the nineteenth century, you see the concern for the churchless among the British churches, but it is always seen as a pastoral crisis: the churches are in the wrong place; we don't have enough ministers; people don't feel comfortable coming to church if they don't have a new set of clothes, so we must have places where they don't feel they need to dress up—all these operations. In fact, it was not that the church had lost the industrial classes in Britain; it had never had them.

The other currents were intellectual. The reading classes in Britain and America now began to read books about Hinduism and Buddhism—not the old accounts that they had read before, about human sacrifice and widow burning, but accounts of profound philosophy and attractive views of life. In 1874, the Royal Institution hosted a body of lectures by one Reginald Bosworth Smith, which was later published as a book called *Mohammed and Mohammedanism*.[6] In this book, Bosworth Smith argued for a positive evaluation of Islam and of its civilizing effect. One can see it, like so much of the intellectual currents of this period, in the context of evolutionary development. In a scale of evolutionary development, Islam is quite high—not as high as Christianity but at the higher end of the scale—much higher, for instance, than the traditional religions of Africa.

This enters into British colonial policy. The Islamization of Africa will be a civilizing effect. You do not ask the question, Are these things true? You ask, What are their social effects? And the social effects of Islam in Africa would appear to be beneficial. And so with the rise of the imperial age, as more and more territories are taken over in which Muslim and non-Muslim people live side by side, direct encouragement is often given to Islamization, and missions constantly find themselves locked out from areas where it was feared there might be conflict with Muslims.

I have been concentrating so far rather heavily on Britain, and at this point, Britain is still the leading player in the Protestant missionary move-

---

5. Henry M. Stanley, *In Darkest Africa, or, the Quest, Rescue and Retreat of Emin, Governor of Equatoria* (London: Low, Marston, Searle, & Rivington, 1890); William Booth, *In Darkest England and the Way Out* (London: Carlyle, 1890).

6. Reginald Bosworth Smith, *Mohammed and Mohammedanism* (London: Murray, 1889).

ment. But let us cross the Atlantic now and see what is happening in the United States over the same period.

Parallel Trends in the United States

By the middle of the century, the young nation of the United States was becoming a world power. Its own size was increasing as it spread across the continent to the Pacific coast. It occupied former French territory in Louisiana, former Spanish territory in Florida, former Russian territory in Alaska. It annexed Texas from Mexico. On the world stage, it began to make a stand, notably in the Far East. It was involved in the opening of China to the West, and it was a missionary, Samuel Wells Williams, who became the first US ambassador in China and wrote a book about China that was much used for a couple of generations by Western readers.[7] The United States set up close relations with the kingdom of Siam (part of modern Thailand) and forced Japan to open itself to foreign influences with a naval raid. In 1898, the war with Spain made it an imperial power as it took over the Spanish colony of the Philippines as well as others in the Caribbean.

All this was bound to make Americans, so long concentrated on affairs in their own continent, more and more interested in the wider world, to make American Christians think more about that world, a world in which in the 1880s, the European powers were consolidating huge colonial empires, with Africa being carved up by Britain, France, Germany, Belgium, and Italy, until only Ethiopia and Liberia were left outside these empires. Much the largest of these empires was the British. Those who studied signs of the times had to ponder what this meant.

One person doing this was a Presbyterian minister called Arthur Tappan Pierson (1837–1911). He began with the background typical of New England Congregationalists and Presbyterians: evangelical, orthodox Calvinist, eager for the gospel to spread, strongly supporting the North in the Civil War, convinced that the antislavery cause was a righteous moral cause, and strongly supporting missions. When he became a pastor in Detroit, he came into a sense of what the American cities were like. The turning point for him, the great deliverance, was when his church was burned down, because this forced his congregation to meet in a theater. He introduced popular hymns of the new style, and the new style of preaching. His theology began to change, too.

---

7. S. Wells Williams, *The Middle Kingdom: A Survey of the Geography, Government, Education, Social Life, Arts, Religion, etc. of the Chinese Empire and Its Inhabitants*, 4th ed. (New York: Wiley & Halsted, 1861).

He became a premillennialist, expecting the imminent return of Christ, and he became more and more concerned with multiplying missionaries before the Lord's return.

Pierson remained a loyal Presbyterian but thought that his mission board was making a mistake by transferring the Presbyterian idea of a learned ministry to the mission field. There were many people, he held, men and women, who could be effective missionaries if they had some proper training. They did not need a college education; they did not need a full seminary course. They needed short courses of systematic Bible teaching of the sort that lay workers in the industrial cities needed, the sort of people he could use as assistants in his ministry in Detroit. He was also reading George Müller and, indeed, corresponding with Müller about the supply of needs by prayer. Pierson, in fact, was passing through the same processes that Hudson Taylor was going through in England and in China.

Then he was transferred to Philadelphia. The trouble was, his church was rebuilt after the fire, and the congregation insisted on building it the way it was before, which meant shutting out the new congregation that had come to the theater. So Pierson left and went to Philadelphia. There he tried to impress on his colleagues and presbytery the urgency of world evangelization, and especially how world evangelization could not wait for the fulfillment of those long ministerial courses. The presbytery should consider recruiting laypeople, with short courses of training. He got nowhere. This was too un-Presbyterian.

Pierson then developed a characteristically American response. America, the enlightened nation, likes to work by applying scientific principles. Identify the problem and solve it. The problem? The problem is how the world can be evangelized before the Lord's return. Scientific calculations—if one in every hundred Christians was to become a missionary and if every Protestant gave one dollar a year, then you would have three hundred thousand missionaries and a missionary budget of $30 million in a very short time; and that would be enough for every person in the world to hear the gospel by 1900. We should notice that evangelization is a matter of people's *hearing* the gospel, not of *understanding* it. They hear words; they do not necessarily hear the gospel. Pierson sketched a systematic plan for carrying out this verbal communication against the background of a world where it seemed there would soon be no countries closed to the gospel.

Pierson took over the editorship of the periodical called *The Missionary Review of the World*. He made it a major journal designed to show the progress of the gospel, and he spelled out his ideas in a book called *The Crisis of*

Missions, which was published in 1886.[8] That same year, he was invited by the great evangelist D. L. Moody to be a speaker at a month-long retreat that Moody was holding for college students. The sponsoring body was the still young YMCA, the Young Men's Christian Association, one of the earliest great parachurch movements. Moody is holding this retreat at his own institution in Mount Hermon, Massachusetts, for students who are associated with the YMCA. It was a conference on prophecy, not on missions, but there was a group of twelve students there who, in the course of the meeting, committed their lives to God as missionaries. They met every day to pray that others would get the same vision of missionary service, and they approached Pierson to give an address to the conference on missions. Their spokesman was a young Princeton student called Robert P. Wilder.

The program had already been designed for the rest of the conference, with no room for this additional lecture on missions, so it had to be made an optional extra to the program. Pierson agreed, and the effect was electric. More students committed themselves to missions; others were obviously wrestling with the idea, and the idea gradually took over the conference. By the end of the conference, a hundred students had offered for missionary service, and the YMCA began to organize mission bands in colleges, missionary libraries for students, and systematic teaching for the study of missions. Over the next two years, two student delegates visited 167 colleges and universities with this challenge: "I am willing and desirous, God permitting [an important proviso], to become a foreign missionary." Over these two years, 2,200 students responded.

The Student Volunteer Movement

Something similar, though on nothing like this scale, had begun to happen in Britain. We have seen that for a long time, it was very hard for British missions to get university-educated missionaries. This changed in the 1880s. In 1885, the year before the Mount Hermon conference, there was a great stir when seven upper-class Englishmen, most of them associated with Cambridge University, and including some of the university's leading sportsmen, the most famous of them C. T. Studd, all offered for service with the China Inland Mission. The Cambridge Seven, as they became known, made a tour

---

8. Arthur T. Pierson, *The Crisis of Missions, or the Voice out of the Cloud* (New York: Baker & Taylor, 1886).

of British universities and colleges, and again there was a major impact. University graduates were drawn to mission service in numbers.

Back in America, the Student Volunteer Movement for Foreign Missions was formed in 1888. It adopted a watchword that was based on Pierson's ideas: "The evangelization of the world in this generation." Now, "generation" can mean several different things; the first interpretation given to it was that of people who were alive at the time. The Student Volunteer Movement held regular conferences so that every student could attend one during his or her college career. Pierson was one of the most favored speakers. It also produced a parallel development in Britain, the Student Volunteer Missionary Union, which in 1896 adopted the American watchword as its own. The people who introduced it were Robert Wilder, who was the spokesman of the student group who got Pierson to give the climactic address in the Mount Hermon conference, and John R. Mott, who also had been one of the hundred students at the Mount Hermon conference who had volunteered for missions.

The first international student conference took place at Liverpool in 1896. It involved a reinterpretation of the watchword: the watchword simply meant that the good news of salvation was intended by God to be made known to all fifteen hundred million of the present human family, and that the responsibility for this gigantic undertaking lies on all who have been redeemed by his Son. This was the declaration adopted by the Liverpool conference of 1896, and they added for home consumption in Britain an appeal to the British churches to adopt the watchword as their own and make it official church policy. The Liverpool conference included delegates from France, from Holland, from Switzerland, from Norway, and from Germany, who pledged to form their own organizations in their own countries.[9]

What happened to all this enthusiasm? By 1912, there were five thousand Student Volunteer Movement members from the United States who had become missionaries. The student missionary movement had become internationalized, with its own organization quite independent of the mission societies. The student conferences were, in fact, preparing the way for the World Missionary Conference in Edinburgh in 1910; but for the moment, the focus was the evangelization of a world that seemed open as it had never been before to the gospel: opened by modern technology, opened by political developments that seemed to point to Britain and the United States as partners in the leadership of world evangelization, opened by cataclysmic changes in Asia. The watchword represents activism, pragmatism, and strategy—all of them, I would suggest, typically American characteristics.

9. *"Make Jesus King": The Report of the International Students' Missionary Conference, Liverpool, January 1-5, 1896*, 2nd ed. (London: Student Volunteer Missionary Union, [1896]), 109–33.

Every arm of the existing mission agencies found impetus from the student movement. Many students went to the new faith missions, but many others went to the older denominational societies. Indeed, Pierson, who remained a loyal Presbyterian even after he was rebaptized in London, took action to ensure that the Student Volunteer Movement did not tie itself to the faith missions, as many people wanted them to do, but would be open to all the mission agencies.

In England, the Church Missionary Society was transformed. There are stories of that transformation—the way, for instance, in which young men in a hurry take charge of the Niger mission and in fact remove all the original African missionaries; how the young Church Missionary Society missionaries in northern Nigeria wear Hausa dress, whereas the earlier African missionaries wore European dress. The spirit of the China Inland Mission is now entering into these other situations. But Hudson Taylor and A. T. Pierson had urged that there was a place not just for university students on the mission field but for others less educated as well; and numbers of such people came forward at the same time, stirred by the same influences. These went mainly to the faith missions, which were usually ready to receive them. New colleges came into being for missionary training, Bible teaching, perhaps some practical training, but no academic theology, and such people were rarely ordained. Missions are getting further from the churches.

The spirituality of the volunteer movement went along with the new doctrines of sanctification now becoming current. Traditional evangelicalism depicted the Christian life as one of struggle, of wrestling with continuing evil and temptation. The new holiness teaching, which in Britain was associated with the Keswick Convention (founded in the English Lake District in 1875), said it should be one of rest and of victory; there was in fact an experience *after* conversion where that victory might be received by faith. The same spirituality called for utter consecration, laying all on the altar. That proved a powerful driver of recruitment for missionary service. What it did not have was the older evangelical commitment to social action that took evangelicals into antislavery movements and got them involved in cotton growing.

CHAPTER 10

The World Missionary Conference and the First World War

Bright Visions, Dark Clouds, Hidden Happenings

It is now widely accepted that the Christian faith is in the process of becoming once again what it was at the beginning, a non-Western religion. It is equally clear that until well into the last century, it was overwhelmingly—though never entirely—a Western one, and had been a Western one for so long that people had forgotten that it had ever been anything else. In other words, during the course of the twentieth century, the Christian church changed its shape completely.

There are various reasons for that change, some more theological, some more to do with politics and demography. By the dawn of the twentieth century, the missionary movement had been in existence for something like four hundred years, first in Catholic form, then Protestant, and then Catholic and Protestant side by side. Yet in numerical terms, Western missions had in 1900 relatively little to show for their efforts. In other words, it took a very long time before the missionary movement effected the sort of change that its champions always spoke about and preached about and prayed for and that their congregations sang about in their hymns.

Over previous chapters, we have been looking at the earlier part of that story: first at the early Catholic missions and then at the cross-cultural encounter of the first Protestant Christians to live next to a non-Christian people in New England; and then the origins of Protestant overseas missions among Christians in Germany and central Europe, how that movement spread to Britain in the late eighteenth century and the infant United States in the early years of the nineteenth; and how this development, by involving powers with maritime capability, transformed the movement, opening up vast new possibilities to it. That mention of the maritime factor indicates that the missionary movement changed when it was taken up by people who had access to ships and were in regular contact with places overseas. That should remind us that the missionary movement did not take place in a vacuum, unaffected by developments in national and international affairs. But let us begin with developments in the sphere of the mind.

In 1907, Bernard Lucas, a Congregationalist missionary of the London Missionary Society in South India, published a book with a title that was typical of that high imperial age, *The Empire of Christ*. "The missionary enterprise," he says, "appeals with less force to the Church as a whole than it did fifty years ago. Then the Church knew less but felt more, now it knows more but feels less."[1] Fifty years ago, fifty years back from 1904, takes you to 1854, not long before his own birth. He seeks to justify this statement in the realm of theology. The essential missionary motivation, he contends, is the same as ever, but the belief and sentiments are not as powerful as they were. Intellectually missionaries in 1904 lived in a different realm from their fathers, a realm that was constituted essentially by the natural sciences and the evolutionary process. The key concept in the new universe had not been able to accommodate the category of sin. He goes on to speak of the recognition of the desperate needs of the industrial masses of the cities of Britain calling out as loudly as those of the slums of Calcutta. The discoveries of comparative religion have revealed how rich are the religious and literary heritage of the East, so that thinking within the church, like thinking outside the church, was beginning to conclude that every nation knows the religion that is good for it and should be left to enjoy it.

The Writing on the Wall That Few Western Christians Could Read

The interesting thing about Lucas's perceptive argument is that in a statistical sense, missions were in fact much *more* significant in British Christianity in 1904 than they had been fifty years earlier. In 1904, Lucas's own society sent out seventeen missionaries, not including wives, who were now becoming missionaries. In 1854, it had not sent any. The great period of missionary enthusiasm did not set in until a little before the time that Lucas's own service began, in the 1880s. And Lucas was probably correct in detecting that when the twentieth century came, that enthusiasm was already fading. The British

---

1. Bernard Lucas, *The Empire of Christ: Being a Study of the Missionary Enterprise in the Light of Modern Religious Thought* (London: Macmillan, 1907), 1.

intellectual climate had set against the missionary movement. What was not yet manifest until long afterward was that it had set in against Christianity itself. The sea change in theological perspectives on other religions was, however, not the only development in the context of the missionary movement that would fundamentally affect its character and fortunes in the twentieth century. Demography also played its part. The twentieth century was remarkable for bringing the end of a vast movement of population that had shaped world history over several centuries. In the course of the twentieth century, this great European migration of population reached its peak, then came to a halt, and finally went into reverse. What's more, over the same period of time, the flow of Christian missions was not so much reversed as made increasingly multidirectional. The twentieth century would see the end of the era in which it could be safely assumed that missionaries all wore white faces.

Nobody in the first decade of the twentieth century had any idea that the Western missionary movement was about to reach its peak and then enter into decline. In order to reinforce that point, let me in this chapter take you to Scotland again, to Edinburgh this time. My former office in the University of Edinburgh stood next to the Assembly Hall where the World Missionary Conference met in 1910 to discuss what was called the missionary problem of the world, which was quite simply how the work of mission could be organized to bring the gospel to everyone in the world. As the leaders insisted at the time, the thing looked possible. I think we can see this as the high point of the Protestant missionary movement. I stress "of the Protestant" movement. For Catholic and Orthodox mission, this is not a particularly significant year, but for all sorts of reasons, 1910 marks the high point of the Western movement. From that time, it becomes something else, and that something else is what I would like to look at in this chapter.

The High Point of the Western Protestant Missionary Movement in Edinburgh, 1910

The twentieth century was the most violent in human history, but for its first decade, there was no sound of the beating of the wings of the angel of death. Despite rivalries and tensions between the powers of Europe, the world appeared stable. Very few countries were absolutely closed to the gospel. Mobilization of Christian resources, and international cooperation in the work of the gospel would under God's blessing bring about the evangelization of the whole world. And the resources to be mobilized were essentially those of the parts of the world that were thought to be fully missionized already, that is to say, Europe and North America, plus Australia and New Zealand.

I do not want to say a lot about the conference itself; I have written on that topic and on the events that led up to the conference in *The Cross-Cultural Process in Christian History*.[2] The third essay in the book, "From Christendom to World Christianity," takes the World Missionary Conference as a point in the transformation of Christianity culturally and demographically. We will come to that in a minute. But if you are looking for the origins of the conference, again we have been talking about these apparently accidental happenings. There was no great plan or strategy behind the Edinburgh conference in its origins. The person who suggested it was John Fairley Daly, a very obscure Scottish missionary in Nyasaland (Malawi). The so-called World Missionary Conference of 1910 was not the first missionary conference, nor was it even the biggest missionary conference; there had been a much larger conference in New York ten years earlier. So there is something else that makes its significance. The World Missionary Conference was not primarily a triumphal celebration of achievement, although it had its moments of triumphalism. Rather it was a serious attempt at a systematic, businesslike analysis of what Protestant missions had already achieved and what remained to be done. The 1910 conference was about business. That is one respect in which it differs from the so-called Centenary Conference of 1888, which was the largest of the mission conferences but was much more a celebration and a free-for-all, anybody-can-come sort of conference.

Immense labor went into the preparatory documents and notably into the *Statistical Atlas of Christian Missions*.[3] This you might see as the first edition of the *World Christian Encyclopedia*,[4] the first attempt to produce comprehensive statistics for missions across the world, and it was done as part of the preparatory work for the conference: a statistical atlas, maps of each part of the world, every known mission station marked, and statistics for each of those stations given. In other words, those attending the conference were supposed to have all the available data about missions at their fingertips.

---

2. Andrew F. Walls, *The Cross-Cultural Process in Christian History: Studies in the Transmission and Appropriation of Faith* (Maryknoll, NY: Orbis Books, 2002), 49–71; see also Brian Stanley, *The World Missionary Conference, Edinburgh 1910* (Grand Rapids: Eerdmans, 2009).

3. World Missionary Conference, *Statistical Atlas of Christian Missions* (Edinburgh: World Missionary Conference, 1910).

4. *The World Christian Encyclopedia* was first published by Oxford University Press, under the editorship of David Barrett, in 1982. Barrett, together with George T. Kurian and Todd M. Johnson, produced a second edition in two volumes in 2001. A third edition, edited by Todd M. Johnson and Gina A. Zurlo, was published by Edinburgh University Press in 2020.

Preparations

No conference was ever better prepared beforehand. Eight commissions toiled for months to produce book-length reports as a basis of discussion of the major aspects of missions. Discussion itself was kept crisp and pointed by limiting participants to seven minutes each. These are people who were used, for the most part, to pulpit eloquence, the days when sermons were really sermons; but you had to get it over in seven minutes at the Edinburgh conference. Similarly, no announcements were made at the Edinburgh conference, just to save time in the meetings. All delegates, the official record of the conference says, received the announcements for the day at their breakfast table.[5]

Some years ago as I was giving a lecture in Dundee, Scotland, an old gentleman in the front row appeared to be asleep the whole time. The Edinburgh conference came into what I was saying somehow. At the end of the lecture, he came to me and he said, "You were talking about the missionary conference in Edinburgh in 1910." I said, "Yes." He said, "I was there." Well, as I say, he was an old gentleman, but I was trying to do my calculations. He said that as a boy of twelve, he had been employed to ride around Edinburgh on a bicycle delivering the daily announcements to the lodgings of every delegate so that they had the announcements for the day at their breakfast table. He received a shilling a day for this, great riches, "which," he said, "I regret to say, I wasted on the new entertainment of the cinema."

The Delegates

Edinburgh 1910 was very carefully regulated as to who came (again, I discuss that question in the essay).[6] Representation at the conference was carefully balanced to reflect the proportional involvement in missions of the main sources of missionaries, that is, Britain, North America, and continental Europe, with a small place reserved for the colonies, that is, the white populations of Australia, New Zealand, and South Africa, which were sending missions on a small scale (they had about fifteen delegates). Great pains were also directed to ensure coverage of the entire theological spectrum represented in non-Catholic missions. The great problem at that point was to involve the

5. World Missionary Conference, *The History and Records of the Conference together with Addresses Delivered at the Evening Meetings* (Edinburgh: Oliphant, Anderson & Ferrier, [1910]), 23–24.
6. Walls, *Cross-Cultural Process*, 55–58; see also Stanley, *World Missionary Conference*, 12–13, 91–97.

whole range of Anglicans who were involved in mission, to enable them to meet with people whose doctrine of the church they did not accept.

The benches in the Assembly Hall in 1910 were packed with European and American missionaries and mission executives. There was a small number, just eighteen, of Asian delegates, mostly from China, Japan, Korea, or India; there was only a single African present—Mark Christian Hayford, a Baptist from the Gold Coast (Ghana).[7]

The Commission I Report

The report that has attracted most attention in later times is the report of Commission IV, called "The Missionary Message in Relation to Non-Christian Religions," with its analysis of the replies received to a detailed questionnaire sent out all over the world. But of all the volumes that contain the record of the conference, the one that perhaps stands closest to the focus of the meeting is the report of Commission I, published under the title "Carrying the Gospel to all the Non-Christian World." The commission was chaired by John R. Mott, who was in fact the dominating figure at the conference. It had twenty members: eight British, eight North American, four continental Europeans, and the list included some of the biggest names in the missionary movement at that time. Its report conveys the drift in the very title of its first main section: "The Opportunity and the Urgency of Carrying the Gospel to All the Non-Christian World." This section of the report began by confidently asserting, "It is possible to-day to a degree far greater than at any time in the past to give the Gospel to all the non-Christian world."[8] For one thing, the report argues, the world was now known and explored. For another, it was now largely open to the gospel—open not only in the political sense of unimpeded access but also in the more important sense of the attitude of its peoples. The decision-making classes in countries like Japan and Korea that had been closed to outside ideas for centuries were now ready to listen. In India, the outcaste and lower caste groups were recognizing the advantages of Western civilization and were taking the Christian message seriously as a result. Africa and the Pacific were at last open to mission enterprise (*Report of Commission I*, 6–10). In Africa, as we saw in the previous chapter, for most

7. Professor Walls wrote that there were *no* Africans present. For Hayford, see Stanley, *World Missionary Conference*, 97–98.—Ed.

8. World Missionary Conference, *Report of Commission I: Carrying the Gospel to All the Non-Christian World* (Edinburgh: Oliphant, Anderson & Ferrier, [1910]), 5.

of the nineteenth century, the mission presence is almost entirely coastal; only with the twentieth century does the continent become fully open, even if colonial governments still placed obstacles in the way of missions in areas with a Muslim presence.

If the commission was impressed by the opportunities that the contemporary situation offered, it was also insistent that the opportunities might be temporary. While it was certainly true that the non-Christian religions were losing their hold on key groups in some countries, it did not necessarily follow that the classes on whom they were losing their grip would turn to the Christian faith. They might turn elsewhere, or the old religions might reform in order to meet the challenges of modern thought, or they might turn to the modern secular education now spreading in Asia, which might make a climate unfavorable to Christianity. Islam, with the aid and protection of European colonial governments, might well become the religion of Africa. Western influences were spreading on a global scale, but the net result might be that the worst, not the best, features of Western civilization would take root in Africa and Asia. The worst face of the West was already displayed among the European and American residents in non-Western countries. Though at present the winds were fair, the commission saw the possibility of unsettled weather ahead. It was another incentive to immediate action.

The second, and the largest, division of the report is a survey, continent by continent, of the non-Christian world. The statistical atlas was meant as a companion to this; you were supposed to read the two together. There are 142 pages devoted to the missionary situation in Asia, followed by 42 on Africa, and 10 on Australasia and the Pacific. Then there is a short section on non-Christians of the Western Hemisphere devoted entirely to the native peoples of the Americas North and South and to Asian immigrants in America. The Caribbean hardly occurs in the report of Commission I, because it was thought of as part of the Christian world, part of Christendom.

This last section that I have mentioned points to a major lacuna in the World Missionary Conference. I have mentioned that the organizers had aimed at theological inclusiveness. There were large numbers of Anglicans involved in missions that belonged to the Catholic end of the Anglican spectrum. They had not been officially represented at any of the earlier mission conferences, and the general theological climate of the time did not make such meetings easy. It is quite hard for us, I think, to think ourselves back into the theological conditions of 1910 and a situation where, certainly in England, for instance, the division between the established and the other churches could often be very deep and mark out many forms of identity. Other controversies were making this a major political issue at the time. So it was something of a triumph to bring Anglicans and non-Anglicans to-gether on the scale that the Edinburgh conference did. One of the things that made it easier was the Student Volunteer Movement, because many Anglicans had gone with the student volunteers, including many, or at least a substan-tial number, from the Catholic end of the Anglican spectrum. So some key bishops were well disposed to the movement because of the involvement of their young men in the Student Volunteer Movement. One of the key Anglo-Catholic bishops, Bishop Edward Talbot of Southwark, had a son, Neville, who was a student volunteer and went on to play a leading role in the Student Christian Movement.

This attempt, then, to be as inclusive as possible, to bring in the Catholic expressions of Anglicanism, had required a great deal of diplomacy on the part of the organizers. The result was that almost the whole spectrum of contemporary Anglicanism was represented at Edinburgh, making it impor-tant to avoid flash points where the traditions might come into conflict. The greatest potential for flash points lay in discussions of Latin America. The ex-pressed concern of the conference was for the unevangelized parts of the world. For the majority of delegates, especially the North Americans, Latin America as a whole could be considered unevangelized. For others, for people at the Catholic end of the Anglican spectrum, the only unevangelized peoples in that continent were the forest and mountain peoples who had not been reached by Roman Catholic missions. The effect of this was really to move Latin America out of the discussions of the Edinburgh conference altogether, and that is why it plays such a marginal part in Commission I.

After the section on the Western Hemisphere comes another on the Jews throughout the world, and there is a final statement about "unoccupied" sections of the world, those with no missionary presence at all. This section first indicates areas of special difficulty of access or sparse population, such as central Asia, and then resumes the theme of the position of Africa:

> To a far greater degree than even in the case of Asia, the heart of Africa constitutes a vast unoccupied field. . . . There are therefore to be found in Africa about 70,000,000 people, more than one-third of the population of the entire Continent, without any existing agency having plans actu-ally projected for their evangelisation. These figures are overwhelming, and they become more so when it is pointed out that the extent of the effective influence of existing missionary agencies has probably been greatly overestimated. The question can be seriously raised, Has the Church more than made a beginning in the evangelisation of the Dark Continent? (*Report of Commission I*, 281–82)

The last division of the report concerns factors to be taken into account in planning for the evangelization of the non-Christian world. It has a substantial chapter on the church in the mission field—which here means the indigenous church—as an evangelistic agency. This is how the report of Commission I sums up its comments on the indigenous church:

> The small native Church, left to itself, is in danger within a generation or two of losing its tone under the influence of monotony, isolation, or ill-success. As a rule, it needs the guidance and stimulus of the spiritual ideas, as well as the spiritual aids, which are supplied through contact by means of missionaries with the life of older Churches. While many noble leaders have arisen among the early converts in the field, it will take time to develop a sufficient number of men of knowledge, gifts, and character to enable the Church to stand with advantage, or even with safety, apart from foreign missionaries. (*Report of Commission I*, 342)

The indigenous church is a delicate plant. You almost feel it is on life support. It is small, and it is going to be a long time before it can do without missionaries.

The impression given by this whole division of the report is that the task of evangelization depends largely on Western missionaries. The factors to be taken into account in carrying the gospel to the non-Christian world are thus how missionaries should be deployed, how historical factors have skewed deployment, what methods missionaries should use, and missionary participation in the spiritual disciplines. The report addresses words to the home church (the home church is, of course, the church in the West) about the danger that increasing luxury and growing materialism may enervate the home church, quench the missionary spirit. Missionaries are represented as overstretched physically, mentally, and spiritually, unable to get time for either the intellectual or the spiritual preparation that their demanding task requires. The thrust of the report is about the responsibility of the home church, that is, the church of the fully evangelized world in Europe and North America. It must produce the missionaries and the resources that are needed to tackle the unprecedented opportunities now being offered to evangelize the non-Christian world before it is too late.

As we read the report over a century later, it is at this point that the greatest difference appears between the conditions under which the older missionary movement sought to fulfill the Great Commission and the conditions of our own day. The best analysts and thinkers of 1910 could take for granted that there was a reasonably homogeneous, fully evangelized world: the home church, and beyond it, a world that was unevangelized or only partly evangelized. From the fully evangelized world of Europe and North America, the home church must send forth its choicest members in order to carry the gospel to the non-Christian world beyond it, where the native church, a tender young plant, stood as an earnest of its future. Here is the report again:

> How to multiply the number of Christians who, with truthful lives, and with clear, unshakable faith in the character and ability of God, will, individually and collectively or corporately as a Church, wield this force [of intercessory prayer] for the conversion and transformation of men, for the inauguration and energising of spiritual movements, and for the breaking down of all that exalts itself against Christ and His purposes—that is the supreme question of foreign missions. (*Report of Commission I*, 360–61)

Will the home church pray? Will it commit itself? This is what it all is going to depend on.

We have seen that the analysts and visionaries of 1910 realized that the hopeful signs they saw in Asia could quickly change to something else much less hopeful for Christian progress. We have also seen that they recognized the possibility of the church in the West losing its missionary zeal under the influence of its rapidly rising standards of living. What they did not glimpse was how soon the West, and Europe in particular, would become part of the non-Christian world. Perhaps the military language that was common at the time of occupation helped to disable them from remembering that Christian history from the first century onward suggests that there are no permanently Christian lands. Christianity is serial in its growth, often decaying in its centers of apparent strength in order to start anew at or beyond its margins.

The analysts of 1910, living in an age of seaborne communications, held a maritime view of the church and of the world. They saw the carriers of the gospel as crossing the seas in order to fulfill their task. Though they lived at the climactic period of the great European migration, which I discussed in chapter 1, and generally agreed that the spread of Western culture was favorable to the gospel, there is little sign in their report of triumphal rejoicing in the Western empires. When the report directly refers to those empires, which is not very often, it is usually to lament the obstructiveness of Western governments toward missions, and there are abundant references to the negative impact of aspects of Western culture.

Further, while recognizing the difficulties that the anti-foreign movements in Asia created for missionaries, the authors do not condemn nationalism. Here is the report again:

This national and racial spirit cannot and should not be crushed or checked. It is a matter of profound concern to the Christian Church. It will have much power to hinder or to facilitate the spread of Christ's Kingdom. Christ never by teaching or example resisted or withstood the spirit of true nationalism. Wherever His principles, including those pertaining to the supreme claims of His Kingdom on earth, have had the largest right of way, they have served to strengthen national spirit, not to weaken it. (*Report of Commission I*, 33)

Even in India, the report goes on, where the national movement gave rise to strong antimissionary dealing, it was important to note that the same national movement also denounced and discarded caste, which up to now had been the main obstacle to Christian preaching. Nationalism should cause missionaries to take their work to a deeper level, to realize in humility that they must decrease, while the native church must increase.

Theology Off-Limits

On mission theology, Edinburgh 1910 had little to say. The conference ground rules excluded the introduction of topics known to be controversial among participants. That was one of the rules you accepted by coming to the conference; you were not going to start arguing about how much water was necessary in baptism or anything of that sort. Even so, it seems remarkable today that so many people representing such a wide range of theological views could take for granted that they were agreed as to what the gospel was. It seems equally remarkable that they could all accept that evangelism, translation, education, medicine, literature, industrial training, and women's work were simply different methods of carrying the gospel. The most notable questioning voice was that of the German missiologist Gustav Warneck. Warneck was not present at Edinburgh, but he sent a long letter to Mott that is reproduced as an appendix to the report of Commission I (*Report of Commission I*, 434–36). Edinburgh 1910 reflects a certain confidence that whatever issues may divide Christendom, there is a consensual theological deposit that is the common heritage of all Christians.

The conference was a time of dreams and visions. The excitement of the delegates is palpable, even in the staid pages of the official report. It appears in accounts of people who were there—for example, the very lively little book by an Anglican missionary in Egypt, W. H. Temple Gairdner, just called "*Edinburgh 1910*," which is a sort of popular report of the conference for ordinary church people in Britain. As you read it, you pick up the excitement that clearly built up over the course of the conference, even though, as noted earlier, this was not intended as a tub-thumping, rabble rousing, cheering event.[9] This was serious business, hard work, with whole buckets of information to deal with.

Not for nothing are the origins of the modern ecumenical movement often dated from this meeting. Although delegates from the non-Western world were few in number, many who were present caught a first glimpse of what a truly world church might be like. But the meeting was not solely visionary. It was severely practical, directed to systematic planning and cooperative effort. For those there, it was an inspiring, for some a transforming, experience, and it ended on a note of high commitment. "The end of the Conference," announced John R. Mott in his closing address, "is the beginning of the conquest."[10] With this in view, the delegates dispersed, pledged to full mobilization of Christian resources, pledged to international cooperation.

What Happened Next

Then came the First World War, sinking many of those hopes of immediate international cooperation. The government of one Christian nation was soon interning the missionaries of another. Then came the angel of death, and much of that young life that was to be mobilized for the evangelization of the world drained away into the trenches of France and Flanders. Then came the Depression, eroding the economic base on which missions had operated for a century. Then came more war, more destruction, the appearance of weaponry of a power unimagined before, and then the dismantling of the European empires that in 1910 had seemed a pledge of political stability and missionary accessibility. Finally came the most shattering realization: that the lands once thought to be evangelized, the home base of missions, the treasure house that was to yield the dedicated resources of the Christian world, themselves needed to be evangelized afresh. One by one, all the props that upheld the world of 1910 were taken away. All the assumptions underlying their vision of the world and of world evangelization were undermined.

All of this might seem to invalidate the whole vision of the World Missionary Conference and the project that it represented, were it not for another

9. W. H. T. Gairdner, *"Edinburgh 1910": An Account and Interpretation of the World Missionary Conference* (London: Oliphant, Anderson & Ferrier, 1910).

10. World Missionary Conference, *History and Records of the Conference*, 347.

extraordinary aspect of twentieth-century church history. This is the extent to which the dreams and visions of the conference about the evangelization of the non-Christian world were in fact fulfilled, though not in the way or always by the means or even in the places that the delegates expected and planned. The fact remains that by a huge reversal of the position in 1910, the majority of Christians now live in Africa, Asia, Latin America, or the Pacific, and that proportion is rising. Simultaneously with the retreat from Christianity in the West in the twentieth century went, just as the visionaries of Edinburgh hoped, a massive accession to the Christian faith in the non-Western world. The map of the Christian church, its demographic and cultural makeup, changed more dramatically during the twentieth century than in any earlier century probably since the first. But it happened in ways that the analysts of 1910 could not have predicted. The most favorable signs that they could observe lay in Asia. They saw multitudes in Japan, in China, and in India turning to new ways of thought and thus, as it seemed to them, becoming open to Christian ideas as never before. The great Asian cultures had long received the heaviest deployment of missionary personnel and effort. Medical missions, the most financially intensive branch of missions, and other specialisms had been developed largely with Asia in mind. Missions were significantly involved in higher education to university level in Asia, in addition to equipping entire medical faculties in the Chinese Empire. But the Christian growth that has taken place in Asia has not always followed the patterns of missionary investment. China has indeed seen substantial if as yet unquantifiable Christian growth, but that growth came in the second half of the twentieth century, in the teeth of official disfavor and often of outright hostility, and it has taken place in the period after missionaries were excluded from the country.

Korea was somewhat cursorily treated in the commission's report,[11] since Protestant work there was so new and the country's long period of isolation from foreign influence was so recent. In this connection, one might recall that in some ways, North Korea's present isolation is a reversion to type; it is going back to the old ways. But the twentieth century, a time of frequent and varied trauma for Korea, saw Korean Christianity becoming a major force in the land, taking shape in the national movement against Japanese colonialism, burgeoning in the times of the dreadful troubles that followed. In recent decades, Korean Christianity, besides becoming a significant force in North America, has produced thousands of missionaries to serve in other parts of the world, including some of the most inhospitable, the places that the 1910

11. See *Report of Commission I*, 71–80.

report called "unoccupied," where Western missionaries never penetrated. If any country can be said to preserve the spirit of 1910, it is South Korea.

Vigorous churches have also arisen among the complex of peoples who live in northeast India and southwest China who are neither Indic nor Han Chinese, and for these, the period of decisive growth was the twentieth century. There are states in northeast India where Christianity is the majority religious profession. The Indian state of Mizoram claims more than 90 percent of the population as professing Christianity. And in this and other northeastern states, large numbers of missionaries have arisen for the evangelization of the subcontinent and beyond. Across the frontier with Myanmar among peoples of similar ethnic origin, Christian growth has accelerated since the expulsion of the missionaries in the 1960s. In each of the countries mentioned—Nepal, India, China, and Myanmar (perhaps one should add Thailand)—Christians are a minority and often a small one, but taken together, they form a substantial Himalayan-Arakan Christian community, of which there was hardly a trace when the conference met in Edinburgh.[12]

Latin America, which ecclesiastical diplomacy led the World Missionary Conference to leave on one side, has now become a theater of Christian operations that no one can possibly ignore. The peculiar history of Latin America has given it an unusual Christian trajectory. The conquest was intended to bring it within the existing Christendom, so Mexico became New Spain, with the expectation that its laws and customs would be those of old Spain.

In the sixteenth century, Latin America received the church settlement adopted in southern Europe, a settlement arising out of the conditions and controversies of sixteenth-century Europe. It received the Catholicism of the Council of Trent without going through the processes and experiences that produced the Council of Trent. For several centuries, there seemed no reason to doubt that Latin America had been successfully incorporated within the Christendom framework derived from medieval Europe. But Latin America was no mere extension of Europe. It was a union of diverse peoples with powerful indigenous religious influences. In the twentieth century, with rapid urbanization and huge social ferment, the lid blew off the religious pressure cooker. A theological upheaval occurred as drastic as any that befell Europe in the sixteenth century, and Latin America's delayed reformation era began. As in Europe, there was a pastoral revolution within the established church. As in Europe, reforming zeal took both conservative and radical ecclesiastical

---

12. However, it should be noted that one of the Asian delegates was Burmese, Professor L. T. Ah Sou, while another, Rev. Thang Khan Sangma, was from the Garo Hills in Assam. Both were delegates of the American Baptist Foreign Missionary Society.—Ed.

forms. As in Europe, popular religious movements burst the bounds of the old church altogether.

Outside immigrant communities, Protestantism had traditionally played no significant part in Latin America. At the time of the World Missionary Conference, it was hardly visible. By the end of the twentieth century, Protestants formed a significant proportion of the population, in some Central America countries perhaps actually a majority of the actively practicing Christians among the population. But the movement took an indigenous form. The overwhelming majority of Latin American Protestants are now Pentecostal. What in the West has been marginal has in Latin America become mainstream. Latin America may be manifestly carrying the impress of European and North American influences, but its potent mix of the cultures of three continents ensures it has a religious dynamic of its own. Liberation theology and Pentecostal preaching and congregational life are alike examples of its effect, and the spread of a huge diaspora from Latin America, with the United States as its main focus, a further effect of the twentieth century, will ensure that its influences spread far beyond Latin America itself.

We have seen that the analysts of 1910 saw inland Africa as a great unoccupied field and questioned whether more than a beginning had been made of the evangelization of the continent. It is perhaps in Africa that the strongest contrast appears between the church today and the church as seen by the writers of the report of Commission I. They said in 1910 that the evangelization of the interior had hardly begun, but think what the twentieth century has brought: at the beginning, perhaps 9.64 million professing Christians in the whole continent. At the end, who knows how many? The current estimate for the year 2000 is 382.5 million.[13] Sub-Saharan Africa has become one of the Christian heartlands and is quietly slipping into the place in the Christian world that was once occupied by Europe.

The meeting in 1910 envisaged the native church, as the churches of Africa and Asia were then collectively designated, as a tender young plant in need of constant supervision. It is salutary to remember the fiery trials, the multiple testings, that many of those churches have endured since then. Is there a parallel in Christian history to the church in China over the past fifty years in terms of what it has endured and how it has emerged? Over the same period, Christian faith in many parts of Africa has been honed on endemic disaster in places where the normal climate of the life of faith has been war, disruption, dispersal, disease, and disappointment. The churches of South Africa were

---

13. The estimate for 2020 is 667.8 million. Todd M. Johnson and Gina A. Zurlo, eds., *World Christian Encyclopedia*, 3rd ed. (Edinburgh: Edinburgh University Press, 2020), 6.—Ed.

called to give moral leadership to their nation in ways the Western church has not known for many centuries.

There are other countries where the churches, sometimes the only functioning forms of civil society where even the state has broken down, have become salt and light to nations in distress. If suffering, persecution, and faithful wrestling with impossible situations are the marks of Christian authenticity, then perhaps God has been training some of the churches of Africa and Asia for leadership in mission, imparting to them accumulated knowledge of God's salvation.

More and more, events and developments in Africa, Asia, Latin America will shape the future of Christianity, for these are the great modern theaters of Christian mission, the scene of crucial engagement between the Christian gospel and what the Fourth Gospel calls "the world." Increasingly this engagement will raise issues for Christian faith and Christian service and define the agenda for the Christian church worldwide. One pressing item on the agenda will be the re-evangelization of the West, the vista the analysts of the missionary situation had no reason to contemplate in 1910. Now the situation of the West has to be pondered not in terms of Christian revival but of cross-cultural primary evangelism, the penetration of a non-Christian culture.

One by one, all the props of the world of 1910 have been taken away. All the assumptions on which their view of the world and of world evangelization were based lost their foundation. But the vision granted at Edinburgh, the vision of a world church, the vision of a gospel spread throughout the world—that was a true vision, and it came to pass; it really happened. But it happened in ways that no one at Edinburgh expected or predicted.

CHAPTER 11

The Missionary as Specialist

Healing and the Gospel

Now we turn to the missionary as specialist, which increasingly comes to mean the missionary as professional. It will confine itself to looking at the issue of healing; education, which I had originally intended to include, raises a whole set of other issues. One of the themes that will emerge is how the consolidation of the medical profession in the Western countries, and in Britain in particular, impacted the missionary movement.

I do not want to repeat too much of what I have said in an essay that appears in *The Missionary Movement in Christian History*, "The Domestic Importance of the Nineteenth-Century Medical Missionary," with the subtitle "The Heavy Artillery of the Missionary Army."[1] I will leave most of that without trying to say it again and will try to approach the issue of medical missions through one particular person.

Early Protestant Missions

The early assumption in most Protestant missions was that a missionary, being a preacher of the gospel, would be a minister of the gospel in the same way as a preacher of the gospel normally was at home. It was a result of this that when people were sent to the mission field who were not ministers, not preachers of the gospel, there was always a degree of ambiguity about their status as to whether they were really missionaries. That ambiguity existed in

1. Andrew F. Walls, *The Missionary Movement in Christian History: Studies in the Transmission of Faith* (Maryknoll, NY: Orbis Books, 1996), 211–20.

the case of missionary wives for a long time. It is very difficult to say who was the first woman missionary; woman missionaries tended to be appointed to fill a gap, which some missionary wife had been covering until she was removed from the scene. You did not really intend to set up woman missionaries, but you had to continue the work begun by the late excellent Mrs. Jones—and Mr. Jones couldn't do it. In India and later in China, it became necessary to recognize that there were whole areas of mission work that men simply could not approach and that you had to have an order of women to do. But you tended to have separate societies for these persons; they did not complicate the mission itself. You set up a society for female education in Bengal or things of this sort to cover this anomalous status. The assumption for a long time is that the missionary is an ordained minister.

Lay functionaries in the early days were usually schoolmasters, and the schoolmaster usually meant a fairly humble person in terms of education who would deal with elementary schooling, usually someone who did not have the educational qualifications for ordination. Again, these are seen as ancillary. They are not real missionaries; they are assistants to the missionary task.

In the early days, medicine is rather in this category. It was always recognized that medical training might be a useful subsidiary skill for a missionary. Many missionary candidates took medical training before their departure to the mission field. For instance, Robert Morrison, the first and for a long time the only Protestant missionary in China, whom we discussed in chapter 8, having completed his theological studies, spent some time in a London hospital; that was his medical training, being attached to a hospital, where he picked up what knowledge he could. Because, in 1807, training of doctors was still very much a matter of apprenticeship. The young Hudson Taylor, whom we examined in chapter 9, received his initial medical training in his father's chemist shop in Barnsley and then became an apprentice to a distant relative who was a practicing physician in Hull. Finally, in 1852–1853, he topped this out with attendance at the London Hospital in the East End of London. Medical training in the mid-nineteenth century was very much a matter of apprenticeship and learning on the job.

Some missionaries took a full medical course; this is usually at a rather later time, though there were a few who did so in the first half of the century. David Livingstone is an example of this. In Livingstone's case, the training was taken in Glasgow. Livingstone's missionary service with the London Missionary Society began in 1841, when things had moved on a good deal from 1807, when Morrison was a candidate for the same society. But Livingstone, while a medically qualified missionary, was never thought of as a medical missionary. When he arrived at his station in what is now Botswana, he carried out normal missionary duties as a preacher and as a pastor in the same way as the other missionaries. Medicine was just an additional activity, which was useful in certain circumstances.

The reason why Livingstone had taken a full medical course before coming to the field was that he had originally hoped to go to China, and it was clear that in China, medicine was playing a crucial part in missions because it was so difficult to get a hearing any other way. Anti-foreign feeling was always strong in China, and it became even stronger following the humiliation of China after the Opium War of 1839–1842, when the country was forced by the power of Western gunboats to agree to treaties that allowed foreign residents. Foreigners were now legally present in the five treaty ports, but this did not make them welcome. They were bitterly resented, and missions were seen as part of the foreign invasion. From this situation, the greatest degrees of success in reducing the prejudice against foreigners and gaining a hearing came from such medically qualified missionaries as began to arrive in the late 1830s and the early 1840s. Most of them began Livingstone-style, just trying to do the ordinary missionary duties. It was only when they opened their houses as clinics that they began to be taken seriously—and so medical missions were invented in China.

The Impact of the Professionalization of Medicine

The conventional identification of the first medical missionary is the American Peter Parker (1804–1888).[2] In China, he gets his nose just ahead of William Lockhart, of the London Missionary Society; but again, it was external factors that set the pace. The first half of the nineteenth century saw a revolution in the medical profession. It happened on both sides of the Atlantic but reached its climax in Britain in 1850 with the establishment of the General Medical Council. From 1850 onward, every medical practitioner had to be licensed by the council, hold qualifications recognized by the council, and be subject to the council's discipline. The council could strike a person off, and from that time, it was a criminal offense to practice medicine.

The effects of the establishment of the council were considerable, even though their writ did not run to the mission field. There was no reason why the ordinary missionary should not pick up a bit of medical training and administer pills and pull out teeth as might be thought necessary as part of

2. Gerald H. Anderson, "Peter Parker and the Introduction of Western Medicine in China," *Mission Studies* 23 (2006): 203–38.

his ordinary work, but he was not a medical practitioner unless he held a diploma recognized by the General Medical Council. Thus standards were set, and anything less than the council's standards was obviously a second best.

Medicine is now a privileged profession, and the status of the profession rises. Its standards rise, too; and over the following years, developments in medicine, particularly the discovery of anesthesia and the general recognition of the sources of septic infection, revolutionized it still further. The 1860s make another considerable advance, with the Crimean War perhaps being a watershed. The Crimean War, among other things, established the nursing profession as a profession in its own right. All this has its impact on the mission field.

The missionary literature gives several reasons for medical missions. I detect four broad categories of justification for them. The first is the example of Christ, who himself said, "Heal the sick," and who went about doing good. Second is the humanitarian call to ease unnecessary suffering. Disinterested benevolence, after all, was one of the tests of Christianity. The third, what one might call a practical argument, was dangers to missionary health. There were many parts of the world where the mortality among missionaries was extremely wasteful. Early on, there had been that episode of the white man's grave at the very time when Sierra Leone had become the main center of missions in Africa and indeed one of the main centers anywhere in the world. At this very time, you had the phenomenon that missionaries lived sometimes only a few months, a few weeks, or a few days. The drain on personnel was extraordinary. There were other parts of the world where this happened also. Toward the end of the century, it was being urged that it was in the interest of missions to have medical practitioners who would care for the health of their staff. This became very important in Congo, for instance, where a new field opened. The first doctors in Congo were not setting up hospitals; they were trying to keep their colleagues alive.

The fourth group of reasons is the situations—we have seen that China was an outstanding example of this—where the gospel would receive no hearing by any other way. In practice, all the arguments are used, and very often more than one of them at the same time; but in determining where medical missions were directed, I think the fourth reason can be seen to be particularly potent. Medical missions become the heavy artillery of the missionary army to batter down the gates of resistance to the gospel by any other means.

For instance, one of the missions that was particularly slow to move to medical missions was the Church Missionary Society. Henry Venn was very skeptical about their value. But in the early 1860s, the missions were finding great difficulty in getting access to Kashmir, but there was some evidence that a medical man might be acceptable there. It was put to the Church Missionary Society in those terms, and the Church Missionary Society approached the Edinburgh Medical Missionary Society, which had been established in 1841 in order to train medical doctors for the mission field. The doctors were trained in the medical school at the University of Edinburgh, with the Church Missionary Society supporting their training; in other words, these are people who would not become doctors by any other way, but they come because they are recognized as having a missionary calling. Now the Church Missionary Society produces a newly qualified doctor, a young man called William Elmslie, and so this Anglican society takes on a Presbyterian from the Free Church of Scotland as its first professional medical missionary.

Elmslie found that there was no problem about his conducting public prayers, no problem about his catechists preaching to patients while they were waiting to see the doctor or moving around the beds in the hospital. And then came the news that a local rajah, the Rajah of Chamba, was very willing to pay for a doctor to work in his own state on the same terms under which Elmslie was working in his part of British India.[3] Here are medical missions as heavy artillery, breaking down resistance, and it is in China, in the most resistant parts of India, that medical missions were concentrated. You find them much less often in Africa, very rarely in the Pacific, not often in the areas that had been particularly responsive to Christian preaching.

Elmslie was fresh from medical school in Edinburgh, and before long, he was engaged in very drastic surgery—surgery about which he remarks in a letter that he was very glad that he had attended Dr. Simpson's lectures.[4] Dr. Simpson was William Young Simpson, the person who developed anesthesia. Here is anesthesia being applied for serious operations in Kashmir at a time when it was very little in use in England. It is the latest medical discoveries that are being applied on the mission field. This is a sign of the future. Medical missionaries were usually young men fresh from medical school, aware of the latest technologies, aware of the latest equipment. And they wanted them; they wanted them on the field.

The first medical missionaries had worked from their houses, just opening a room as a clinic. This was soon impossible. Medical missionaries wanted a hospital; they wanted anesthesia. In time, they wanted X-rays. They needed skilled assistants: nurses, technicians, and pharmacists. The people who looked askance at all this were the mission society treasurers, because with the new

---

3. [Margaret Jackson Elmslie], *Seedtime in Kashmir: A Memoir of William Jackson Elmslie* (London: Nisbet, 1875), 153–54, 161–62, 165–66.

4. I have been unable to trace this letter.—Ed.

professional status and the General Medical Council monopoly, these things led to another dislocation of the way that missions had worked. The doctor was lord in his hospital, not the mission superintendent. It is the doctor who determines whether the patient is well enough to hear the gospel. It is the doctor who says when the evangelist can come into the ward. It is the doctor who has command of the Sunday services. With the advent of the "professional" medical missionary, a whole series of new configurations has come about.

Dugald Christie of Manchuria

We will now examine some of the issues that arose through the life and experience of one missionary, whom I have come rather to enjoy as I have gotten to know him. His name is Dugald Christie. He was born in 1855 in the Scottish Highlands where his father was a sheep farmer and an innkeeper. His father died when he was an infant; his mother died a little later, so he had a very disrupted childhood, moving from place to place, with an elder sister as his principal caregiver. As a result, he had a rather disrupted and patchy education. The family eventually moved to Glasgow, where as a teenager, he became apprenticed to a draper. In 1874 (Christie was now nineteen), D. L. Moody conducted a famous mission in Glasgow, and the young draper's apprentice was one of those who responded to the call. One result of it was that he was now eager to engage in Christian service, and, despite his rather patchy education, he resolved to be a medical missionary.

A young man of patchy education and very little money had only one hope of becoming a doctor: the Edinburgh Medical Missionary Society existed exactly for people like him with a missionary calling and no other way of becoming qualified in medicine. He applied to the society, was accepted, and carried out the medical course at the University of Edinburgh. One of the ways in which the Edinburgh Medical Missionary Society trained its candidates for missionary service was to get them to work on weekends in the Edinburgh slums, so Christie became attached to the Cowgate Mission, where he worked enthusiastically; indeed, when he qualified, he stayed on for a time as the resident physician in this Edinburgh slum mission.[5] In addition to his medical training, he had been attending theology classes at New College in Edinburgh, at this time the theological faculty of the Free Church of Scotland, which was his own church. And just to fill in the time, he was

---

5. [Elizabeth Hastie Christie], *Dugald Christie of Manchuria: Pioneer and Medical Missionary; The Story of a Life with a Purpose, by His Wife* (London: Clarke, [1932]), 25.

also attending astronomy and navigation classes at the Navigation School in Leith, since that would obviously be helpful in China, where, by all accounts, astronomy was avidly studied.[6]

Christie's church background, as I have said, was Free Church of Scotland; but he had already developed a theory about medical missions, a theory that the Free Church of Scotland mission was not prepared to accept: that a medical missionary could not work effectively without a hospital, or at least a dispensary. The Free Church are again thinking very much in terms of ordained missionaries; they are not averse to ordained missionaries having medical qualifications as well, but moving into the sphere of setting up hospitals is an entirely new thing. That concept of the necessity of hospitals for effective medical work never left him. He changed his allegiance to the United Presbyterian Church, who were more open to the idea, and he joined their fairly new mission in Manchuria in 1882.

Manchuria, the northeast region of the Chinese Empire, was, of course, China beyond the wall, a sensitive area politically and internationally because it was surrounded by predators. To the north, it had a frontier with Russia; Japan, another predator, was just across the water. Not surprisingly, the suspicion of foreigners, always strong in China, was especially strong in Manchuria, and Christie's arrival made people apprehensive that this was the forerunner of a British invasion.

The next year, in 1883, Dr. and Mrs. Christie moved to the Manchurian capital, then called Mukden, now called Shenyang, where his senior colleague was John Ross, who was later to be very significant in the Christian history of Korea. They initially set up their home in Ross's compound before purchasing the adjoining property, where they held regular clinics in an outhouse at the front gate of their home.[7] Christie got down to learning Chinese and to the study of traditional Chinese medicine. On this, he was not as dismissive as most Westerners were, though he was horrified at some of the treatments, especially those for setting broken bones, which included covering with the so-called black plaster that often induced gangrene. He was also very observant of the courtesies of Chinese life and built up good relations, in some cases genuine friendship, with government officials, who were often, if not very interested in Christianity, at least interested in technology and in scientific developments. This remained a lifelong aspect of his policy.

Christie discovered that it was surgery, particularly cataract operations, that broke down much of the prejudice. He carried out the operations outside

6. [Christie], *Dugald Christie of Manchuria*, 25.
7. [Christie], *Dugald Christie of Manchuria*, 40–41.

so that everybody could see him. A crowd would always be around watching, because there were constant rumors that foreigners stole body parts to use them for vicious purposes. Come and see what actually goes on. And with the unheard-of development of people getting their sight back, the acceptance of the mission steadily increased. By 1885, he was able to open his first hospital in a dilapidated building they were able to acquire. It soon fell down, but soon afterward, he obtained a bigger building, and subsequently that was enlarged. By 1893, the hospital was treating 593 inpatients in a year and had seen 20,000 outpatients and carried out 954 operations. By this time, too, Christie had set up a training program for local people, not yet a full medical course (these were going to be medical assistants), but it was still a training program in this form of medicine.

Manchuria, as we have seen, was a politically fragile environment. War broke out between China and Japan in 1894, and Manchuria was a battlefield. Christie worked under the Red Cross and received a Chinese government decoration for his work. Then in 1900 came the Boxer Rising and the boiling over of anti-foreign sentiment in many parts of China. The hospital, as with other buildings associated with foreigners, was burned down. Christie and his wife escaped only just in time. They returned at the end of the rising to rebuild the hospital and open a new women's hospital. But just as the hospital was ready, war broke out again, this time between Russia and Japan, and Manchuria, as the area between the two, once again became the battlefield. The hospital, newly reopened, was taken up by caring for the wounded.

After the war came famine, and after the famine came plague. Pneumonic plague broke out in the severe winter of 1910–1911, a plague that killed nearly everyone who was infected by it. Christie was appointed medical advisor to the government of Manchuria and had to work out a strategy for plague prevention: isolation, disinfection, and early burial of the dead—public health arrangements that were unprecedented in the past. Christie's central place in service to the community during these dreadful years led to numerous donations from Chinese officials to the project closest to his heart, what he had always wanted to do, the apex of medical missions. You start with a clinic, it becomes a dispensary, the dispensary becomes a hospital. What is the next step? A medical school. And so he moves toward the setting up of the Mukden Medical College. He is able to show a good deal of local support and local finance for it, and he hopes that this will act as a sweetener with the fathers and brethren back in Scotland.

The Mukden college was opened in 1912. It offered a five-year medical training based on the Edinburgh curriculum, demanding the same standards as in Edinburgh. The difference from Edinburgh was that the teaching was entirely in Chinese. Christie became the first principal; the five-year course became six years and then seven years. In 1934, the University of Edinburgh recognized the college as qualifying for its postgraduate studies in medicine. The United Presbyterian Mission had supported Christie loyally so far, but the college was one step too far. They said the college must raise its own funds. Christie retired (he was 68) in 1923. He spent his remaining years (he died in 1936) seeking to build up the funding for the maintenance and development of Mukden Medical College.

Christie had, as we have seen, taken a certain amount of theological study in Edinburgh, and he was ordained on the field by the presbytery of Manchuria during his service, so he had been adopted into the official structures of the church. Manchuria was unusual in having a single church; there were two missions, both of which happened to be Presbyterian, which, though they remained separate missions, produced a single indigenous church. But Christie came to argue strongly for a special ordination for medical missionaries, for they, he argued, were a special branch of ministry. The pulpit ministry, as it were, receives ordination in one way; the other people are waved off at some valedictory service. But this is the ministry of the church; this is a solemn setting aside. Should not there be a solemn setting aside to the ministry of the church for people who are called to this branch of service?

The China Centenary Mission Conference

It was at the China Centenary Missionary Conference held in Shanghai in 1907 that Christie took the chair at a committee concerned with medical missions. There were eleven missionary doctors on this committee, and he presented a sort of position paper on the topic.[8] It is a good expression of his mature thought on the theory and practice of medical missions. The interesting thing is the high degree of space that he gives to the theory, and the deductive process by which he moves from theory to practice. There is no need for him to justify medical missions, he says, and goes on, of course, to justify them.

Christie's paper reported that virtually every mission in China now uses medical missions. There are no less than three hundred missionary doctors in 250 hospitals and dispensaries treating at least 2 million patients a year (*Records*, 267). Their effectiveness as a pioneering agency (that's the heavy artillery side) is universally recognized, so much so that there is a tendency

8. *Records: China Centenary Missionary Conference Held at Shanghai, April 25 to May 8, 1907* (Shanghai: Centenary Conference Committee, 1907), 247–68.

in some quarters to think that this is what they are really for, and therefore, medical work becomes secondary once you have established a church. You move the heavy artillery away once you have got some sort of response. But it is also recognized that even a hospital can be a valuable evangelistic agency. An outpatients' waiting room provides a captive audience, many of whom will not hear the gospel any other way. But in addition to the direct contribution that medical missions make to the evangelistic task by gaining a hearing and gathering an audience, medical missions should be recognized as demonstrating Christian love and mercy. There are indirect advantages as well from this demonstration: it predisposes practically minded Chinese people toward the doctrine that produces results like that, and it affords a model for the Chinese church to work out its own schemes of disinterested benevolence.

The China missionary conferences took place every ten years, with the first of them in 1877; they also discussed medical missions, and you can see the difficulty that they have integrating the view of medical missions between the philanthropic duty of benevolence and the manifest evangelistic benefits. You can recognize that, yes, we have a duty to show love and compassion in medical work, but there is concern on the part of some that medical work will distract from the evangelistic imperative. Christie tries to present an integrated view of medical work from first principles, setting aside all the three usual grounds as inadequate. There is a rumbling argument going on underneath about the status of medical missionaries and this suspicion that they are moving into the domain of the ordained minister.

The basis of Christie's theological argument lies in the healing ministry of Christ. What was the healing ministry of Christ for? It was not to gain a hearing; he manifestly had abundant hearers without the healings. All the evidence is that the healings created problems and scandals and opposition. It was not to gather a crowd; Jesus's teaching itself secured the crowd, and he often told people who were healed not to tell anybody. It was not to prove his identity as Messiah; he constantly resisted invitations to prove his mission that way. It was not to produce faith; faith was the result, not the motive, for healings. It was not to convey teaching, even if healings are often parables. The whole point is that the gospel healings are not instrumental at all. They have reality in themselves. They are not casual; they are not incidental. They were clearly costly to the Lord. Remember after the woman touched him in the crowd, he knew that something had happened, that power had gone out from him. That is, the healings were a deliberate and major part of his ministry—and so they should be a major part of the ministry of the church. All the arguments that operate in the case of the Lord operate for his servants: "As the Father has sent me, so I am sending you" (*Records*, 249–50).

When Christie turns to the more practical matters, he is again insisting on his theme that the hospital should be the nexus of a medical mission. Other means have limited use. Moving around, itineration, may be essential in the early stages—you've got, as it were, to advertise your presence—but it is never satisfactory from a professional point of view, because you can't follow up; you can't see how a patient is getting on. There is also a danger that it can be counterproductive: if a patient's condition gets worse, he blames the foreign drug. Dispensaries are one step better than itinerant treatment, but do not be misled by the large attendance that you get at many dispensaries. The test of their effectiveness is how many people come back. A large number of first-time visits is a sign of failure, however much preaching they have heard. The other test is whether, after receiving the dispensary treatment, they are prepared to go to the hospital. It is the hospital that has to be the center of treatment, and the hospital should be up to date; it should be at as high a standard as it is in the West. Avoid the trap that anything is good enough for China. The Chinese will not look at it that way. Do not overstretch; place two doctors together as far as possible (*Records*, 255–58).

Then Christie returns to the question of where the medical missionary fits into the general work of ministry. The medical missionary is not a secular worker. Surgery or nursing are forms of preaching, and they need prayerful preparation in the same way that preaching does. Medical assistants should also be preachers. One of them should be a hospital chaplain; this person should have some sort of medical training and should be responsible to the doctor, not to the ministerial missionary. In other words, the medical missionary is responsible for the whole pastoral impact of the hospital, from prayer with the staff to preaching to seeing outpatients and doing bed-to-bed visiting. If you can get a minister to help, that is fine, but clearly the hospital is an autonomous unit of the church.

The most difficult aspect of the paper for the audience was the part dealing with support, especially the issue of charging fees, for missions had differing policies and differing philosophies on these. Christie's own underlying conviction is that healing should be as free as preaching. This perspective arises naturally from his view of healing as part of mission: it is as free as the gospel. But the principle of charging was already well established in most missions; even where missionaries would gladly avoid it, home boards made no provision for funding, and they were forced to charge. The answer, then, is to assert the true place of healing in the mission of the church, and then the church will recognize its obligation to support it fully. Christie, though opposed to charging, does recognize local sources of funding. There is no reason, for instance, why you should not charge patients for food and encourage thank offerings for healing. When this happens over a period, Chinese officials and Chinese merchants are usually ready to give generously. Much more comes from this source than you would get by charging them fees; they will give more than you would charge them. Encourage the church to support the local hospital, to support local evangelists there, and so on (*Records*, 261–63).

All this requires well-trained indigenous staff. The medical missionary must reproduce himself as far as possible. Central medical schools will be necessary to maintain a high standard. Already the government has sanctioned one; central institutions might absorb smaller scattered ones. But it is recognized that this is expensive. Few missionaries can pay the salaries of trained people. So the job will continue. Even so, local sharing of resources could be carried out by several missions joining in producing intermediate-level training schools for nurses, for dispensers, for midwives, and so on. A whole series of medical textbooks is also necessary, so teachers in medical colleges will have to produce these and must have the time and the space to do so (*Records*, 263–65).

The Cost of Professionalization

I conclude this chapter with some general observations. First, it was clear that medical schools were going to be more and more expensive. Eventually they proved beyond the capacities of either Western missions or any realistic fee charging. Whether this was the failure of the church to grasp the vision of healing as ministry or some other cause is another matter. Almost all Western mission agencies in the 1930s were confronted with serious crises of financial sustainability, crises that greatly accelerated processes of devolution to the indigenous church. In an age of severe economic depression, maintaining sophisticated medical institutions proved beyond their capacity. The same applies to the Christian colleges and universities that the missions (especially American ones) had established in China, but that is another story. Second, there was in fact no possibility of the Chinese church, composed as it was mainly of those of limited means, inheriting this financial and institutional burden. Third, setting up within China a system of scientific medicine based in indigenous society and based on indigenous people produces a national medical service—a Christian, a missionary, creation but perhaps continuing independent of its origins. And the whole theory is based on a challenge to traditional Chinese medicine; while integrated with theology, the theology and the medicine could part company again as they had done before.

Professionalization thus came at a high cost to the missions. But the contribution of these Christian medical institutions has not been forgotten in

China. Perhaps I could add a little story as illustration. The Centre for Research Collections in the University of Edinburgh holds the records of the Mukden Medical College and a substantial number of sets of papers by people who worked there.[9] A few years ago, I was visited by a gentleman from the Institute of Social Sciences, from Shenyang, who was a historian of science working on the history of the medical services of northeast China. He was aware that Mukden Medical College, which incidentally was closed in 1947 by the new People's Government, had played a key part in the early provision of these services, and so he wished for access to the papers. He worked for some time on this, became very enthusiastic about it, and proposed that it would be a very good thing if I could come and talk about Dugald Christie in Shenyang. After all, it is Scottish cultural relations with China. "And we have so much in common. We are China beyond the wall, you are England beyond the wall."

I was very interested to receive some time afterward a letter from the professor, head of the medical school, announcing that they were having a special day (now, one of these wonderful names; I've forgotten for the moment what the day was going to be called, but anyway, a sort of day of reflection and aspiration), and one of the things that they had done in celebration was to restore the bust of Dr. Dugald Christie that they had found and that had been damaged by the Japanese (I suspect actually in the Cultural Revolution, but we need not worry about that). They had now restored the bust and had set it up as the pioneer of the medical services of northeast China. He renewed his invitation, which I deeply regret I was unable to accept, to come and join them on that day, "that we may celebrate and emulate the spirit of selfless service as demonstrated by Dr. Dugald Christie."

9. University of Edinburgh Main Library, Centre for Research Collections, Church of Scotland China (Manchuria) Collection, Centre for the Study of World Christianity 40. This collection (which Professor Walls assembled) includes annual statements and reports of Mukden Medical College between 1911 and 1948. Other collections assembled by Professor Walls in the same location include the papers of a good number of individual medical missionaries who worked at Mukden.—Ed.

CHAPTER 12

Before the Volcano Erupted

The Tambaram Meeting and the Eve of the Second World War

This chapter concludes a series of four chapters that have surveyed the history of the missionary movement in the West, more particularly its Protestant manifestations, from somewhere near the middle of the nineteenth to somewhere near the middle of the twentieth century. Our course has not been on the history of missions, still less on the history of *the Christian* mission; it has been specifically on the history of the missionary movement from the West. We began with a study of what I called the midlife crisis in Western missions, located in the nineteenth century; and by chapter 10, we reached what we designated the high-water mark of Western missions in the World Missionary Conference at Edinburgh in 1910. If 1910 is the high-water mark, then anything after that indicates an ebbing tide; and if that is tied to a midlife crisis, then the subsequent story must reveal the onset of old age. In the present chapter, as we reach 1938 and the conference of the International Missionary Council that met that year in Tambaram, Madras (now Chennai), we are seeing the Western missionary movement—not, I stress, the Christian mission as a whole, only the Western and especially the Protestant form of it—enter its twilight years.

In 1826, a leading British statesman, George Canning, seeing the significance of the developments in the Americas at that time, and seeing that these were going to overturn traditional European ideas about the balance of power, spoke of bringing the New World into existence in order to redress the balance of the Old.[1] In the twentieth century, God called a new Christian

---

1. George Canning, "Address on the King's Message Respecting Portugal," *Hansard*, n.s., 16 (1826): 397.

world into existence to redress the balance of the old, and it is within that new world that my own ministry is set. The center has shifted. Lands that were once at the center are now on the margin. Others that were once on the margin are now at the very heart. I am old enough to recognize that old age still leaves one plenty to do, and some of it may even be useful. The Western missionary movement has had quite a vigorous old age so far. But old age is also the time when you see other people taking up your work and doing it better than you ever did or could, identifying new tasks that you never noticed. This is the time, also, when you realize that some of the things that you dreamed of doing are going to belong to somebody else.

The Great Migration Going into Reverse

The twentieth century was an extraordinary period in human history. As far as recorded history goes, it was extraordinary in its violence, though the record of the past few years suggests that in this respect, it might be outstripped by the twenty-first century. In geopolitical terms, it was remarkable for bringing the end of a vast movement of population that had shaped world history over several centuries. In the course of the twentieth century, this great European migration of population reached its peak, then came to a halt, and finally went into reverse. By the middle of the century, the migration had itself ceased, or at least been reduced to a trickle; the formation of the State of Israel in 1948, consisting mainly in the early days of Jewish immigrants from Europe, was its last great creation. In the second place, from the mid-1950s, the European maritime empires that had been established by the great European migration were progressively dismantled. Finally, from 1989, even the Russian land-based empire was substantially reduced. Patterns of international trade became more complex, their relation to the power of nation states less evident, though still real. The rise of Asian powers—India and especially China—began to hint at new patterns.

However, the twentieth century was also notable for the beginning of another movement of population, one that may turn out to determine world history just as much as did the great European migration itself. In the middle of the century, the great European migration not only came to an end but actually went into reverse. Numbers of people from Africa, from Asia, and from Latin America began to move to Europe and North America and to set down roots there. Numbers have steadily grown, and as United Nations population studies indicate, the process looks set to continue. On the one hand, pressures for movement from the non-Western world are inexorable; on the other, though the nations of the West may not want more immigration, they can sustain their economies in no other way.

This great reverse migration alters the dynamics of cultural and religious relations. Africa and Asia are now part of Europe and part of North America, too, where once they lay at the end of a long maritime journey. Latin America is part of North America as well. The religious traditions of the migrants have come with them; Islam and Hinduism have become religions of the West in a period when Christianity has become more a non-Western than a Western religion. And the migration has brought substantial numbers of Christians from Africa and Asia and Latin America to the West, often bringing with them Christian forms and expressions new to the West. There are people in this migration who are well placed to be cultural brokers and mediators. There are academics and theologians among them who can open up new channels of understanding. The meeting of the International Missionary Council held in December 1938 in Tambaram was the first occasion when these non-Western voices spoke with clarity and authority in a forum convened by the representatives of the older missionary movement from the West. The Western missionary movement was about to enter its old age.

The Tambaram Meeting of the International Missionary Council

The chairman of the Tambaram meeting, the now venerable John R. Mott, called it "the most widely representative meeting of the World Mission of the Christian faith ever held."[2] The International Missionary Council was a product of the World Missionary Conference at Edinburgh, where Mott had been a dominating figure twenty-eight years earlier. It was one of three main strands of ecumenical activity that had emerged from the years that followed World War I.

Edinburgh 1910 had provided a glimpse of what a truly world church might look like. The Faith and Order Movement, pioneered by Bishop Charles H. Brent of the Protestant Episcopal Church, had held its inaugural conference in Lausanne, Switzerland, in 1927. Its goal was to tackle the unhappy fragmentation of the world church along confessional and denominational lines. The second strand was represented by the Life and Work Movement, established in 1920, which aimed to promote coordinated thinking in the world church about its proper place and role in society. The third strand, the International Mis-

2. International Missionary Council, *Addresses and Other Records*, Tambaram series 7 (London: Oxford University Press, 1939), 1.

sionary Council, established in 1921, was perhaps closest to the original vision that had brought Edinburgh 1910 into existence. Its purpose was to achieve more permanent and substantial ecumenical cooperation in the mission of that church, a task the principal agents of which was still seen as the organizations forged by the missionary movement from the West. Those same organizations, however, the mission societies that had provided most of the delegates at Edinburgh 1910, were now inextricably linked with other entities in Asia and Africa. "What is the International Missionary Council?" asked Mott (rhetorically, of course). "It is the body which weaves together for united thinking, planning and action the various National Christian Councils throughout the world, and these in turn are the creatures and servants of the churches."[3]

I do not propose to explore the theological debates most often associated with Tambaram. The Edinburgh delegates studied book-length reports on aspects of the Christian mission; Tambaram delegates studied, or were assumed to have studied, a major theological text, Hendrik Kraemer's book *The Christian Message in the Non-Christian World.*[4] Debate on it was joined by such luminaries as A. G. Hogg, Karl Ludvig Reichelt, T. C. Chao, Karl Hartenstein, and H. H. Farmer. This debate has been well described in various places. All I will add is the discovery among some Tambaram papers in Yale Divinity School's Day Missions Library of a little pamphlet by the Scottish missionary Nicol MacNicol giving a handy summary of Kraemer's great book specifically designed for Tambaram delegates.[5] We may picture all the delegates poring over Kraemer; I wonder how many contented themselves with MacNicol's twenty-page summary, for much happened at Tambaram apart from Kraemer's restatement of mission theology. In any conference, some of the most important business is done in the coffee breaks. Frieder Ludwig's published study of the conference shows how important the conference was in ways that never reached the official reports.[6]

Edinburgh and Tambaram Contrasted

We saw in chapter 10 that at Edinburgh, there were only eighteen Asian delegates and only a single African. At Tambaram, there were no less than 149

3. International Missionary Council, *Addresses and Other Records*, 3.

4. Hendrik Kraemer, *The Christian Message in a Non-Christian World* (London: Edinburgh House, 1938).

5. Nicol MacNicol, *A Shortened Version of Dr. Hendrik Kraemer's* The Christian Message in a Non-Christian World (London: International Missionary Council, 1938).

6. Frieder Ludwig, "Tambaram: The West African Experience," *Journal of Religion in Africa* 31 (2001): 49-91.

indigenous delegates from Asia (including the "Near East" or west Asia) and sixteen from Africa (including one from Egypt).[7] Ludwig shows how important the conference was for bringing together the African leaders, who came from different countries, and they had a long sea voyage to get to know one another still more. One of them, incidentally, was, one might say, "the first Nelson Mandela," Albert Luthuli, who would become president of the African National Congress in South Africa from 1952 to 1967. Also striking was their meeting with Indian Christians, their encounter with a Christianity that shared in the aims and sometimes the activities of the national movement in India. African Christians were able to catch from their Indian brethren a sense of their own responsibilities, in an Africa that was still colonial, to move toward leadership in both church and state.

Ludwig also charts the fortunes of the German delegates, whose participation in the conference had been in doubt till the last minute. Most of them were close to the Confessing Church. The conference itself heard heart-rending accounts of the persecution of German Jews, and there were many references to the emergence of the totalitarian state brought about by Nazism. The conference "Message to All Peoples" referred to race hatred, the ugly parent of persecution, being set up as a national idol or household god.[8] As Ludwig shows, when they got back to Germany, the Tambaram delegates were under deep suspicion and had a hard time.

In placing the Tambaram conference report alongside the Edinburgh one, we are conscious of a considerable difference in tone. Edinburgh was full of hope, of urgency, and of the sense of opportunity. The whole world seemed to be open to the gospel as never before. The task was to seize the moment, mobilize the resources of the Christian world to evangelize the non-Christian world. In fact, the First World War was only four years away; but at Edinburgh, no one seems to have heard the beating of the wings of the angel of death.

At Tambaram, in contrast, there is a sense that the world is living in the path of a rumbling volcano. The smell of the lava is everywhere. The meeting had been planned not for India but for China, but the Japanese invasion of China had put Hangchow (Hangzhou), the proposed venue, into a war zone. There was civil war in Spain, ugly violence in Palestine. There was violent, systematic persecution of the Jews. "Woe, woe, increasing woe is the lot of these poor people," announced George Sloan, the Tambaram speaker on the Jewish problem.[9] The international order set up to maintain peace after the

---

7. International Missionary Council, *Addresses and Other Records*, 181–201.

8. International Missionary Council, *Addresses and Other Records*, 175.

9. George L. B. Sloan, "Relation of the Christian Church to the Jewish Problem," in *Addresses and Other Records*, 100–108.

First World War had manifestly broken down. Totalitarian states, Nazi Germany at their head, had arisen that exalted the claims of the nation-state to an infinite plane. It was the year of the Munich pact, which had averted war over the fate of Czechoslovakia, but no one could be surprised when nine months after Tambaram, the German invasion of Poland marked the beginning of total war.

The delegates were conscious of all this, and they felt their powerlessness. "We must ... frankly recognise to one another," said William Paton, secretary of the International Missionary Council, "that we, like most other Christians to-day, are burdened by a certain sense of futility."[10] One catches the sense that this is indeed the twilight of Western, or at least of European, Christendom. The word Christendom appears again and again. "Never has Christendom had such an opportunity of showing to Jewry what God's love in Christ really means," says Sloan. "Let Christendom fail, and Jewry in bitter disillusionment will reject once more and perhaps for all time the good news of salvation."[11] By Christendom, he means the nations that profess the Christian faith. But it was clear to most delegates that the churches could now do little or nothing to restrain the forces that would cause the volcano to erupt.

Edinburgh had been essentially an assembly of white missionaries and white mission executives. A symbolic selection of Asian church leaders had been present. At Tambaram, we hear a crowd of significant voices from Asia, and it is often they who speak with the greatest hope and point to immediate duties. Toyohiko Kagawa, of Japan, addressed the conference on the meaning of the cross, the centrality and completeness of the atonement, and the way that it pointed to the path of sacrifice. "If Christ did die for us, we ought to die for Christ's sake" is his conclusion.[12] D. T. Niles, of Ceylon (Sri Lanka, as it is now), spoke powerfully of the risen Christ.[13] Bishop V. S. Azariah, of South India, who as a young man had electrified the Edinburgh conference twenty-eight years before with his assertion that what the indigenous church needed from the West was not leadership or money but friendship, now, near the end of his course, spoke about evangelism and mobilizing the church for evangelism. Every person baptized should be a witness, not ashamed of Christ. Otherwise he denies his baptism. He described how he would get Christians to go and stand together in a non-Christian crowd. Let somebody

10. William Paton, "The Church and the World Community," in *Addresses and Other Records*, 125.

11. Sloan, "Relation of the Christian Church," 108.

12. Toyohiko Kagawa, "The Meaning of the Cross," in *Addresses and Other Records*, 23–27, at 27.

13. D. T. Niles, "Jesus, Whom God Raised Up," in *Addresses and Other Records*, 14–22.

else do the talking, let somebody else do the singing; just standing for Christ would drive them to their knees. "I used to go around among the churches and have the baptised members place their hands on their own heads (as if in the act of baptism) and repeat after me, 'I am a baptised Christian. Woe unto me if I do not preach the Gospel!'"[14]

At Edinburgh, the native church appeared to be a tender plant. The best analysts then believed that missionaries would be necessary for a long time to come in order to enable it to stand alone. The evidence of Tambaram less than thirty years later was that the indigenous church was showing maturity, confidence, and a sense of vocation and direction. In the group discussions, it is clear that tensions were very evident between Western missionaries and indigenous church leaders over the proper relations of the two. "We all know quite well," says William Paton, "that in many of our countries the work is impeded and spiritual progress held up because of unsolved problems in this realm." He asks, "Might it be said to missionaries . . . who hear hard things, and things which they may hold to be unjustified . . . that they should not listen in a stoical calm, but try earnestly to see whether there be truth in what is said." And perhaps those of the younger churches "might remember the judgment of God in Christ and should not be righteous overmuch. We cannot make progress together until we have learned to forgive one another, as God in Christ has forgiven us."[15]

In his opening speech, John Mott had said that the central objective of the conference was "that we, trusted representatives of the older and younger churches of the world, should arrive at a common mind as to God's will concerning the next steps in the realm of attainment and achievement which should be taken by us and our constituencies in the years right before us for the building up of the Church and the spreading of the Christian religion."[16] By any standards, that is a terrible sentence, but it sets out something that Edinburgh said little about: that the next steps did not depend on organizing and mobilizing the Western churches for mission but on what were now being called the older and younger churches' working together.

Of world figures, the one who receives the most attention in the conference is undoubtedly Mohandas K. Gandhi. Mott says, "It would be hard to find a modern parallel to the moral influence of that one person."[17] He asks whether

14. V. S. Azariah, "The Church and Its Mission," in *Addresses and Other Records*, 41–42.

15. Paton, "Church and World Community," 128.

16. John R. Mott, "The Possibilities of the Tambaram Meeting," in *Addresses and Other Records*, 4.

17. Mott, "Possibilities of the Tambaram Meeting," 5.

Gandhi by nonviolent advocacy may be creating a new way for humanity. And where indeed does Gandhi get his doctrine but from Christ? An Asian leader in the YMCA, Dr. T. Z. Koo (Gu Ziren; 1887–1971), puts suffering love as the mode of life for Christians after frankly analyzing his own feelings as a Chinese toward Japanese in the light of Japanese atrocities in China. But he warns against too easy assumptions that the Gandhian way will always bring success in the face of organized brutality. Would Gandhi, he says, be alive if instead of representing Indian liberty against British imperialism he was representing Korean liberty against Japanese imperialism? All the same, success or no success, he concludes, suffering love is the proper path for Christians.[18]

The topic of imperialism is tackled head-on by the veteran anti-imperialist missionary, and friend of Gandhi, C. F. Andrews:

We of the West have been an imperial race for the most part. Africa knows what that means. Asia also knows what it means. We have divided the world into the white and the coloured races, and we have often thought that we who belong to the former are the world conquerors, and that we of the white race must rule and others must be subject. The terrible tragedy of imperialism is two-fold. It sets aflame a burning indignation in the subject races of the world, and it engenders a racial arrogance that few imperialists can escape. Jesus was not born of an imperial race nor in an imperial palace, but in a manger in a little town in despised Judea. He was brought up in the land of the despised race.[19]

Interracial reconciliation, the actual theme of his address, depends on forgiveness. "I have learned from Africa that forgiveness. Oh, how terribly have we treated Africa! Of all people in the world, we white people have done the most dastardly wrong to those dear Africans. And how they have forgiven us!"[20] He details that forgiveness from his own experience in South Africa and in the life of the Ghanaian Christian educationist J. E. K. Aggrey.

Tambaram's Neglect of the Growth of the Church in Africa

Africa is the missing piece in much of the Tambaram discussion. We have seen that in 1910, the best analysts raised the question whether the evangeli-

18. T. Z. Koo, "The Church and the International Order," in *Addresses and Other Records*, 86–91.
19. C. F. Andrews, "Inter-racial Reconciliation," in *Addresses and Other Records*, 93.
20. Andrews, "Inter-racial Reconciliation," 98.

zation of Africa had more than begun at that point. Going further back and looking at nineteenth-century patterns, we find in the first half of that century that Wesleyan missionary Thomas Birch Freeman could publish a whole book describing his successive visits to the rulers of Ashanti, Abeokuta, and Dahomey, all powerful independent states.[21] The Ashanti in particular had taken on the British with relish, and the Asantehene's drum was believed to be still decorated with Sir Charles MacCarthy's skull and his inner sanctum with MacCarthy's red jacket. The penny-a-week collectors who read the missionary journals and distributed them knew from the missionary magazines that all Freeman's predecessors and most of his colleagues had died of fever within a year or two of arrival in Africa.

The twentieth-century missionary was durable through quinine, and the British administration of the Gold Coast Colony and Protectorate meant that there was little chance of his skull joining MacCarthy's. But if his life was less adventurous than Freeman's, he was seeing a totally different kind of response. In Ashanti, he saw, for practical purposes, none at all, but between 1917 and 1922, the Wesleyan mission saw twenty thousand people in Ashanti coming under pastoral care for the first time. The reason was the preaching of someone who had had nothing to do with them and of whom they knew nothing, an illiterate, charismatic jailbird called Samson Oppong, walking through the country with a bamboo cross. He had become a preacher following a dream that itself had followed a series of apparently casual contacts with African Christians in and out of prison. There was no doubt about the effect of his preaching. Powerful chiefs trembled; whole households burned their fetishes. Whole crowds of people came asking to be taught the Christian way.

The Methodist church in Ashanti came into being ninety years after its famous pioneer. But what on earth in Wesleyan polity could you do with Saint Samson Oppong? He could never be recognized as a minister. He did not fit the rules for a local preacher or an exhorter. He knew nothing about leaders' meetings and would not be likely to attend one if he believed God was calling him to preach somewhere else. It was God from whom his commission came. It was for him to preach, for the mission to instruct those who responded.

Figures like Oppong pop up in many parts of west and central Africa and as far south as Lesotho in the crucial years for African Christianity during and after World War I. The areas of rapid response over these years put missions into a reactive rather than a proactive mode.

I remember being involved in a survey of the origins of the Christian congregations of one such area of southeast Nigeria. It was an area where such

---

21. Thomas Birch Freeman, *Journals of Various Visits to the Kingdoms of Ashanti, Aku, and Dahomi in Western Africa*, 2nd ed. (London: Mason, 1844).

congregations were thick on the ground, 332 of them in a five-mile radius of one small town. The striking thing about the survey was that according to congregational memory, at least, not a single congregation had been founded by a missionary. Very few had been founded by any official representative of the church, Black or white. What people remembered was the first Christian coming to the village, a trader, often a tailor with his sewing machine on his head, a ganger building the railway, a clerk to the colonial administration. These people had family prayers on their veranda, sang hymns, stopped work on Sunday, and answered questions. Or it may have been people going *from* the village to trade, to work, to school, in more than one case to jail, who brought back what they had found to their own village. Where were the missions in all this? Usually desperately trying to catch up, saying, "Sorry, we can't send a teacher now; we'll remember you as soon as we have someone."

Such growth of the church in the period between Edinburgh and Tambaram underlies how much Tambaram was concerned with evangelization—how much more so than was the previous International Missionary Council conference at Jerusalem in 1928. Much of the stress on this was coming from those who were called the younger churches.

The First Signs of the Decolonization of the Church

Of course, the volcano erupted, and with it the world order set up by the great European migration fell apart. The empires were dismantled; the superpowers were reduced for a time to two. The great reverse migration of the non-Western to the Western world began. Christendom in Europe went into steep, perhaps terminal, decline. By the end of the twentieth century, the Christians of Africa, Asia, and Latin America were outnumbering those of Europe and North America. The world church had arrived. And what of the missionary movement?

The missionary movement was at no point, even at its highest, a major concern of the Western churches. It began among the enthusiasts; it ended among the enthusiasts. For a substantial time between, it gained recognition, so that all in the church spoke well of it and paid their modest tribute when the collector called, and even bought the magazine. But the movement depended on the narrow base of volunteers who became the collectors or the missionaries. Bernard Lucas's *The Empire of Christ*, which was cited in chapter 10, recognized how people, though remaining regular worshipers, now with a smattering of comparative religion, were giving up on the earnest missionary speaking with the magic lantern.[22] Before very long, they were giving up on the church, too. The constituency of the missionary movement was receding, its personnel and its economic base eroding. Soon after the middle of the twentieth century, its senescence was plain. The old age of the missionary movement had begun.

The late nineteenth century was an expression of the dominant role of Western Christianity, which had made some impression, modest but still recognizable, on other parts of the world. By 1910, it was mobilizing and organizing for the task of world evangelization, which seemed to be its own responsibility. Hardly had it begun when circumstances wrested the steering wheel out of its hands, and for the rest of the century, it never quite succeeded in getting the car under control. Tires blew, there was endless trouble with the clutch, the petrol was always running out. Yet by the end of the century, the task for which the car had been commissioned had been accomplished to a quite remarkable extent. It had not been the planned progress, but the battered old vehicle had been essential to what happened. Often unknown to its occupants, there had been other vehicles involved.

The twentieth century has been the prologue to the decolonization of the church. The long ecclesiastical empire of the West is over. The decolonization process began in the missionary movement, and it was the missionary movement that has had to mediate it to the rest of the Western church. For the balance of the church has shifted. It has, as in other periods of church history, been redressed. Lands that once were at its heart are now on the margins; others that were on the margins are now at its heart. It has no single center. Above all, the idea of a home base in Europe and North America, such as the Edinburgh fathers took for granted in 1910, is long past. The church now has not one but many centers. New Christian impulses and initiatives may now be expected from any quarter of the globe. Christian mission may start from any point and be directed to any point.

The global character of Christianity, now so obvious, is not a new feature. In principle, the faith has always been global, and earlier centuries saw it spread across the whole Eurasian landmass and deep into East Africa. The exceptional period of Christian history, when Christianity seemed to belong essentially to the West, is the one from which we have just emerged: the period of the great European migration and that immediately preceding it. With its return to being a non-Western religion, Christianity has reverted to type.

22. Bernard Lucas, *The Empire of Christ: Being a Study of the Missionary Enterprise in the Light of Modern Religious Thought* (London: Macmillan, 1907), 132-33, 141-42.

Implications for Theology

In the multicentric Christian church, there can be no automatic assumption of Western leadership. Indeed, if suffering and endurance are the badges of authenticity, we can expect the most powerful Christian leadership to come from elsewhere. The same may be true of intellectual and theological leadership. Multicentric Christian mission has the potential to revitalize theological activity and revolutionize theological education. Theology springs out of mission. Its true origins lie not in the study or the library but arise from the need to make Christian decisions, decisions about what to do and what to think. Theology is the attempt to think in a Christian way, to make Christian intellectual choices. Its subject matter, therefore, its agenda, is culturally conditioned, arising out of actual life situations of active Christians. This means that the normal run of Western theology is simply not big enough for Africa, or for much of the rest of the world. It offers no guidance for some of the most crucial decisions, because it has no questions related to those situations.

The reason is that Western theology rests on an Enlightenment view of the universe. The Enlightenment universe is a small-scale one. Witchcraft or sorcery, for instance, do not exist within it. Its family structures have no place for ancestors. The frontier between the empirical world and the realm of spirit, the natural and the supernatural, is closed. There is no space for those principalities and powers that Paul sees as world rulers routed by the triumphal chariot of the cross of the risen Christ.[23] The Bible is not an Enlightenment book.

Much of humanity lives in a larger, more populated universe, with constant activity across an open frontier between the empirical and spirit worlds, and faces issues for which Western theology has no resources. For assured Christian living, Christ must fill the world as people see the world, and this is the province of theology. Christian mission in and from Africa is likely to widen the theological agenda, and the consequent benefit to be of more than African significance. The same applies even more to Asia.

A wider theology of the principalities and powers might deepen our theology of evil, illuminating the nexus between personal sin and guilt, on the one hand, and systemic structural evil, on the other, that has stalled much Western theological discussion. The engagement of biblical thinking and the Christian tradition with the ancient cultures of Asia and Africa could open an era of theological creativity to parallel the encounter with Hellenistic culture in the second, third, and fourth centuries. That early encounter, by following

---

23. Professor Walls appears here to be quoting Colossians 2:15, with a possible allusion also to 2 Corinthians 2:14, although in this latter text, it is Christians, rather than the principalities and powers, who are the captives in Christ's triumphal procession. —Ed.

out issues raised for Christians within the culture and using the intellectual materials to hand, gave us the great creeds and the beginning of classical theology. Who can say what the encounter with Africa and Asia will be and whether it will not be equally enriching?

Church and mission are multicentric, but the different centers belong to a single organism. Christian faith is embodied faith; Christ takes flesh again among those who respond to him in faith. But there is no generalized humanity. Incarnation always has to be culture specific. The approximations to incarnation among Christians are specific bits of social reality converted to Christ, turned to face him, and made open to him. All our representations of humanity are partial; complete humanity is found only in Christ.

The relation to each other of the different pieces of converted social reality was central to the life of the New Testament church. Cultural diversity was built into the church forever when the decision was taken to abandon the Jewish proselyte model that would have turned a gentile follower of Jesus into a Jew. From that time, there were two converted lifestyles in the church, and the Epistle to the Ephesians shows how the two have been made one through Christ's cross. Here are not two races but two lifestyles, two cultures; different as they are, they belong to each other. Each is a building block in a new temple that is in process of building; each is an organ in a functioning body of which Christ is the brain. The temple will not be completed, and the body will not function, unless both are present. Christ is full humanity, and it is only together that we reach his full stature.[24]

There are now not two but an infinite number of segments of partially converted social reality within the church. They include representatives of some of the richest and some of the poorest peoples on earth. Their human relations are shaped by the events of the great European migration; the conditions of the great reverse migration bring them as close together as the representatives of the two converted lifestyles in the New Testament church. Like them, each is a building block belonging to a new temple still in process of construction. Like them, each is an organ, necessary to the proper functioning of a body under Christ's direction. Only together will they reach the fullness of Christ, which is the completion and perfection of his humanity.

24. Professor Walls expounded this theme more fully in his essay "The Ephesian Moment: At a Crossroads in Christian History," in *The Cross-Cultural Process in Christian History: Studies in the Transmission and Appropriation of Faith* (Maryknoll, NY: Orbis Books, 2002), 72–81.—Ed.

PART 4

Old Age

*The Second World War and
the Western Missionary Movement*

CHAPTER 13

The Seventh Chapter of Daniel Continued

The Legacy of World War II and the Birth of the Indian Nation

We observed earlier that the second half of the twentieth century saw the gradual breakup of the world order that had been established by the great European migration, and the beginnings of a great reverse migration that may turn out to determine world history just as much as did the great European migration itself. Our story in this final section of the book is about the progress of Christian mission as the Western maritime empires crumbled, as new world orders took shape, and as the political and economic power shifted first toward America and then toward Asia, a period in which the demographic and cultural balance within the church shifted, until Christians from Africa and Asia and Latin America actually outnumbered those of Europe and America—in which Europe moved steadily further from its historic Christian profession and adopted post-Christian assumptions.

In this final section of the narrative, we will examine three great theaters of mission in particular, how these changed over the era of World War II and the generation that followed, and what effect this has had on Christian mission as a whole. In each case, we will see the Western missionary movement, which has been our theme over the past years, reacting to outside events. It is clear throughout this story that the missionary movement is not in charge: it is carried along by events. But it is a major period of Christian history, a period when Christianity returns to what it was in its early centuries, a truly transcontinental faith, stretching across Europe, Asia, and Africa, with no single center but multiple centers, and greater and grander than the early church model since it now includes the Americas and the Pacific as well. The twentieth century in fact turns out to be the most remarkable century of all for Christian expansion, save possibly the first.

Our survey will have to leave out a great deal. I would have wished to include at least one chapter on Latin America and one on Southeast Asia and one on the Pacific and one on the Middle East. Korea, too, has an unusual Christian history, which we will be able to refer to only incidentally. The same is true of great events in the church at large, such events as the Second Vatican Council of 1962–1965 and the organization of global evangelicalism with the Lausanne Congress on World Evangelization in 1974.

World History Seen through the Eyes of the Prophet Daniel

The title of this first chapter in this section is "The Seventh Chapter of Daniel Continued." The point of that title is that Daniel 7 deals with the heart of our topic: that is, how the mission of God is carried out amid changing and often cataclysmic and tragic world events. For the Bible, there is no such thing as secular history. There is only history, and history is the stuff within which God works out human salvation.

In Daniel 7, the prophet watches a succession of large animals, each different in color or shape from its predecessor, one by one taking center stage. The prophet realizes that he is watching the drama of the superpowers. He belongs to a small, marginal people. He lives in an area that superpowers fight in or over, and he lives at a time when his own people are undergoing the most savage and destructive treatment from the superpower of the day. He watches, fascinated, as one of the beasts sprouts a new horn; then he sees a face on the horn, and he recognizes the face of his people's persecutor. Then he sees a far greater drama in action. The Ancient of Days, in blazing light, presides at a grand judgment where the books are opened that record the deeds of humans and nations, and the books are read in court, and one like a son of man, incorporating all the saints of the Most High, comes before the Ancient of Days and is given power and authority over all. This drama cuts all the superpowers down to size. Their authority is only temporary. They give place to one another in turn. Sometimes, like the ghastly persecuting beast with the little horn, they are utterly destroyed with their evil deeds and by those deeds. More often, like the first three beasts mentioned, they are allowed to live, but they lose their authority, just as Britain and France and Spain, all of whom once strutted on the world stage, continue to exist but can strut no longer. All superpowers have only temporary authority; permanent rule belongs to the son of man, who incorporates into his body the saints of the Most High.

The beasts that Daniel saw are the beasts that Daniel knew, the superpowers of his own day and the recent history of his people. But the chapter has a long continuation. Other beasts come onto the stage, each of a different stripe from its predecessor; but each has only temporary authority, and each time, the thrones are set up and the books are opened and the judgment is given, and that beast passes, leaving only the son of man and the saints of the Most High. We will see beasts of a different stripe yielding up their authority, and we can see other beasts waiting in the wings of the stage ready for their turn. We are bound in this survey to take account of the beasts and their doings; that is the stuff of human history. But never forget the greater drama behind and within that history: the overall rule of the Ancient of Days and his committing that rule to one like a son of man, who takes unto himself the saints of the Most High.

I have suggested in this book that the missionary movement from the West is about five hundred years old and that the Catholic and Protestant missionary movements make up a single story, and each suffers if we neglect the other part of what is a single story. And we cannot separate that story from the rest of the story of the interaction of the West and the non-Western world. The mission story I have sought to tell goes on against the background of this other story, the domination by European powers of the world, building up over five centuries, reaching a climax of activity perhaps in the nineteenth century, at its high point in the early part of the twentieth century, and then suddenly, in the middle of the twentieth century, coming undone. The First World War, you might say, is the warning bell; the Second World War is the sign of the destruction of that order. As already noted, from a biblical perspective, there is no such thing as secular history. All history is part of a great drama watched by the Ancient of Days, who takes account of the books that record its deeds, a drama in which the final and permanent ruler is the one like a son of man.

The First World War made little difference to the colonial map except that Britain, France, and Belgium gained some extra colonies or space at the expense of Germany. The period following World War I, however, was the time when the Middle East map was redrawn, following the breakup of the Turkish Empire. A general understanding existed that the French influence would prevail in the north of the region, hence Syria and Lebanon, and the British in the south, hence the British mandate in Palestine. The British, however, who had entered Mesopotamia during the war with the Indian army and were interested in the Mosul oil field, secured the invention of a new state called Iraq, to be ruled by an Arab prince who had been a helpful ally in Arabia during the war. The postwar settlement left the Middle East and most of the Muslim world in colonies or client states of the Western powers.

The great European migration thus produced a beast of Western imperial power whose rule, demographically, politically, economically was extraordinarily comprehensive and was remarkably long-lived. During World War II and its aftermath, this beast was shorn of much of his authority. Perhaps the first sign of what was to come took place at the very beginning of the twentieth century when the Japanese destroyed the Russian fleet and showed that it was possible for a nation power to defeat the powers of the West. It was sealed in 1942 when Singapore fell to the Japanese, and made clear throughout Southeast Asia that British power would not be reestablished. The end of the war indeed led to the maritime powers dismantling their overseas empires, beginning with Italy, and then France, Britain, Belgium, and finally Portugal. The parts that proved most difficult to dismantle were not surprisingly those like Algeria and Zimbabwe, where Europeans remained as settlers in substantial numbers. The other colonies moved to independence far more quickly than had been expected or might have been intended.

I remember talking with an old colonial officer from Nigeria who had gone to Africa as a young probationer, in 1947 I think it must have been. He was just taking up his duties, and the colonial service probationers at the university where he then was were addressed by Arthur Creech Jones, the British colonial secretary of the day, a man enlightened by all the standards of that time, who told them of the important responsibility before them. They had to prepare these colonial territories for self-rule, and they had only a hundred years to do it in. How quickly after the initial step in India in 1947 that dismantling process took place!

If government was not prepared for self-rule, how about the missions? The British prime minister of the day, Harold Macmillan, made a famous speech to the South African Parliament in February 1960 about the winds of change. The history of one of the oldest British missionary societies of this period has the title *Gales of Change*; "winds of change" is not enough to describe what happened to missions in the time.[1]

For a time, it seemed that two great beasts would contest the postwar world from which the Western European powers had largely withdrawn. Both of these great beasts were products of the great European migration: the United States and the Soviet Union, which represented the landward expansion of the Russian Empire. In 1989, that land-based empire itself began to break up, and there were signs and hints of the growing weakness of the remaining beast. The process of the disappearance of one of the superpowers did not bring about, as some thought at the time, the end of history. The second half of the century witnessed the rise of two new great beasts in Asia: India, an independent nation from 1947, and China, under Communist rule from 1949.

1. Bernard Thorogood, *Gales of Change: Responding to a Shifting Missionary Context; The Story of the London Missionary Society, 1945–1977* (Geneva: WCC, 1994).

The period saw the end of large-scale migration from Europe except for one major factor, the creation of the State of Israel in 1948. As emphasized in the previous chapter, not only did the migration cease, it went into reverse. First of all, the countries that had had metropolitan empires found that they could not remove the legacy of empire by dismantling their immediate responsibilities of rule. Huge populations from the former colonies began to arrive in Europe. The United States proved an even more popular target. What has happened since the Second World War is not merely the end of large-scale emigration from Europe but a movement *to* the Western world from the non-Western world in vast numbers, so that Asia, Africa, and Latin America are now part of Western experience, part of the context of world mission.

The Indian Empires of the Mughals and the British

The remainder of this chapter will examine the course of decolonization in the subcontinent of India, and its implications for Christianity. India was the first territory in Asia to fall under British imperial sway, and the first to throw off the shackles of colonial rule in 1947, just two years after the end of the Second World War. Before embarking on this narrative, we will need to backtrack and attempt a brief summary of the history of the subcontinent, something that so far has not made an appearance in this book.

The subcontinent of India—the whole vast area cut off from the rest of Asia by the vast ranges of the Himalayas—includes what are now Pakistan, Bangladesh, Nepal, indeed for these purposes Burma and Ceylon, or Sri Lanka, containing some of the oldest civilizations known to humanity. Only China can produce anything of comparable antiquity. India still has institutions that so far as archaeology can reveal were functioning before Israel came out of Egypt. It has had many invaders over the ages; three of these invaders made a continuing mark. The Aryans, coming from Iran in perhaps 1500 BC, brought social and religious ideas and structures, the body of religious writings that have shaped Indian society. Then the Mughals, who, beginning in 1526, set up a vast empire in north and central India that fell into decay only as late as the eighteenth century, brought Islam. Islam triumphed in the northern part of the subcontinent and in patches elsewhere, but was not enforced over the whole area, and developed a high degree of tolerance of other religious traditions. The third invader, the British, who arrived as traders in the seventeenth century, took over administration of the greater part of the subcontinent incrementally during the eighteenth and nineteenth centuries, initially in order to eliminate other European trade rivals.

Until 1858, British government and administration in India was vested in a chartered company with a monopoly of trade, the Honourable East India Company. The company was in fact in charge of all dealings with the East, so that the China trade was also held by this monopoly company until its dissolution in 1858. The official policy of the East India Company was to avoid all interference in religious matters. Although the company appointed chaplains, and in the early eighteenth century gave support to the Lutheran Halle missionaries in Madras presidency, in practice the company did little to further and much to impede Christianity. The first governor of Bengal presidency, Job Charnock (c. 1630–1693), married a Brahman and is said to have sacrificed a cock annually on her grave, which indicates, I think, his eclectic religious outlook. For a long time, the Bengal administration resisted British dissenting missionaries as likely to enflame local religious feeling and upset trade; zealous evangelical missions were bad for business.

After a major rising by the company's troops in 1857, called in Britain the Indian Mutiny, called by some contemporary Indian historians the First War of Independence, British India was put directly under the British crown, with a viceroy, literally a "deputy king," representing the British monarch. There were states that were not formally part of British India but ruled by princes; these received British residents as advisors and thus were linked in to British India. In 1877, Queen Victoria was declared to be Empress of India, and India thus once again became an empire. The British invasion, therefore, set up the conditions for a politically and administratively unified nation. It provided the conditions for a national consciousness that transcended regional, ethnic, linguistic, and religious differences—and of all those things India has plenty.

The British did not bring Christianity. That had come long before in the early centuries; there is good evidence that it was as early as the first century AD. Certainly all Indian Christians see the apostle Thomas as the first missionary to India, and the evidence for his being in India is at least as good as the evidence for Peter's being in Rome. Further infusions from the Syriac world came in the fourth century, and today this ancient Christian community forms a substantial part of the population of the state of Kerala, a state where Christians account for more than a quarter of the population as well as being spread over the rest of the country. Pandit Nehru, the first prime minister of independent India, accepted that Christianity was one of the indigenous religions of India. It had been there from its earliest times; it was not a colonial import.

Catholic missions came in the wake of the Portuguese presence in the sixteenth century. Their early effect was felt first in Goa, where they set up a colony, a bit of Portugal in India, which lasted until 1961, when the Indian government incorporated it into its own territory. Some low-status communities in the far south became Christian in order to get Portuguese protection from Muslim invaders and have remained in Catholic Christianity. The remarkable if controversial Jesuit missionary Roberto de Nobili (1577–1656) set up a mission to Brahmins, the high-status priestly caste, in Madurai, developing a deep scholarship and knowledge of the language and a pattern of identification that involved adopting the dress, diet, and lifestyle of a Hindu holy man, a Sanyasi, and bringing substantial numbers of Brahmins to the Christian faith.

As described in chapter 3, the first Protestant mission arrived in 1706, significantly based not in East India Company territory but in the small Danish colony of Tranquebar, staffed by German Pietist missionaries, translating the Scriptures into Tamil, eventually reaching East India Company territory in Madras. This is the beginning of Protestant overseas missions, this group staffed by Germans from the University of Halle, Pietists, maintaining itself, eventually taken over by the Society for the Propagation of the Gospel in the 1820s but maintaining its work right through the eighteenth century.

Indian Christians and Their Aspirations

By the time of the Tambaram meeting of the International Missionary Council in 1938, there was a substantial Christian community across India—still only a small proportion, perhaps something over 2 percent of the vast population. The Christian community was unevenly spread, concentrated in the south and in the northeast. Leaving aside the old Christians of Kerala, many of the newer Christians were from the Aboriginal peoples of India, tribal peoples who had not participated in Hindu culture. Many more were from the lowest sectors of Hindu society, the people now called Dalits, formerly known as Untouchables or by the term that Gandhi gave them, Harijans, literally "men of God." Many had become Christians in mass movements in South India where whole villages or whole social groups decided at the same time to become Christian, finding in the process a new dignity and assurance, and raising enormous pastoral problems with huge communities coming into the church at the same time.

Some missions, notably the Scottish, had directed attention to higher-caste Hindus, seeking intellectual engagement with Hindu thought. This led to an investment in higher education to university level and major institutions such as Madras Christian College or Wilson College in Bombay, now Mumbai.

These institutions were intended to bring Christian influence into society, to penetrate the intellectual climate, rather than as a means of direct evangelism. A good deal of missionary scholarship had been directed to the study of Hindu Scriptures. In the late nineteenth and early twentieth centuries, there developed a school of missionary thought that described Christianity as the fulfillment of the aspirations of the Hindu sages.

In the early twentieth century, the desire for Indian self-rule was becoming more and more acute, especially among Hindu intellectuals educated on the British model and often in Christian institutions, where they had imbibed the political ideas of liberty and democracy and Christian ideas of justice and fellowship. In the church, the lack of these qualities was sometimes acutely felt. In chapter 10, we took note of V. S. Azariah's controversial appeal at the 1910 World Missionary Conference to missionaries to relate to Indian Christians on an egalitarian basis of love and friendship. What Indian Christians wanted most was not leadership but friendship. A friend is somebody you want to spend your spare time with, to be accepted on equal terms.

Twenty-six years later, a young missionary of the Church of Scotland, called Lesslie Newbigin, having recently arrived in India, wrote in his diary this:

> I must say I couldn't help being horrified by the sort of relation that seems to exist between the missionaries and the people. It seems so utterly remote from the New Testament. . . . We drive up like lords in a car, soaking everybody else with mud on the way, and then we carry out a sort of inspection, finding all the faults we can, putting everybody through their paces. They all sort of stand at attention and say "Sir"—it's awful. . . . But one thing is as sure as death: surely they won't stand this sort of thing from the white man much longer.[2]

This was 1936. Missionaries had been sucked into the attitudes of a ruling caste, had become part of the Raj.

This attitude was often reflected in the leadership of the church. Anglicans, for instance, did not receive their first Indian diocesan bishop (Azariah) until 1912, and their second one until 1946,[3] despite the large number of highly educated candidates. The year 1912 was twenty-one years after the death of the Nigerian bishop Samuel Crowther. It is the period of high empire. You can do this before the high imperial period in the 1880s, you can do it as the empire begins to crumble, but to appoint the first Indian bishop at the high noon of

---

2. Lesslie Newbigin, *Unfinished Agenda: An Autobiography* (London: SPCK, 1985), 41.
3. Nirod Kumar Biswas was consecrated bishop of Assam in 1946.—Ed.

empire, in 1912, was a remarkable act, not repeated for another thirty-four years. In that year, Azariah was made bishop of the new diocese of Dornakal, in Andhra Pradesh, where he led a remarkable pastoral program among mass movement Dalits to make them Christian disciples, evangelists, and dignified, engaged citizens. The material legacy of that today is the extraordinary cathedral in Dornakal, a splendid building intended to reflect India. What is an Indian building style? Is it Hindu? Is it Muslim? Well, you have Hindu architecture with Muslim minarets, and no foreign funding at all in this remarkable building. Azariah wanted a grand building, because these were very, very poor people, desperately poor people, who had very little to show. Here was one thing they could show: their house of God. For one thing, they were showing that Christianity was there to stay; for another thing, these people were getting something to be proud of, something that belonged to them. It was all being done by their small coppers or by this one bringing a few eggs, that one bringing some rice, that sort of small offering.

The Road to Indian Independence

The movement of national consciousness, demanding self-rule, developed through the twentieth century. Some leading Christians were part of it; some missionaries, Americans and Danes being notable among them, favored it. Most missionaries probably were not greatly involved either way; they were too busy. Dalit Christians were probably not especially concerned either, because their pass to advancement lay through the Christian faith: this was what was giving immediate benefit. Young Hindu intellectuals, who were the mainspring of the national movement, tended to see Christianity as both foreign and unnecessary. It was not necessarily untrue, except in any claims made for its being exclusive or unique. It was simply a European way of saying things that were already known in India.

The political leadership of the national consciousness lay with the Indian National Congress, formed in 1885, and a substantial force in Indian politics throughout the twentieth century and indeed to the present day. In 1920, the remarkable lawyer Mohandas K. Gandhi became its leader. He had spent time in South Africa from 1893 to 1914, was deeply influenced by Christian teaching, especially by the Sermon on the Mount, and was appalled by the racial divisions in South Africa and the behavior of the white population. He was working as a lawyer in the Indian community in South Africa, which found itself heavily discriminated against quite apart from the treatment of Africans. Returning to India, he led a massive protest against British rule with nonviolence, noncooperation, and what he called *satyagraha*, soul force, as its weapons. The movement for independence grew, and the British authorities were constantly wrong-footed. Imprisonment of Gandhi always made things worse.

In Britain, it was widely recognized that Indian independence was only a matter of time. There were successive movements toward it even in the early part of the twentieth century. Then there would be a change of government and things would move back a bit, and then there would be another change of government and things would move forward a bit. A new constitution in 1935 allowed limited elections at provincial level, and Congress triumphed at those elections. There was not yet a central Indian government, but in each of the provinces, there was a provincial Indian government, directly elected.

Then came World War II, in 1939; and the viceroy, without consulting the ministries, declared that India was at war with Germany. The ministries resigned in protest at not having been consulted. They had been prepared to cooperate with the British government in this matter; they were not ruling out the state of war, but they would have wished to be consulted. It led to an intensification of what now became known as the quit India movement, and this in the middle of a major world war, with Britain in 1940 and 1941 in sore straits and in 1942 facing the entrance of Japan into that war, with the Japanese invasion of Burma and complete hold on Southeast Asia. It was a very anxious time if India should in fact become hostile.

Attempts were made at compromise on both sides (it is very interesting to see how both sides moved a bit in this from 1942 onward), and the crisis passed. One thing perhaps that caused it to do so was a new problem for Congress, or at least the intensification of an old problem. Muslim intellectuals feared being submerged in a Hindu India. The triumph of Congress at elections scared them still more; if this happened at national level, an independent India would be under Hindu rule. They began to demand the creation of a separate Islamic state in Pakistan, a partition that would give the Muslims self-rule in their own territory. The latter part of the war was taken up with this argument, with the Muslim line becoming harder and therefore the path to independence becoming more difficult.

Then 1945 brought a change of government in Britain; it had been a wartime coalition. The new Labour government of Clement Atlee had clearly decided very early on that the only future lay in withdrawing from India completely and decided in favor of independence. The cost of independence, however, was partition. And so in 1947 came the creation of two huge new nations, not one: India and Pakistan, Pakistan consisting of two parts, west and east, separated by a vast swathe of Indian territory between them while still leaving large numbers of Muslims within India itself. Independence began with tragedy. Ghastly violence broke out as refugees by the million moved, Hindus from what would now be Pakistan to India, Muslims from India to Pakistan. Thousands were killed. Distress was immense, and a legacy of bitterness was left that continued and brought attention and was made worse by arguments over Kashmir, a princely state whose Hindu ruler opted to bring it into India despite its having a largely Muslim population. Tragedy came again when Gandhi was assassinated—not by a Muslim but by a Hindu extremist—in 1948.

As the British flag went down in 1947 and the flag of the new India went up, it is said that one of the Congress leaders remarked, "Vasco da Gama sails home."[4] It was the beginning of the end of European hegemony in Asia. Where India led, others would soon follow. Ceylon and Burma and Malaya soon did. The Japanese invasion had already signaled the end of Dutch colonial rule in the East Indian possession now called Indonesia. Nothing was said about African independence yet, but Africans were taking note of what had happened.

The Solution of a Secular State

What was the effect of all this on missions? India, under the leadership of Jawaharlal Nehru (1889–1964), a rather secular man influenced by European philosophies and European socialism, adopted a secular constitution—that is, one that made no religious statements but allowed for complete religious liberty. The point was to give space to all the religious communities embraced within the new nation—Hindu, Muslim, Sikh, Jain, Parsee, Christian, and Buddhist. Christians have held to this as the charter of their freedom. The Indian theologian M. M. Thomas produced in 1966 a book called *The Christian Response to the Asian Revolution*, making the important point that secularism enables choice. Instead of preserving religious communities in themselves, it enables people to negotiate their own religious identity.[5] In other words, it permits conversion. It is the very fear of conversion that has led recent Hindu activists to seek to replace the idea of secularity with something that would cut off that possibility and be, as it were, more indigenous.

---

4. I have been unable to verify this statement or identify the Congress leader concerned.—Ed.

5. M. M. Thomas, *The Christian Response to the Asian Revolution* (London: SCM, 1966), 31–32. The book published Thomas's Duff Missionary Lectures delivered in Glasgow and Edinburgh in September–October 1965.

Foreign mission agencies now faced a situation that was to become increasingly familiar; but remember, this was 1947, and there were not too many precedents for it: the business of getting visas for work and the recognition that there was no certainty that the visa would be granted or, if it were, that it would be renewed on expiring. It was the end of the old concept of the lifetime missionary. No one got a thirty-year visa. Attitudes such as Lesslie Newbigin had described in 1936 were also bound to change, whether consciously or unconsciously. The idea of a foreign religious caste faded, and actual power was in the hand of Indians in society as a whole. The idea of a secular state came with a price tag attached.

The Search for a National Church of India

If Indians were in charge of society, should not they also be in charge in the church? Long before this, Azariah had pioneered two indigenous missionary societies, the Indian Missionary Society of Tinnevelly (Tirunelveli) in 1903 and the National Missionary Society in 1905, both of which were staffed, led, and financed by Indians.[6] He had also become the apostle of a movement for church union in India. He was led to this partly by his own experience of interdenominational cooperation in the Indian YMCA and the National Missionary Society (which was interdenominational), but even more by his conviction that a united church was necessary to combat the inherent divisiveness of the caste system.[7] Negotiations to get beyond the existing missionary principle of comity to ecclesial union took many years, but eventually a Church of South India was born, including Anglicans, Methodists, Presbyterians, and Congregationalists. It was inaugurated in 1947, just six weeks after the inauguration of Indian independence. The union was even more comprehensive than may sound from that list of denominations, since it included Anglicans of quite different traditions: the evangelical Church Missionary Society and the High Church Society for the Propagation of the Gospel, as well as missions of German and American background and theological tradition.

A great deal of theological argument had gone into producing a liturgy that all could accept and that united the traditions, but the most difficult is-

6. Susan Billington Harper, *In the Shadow of the Mahatma: Bishop V. S. Azariah and the Travails of Christianity in British India* (Grand Rapids: Eerdmans; Richmond: Curzon, 2000), 72–90.

7. Harper, *In the Shadow of the Mahatma*, 47–75, 235–41.

sues arose over ordination. High Church Anglicans insisted that true ordination lay in succession from the apostles and that the succession was conveyed through laying on of hands by a bishop, himself ordained in that succession. Others rejected that idea, and the idea of requiring that those who had already been serving—perhaps for a lifetime but who had not been ordained in this way—to be reordained was particularly repugnant. The Church of South India devised a form that included ordination by laying on of hands by bishops. Bishops were chosen from different participating traditions. Some of them would have been ordained by laying on of hands in notional apostolic succession, some not, but the act of union included mutual recognition of the bishops and mutual recognition of the ministry. The effect of this was that the Church of South India would include numerous presbyters (what the Anglicans called a "priest" and other denominations a "minister" was in the Church of South India referred to as a "presbyter") who had not received the form of ordination required by Anglican priesthood. But over time, future ordinations would conform to it.

The ordination question caused much agitation, some from strongly Reformed people who objected to making any sacramental requirement a test of validity of ministry, but most of all within the Church of England. It was a time when Anglo-Catholics were particularly strong in the English church, and many Anglo-Catholics feared that the Church of South India would be a blueprint for future church unions elsewhere. Yet there were Anglican dioceses participating fully in the new church. There was a movement among Anglicans to withhold communion from the Church of South India, which would mean withholding it from existing dioceses. The crisis passed. Newbigin writes of the opening service of union, "It was as though all the agonizing fears and delays of twenty-nine years had dammed up a flood that was now bursting through. I have never heard such singing. I think there were very many like myself who found it hard to keep back tears of joy as we remembered all that had gone before and all that might be ahead."[8] Azariah, alas, did not live to see the fulfillment of the story to which he had made such a signal contribution.

South India had led the way on one of the matters of the hour. Church union was very much on the agenda of the ecumenical movement as a whole. This, too, had been a fruit of the World Missionary Conference of Edinburgh, which had led to three separate developments. These were the International Missionary Council, which we have mentioned several times, the Faith and

8. Lesslie Newbigin, *Unfinished Agenda: An Updated Autobiography* (Edinburgh: Saint Andrew, 1993), 90.

Order Movement, which sought closer unity between churches, and the Life and Work Movement, which considered issues of society. The three streams had developed side by side. It had been agreed that Faith and Order and Life and Work should be joined in a new World Council of Churches, but the war held back the institution of this council, which was constituted only in 1948. And it appeared to be India that was pointing the way to the future, a new church born out of the union of churches that had themselves grown out of the work of missions. It raised the issue whether the International Missionary Council itself should not also be part of the World Council of Churches. Surely mission was above all the business of the church and therefore of churches. That question was to rumble on for some years yet.

The Church of South India gave rise to many other attempts at union churches and provided something of a model for them. The earlier successors came in the Indian subcontinent; a Church of North India, where Christians were much weaker both in numbers and in resources, was to follow in 1970. In Sri Lanka, a united Church of Lanka seemed within reach, but the union negotiations twice collapsed, in 1972 and 1975. In Africa also, a Church of Nigeria, very much on the Church of South India model, was on the point of coming into being in 1966 when it was torpedoed by a lawsuit. The Nigerian Civil War followed shortly after, and the united church sank without trace. I have the copy of the inaugural service, but alas, that inaugural service never took place. (It just shows, documentary evidence is not always exactly what it seems.) A United Church of Zambia, without Anglican participation, came into being about the same time, in January 1965. But generally speaking, there has been little enthusiasm for schemes of church union in Africa. The United Church of Zambia was very much a missionary creation. More recent developments everywhere, the plethora of new churches, the rise of the charismatic movement and Neo-Pentecostalism, and the quantity of new ministries suggest that future church unions will have to follow very different models.

The Shape of Indian Theology

Finally, a word about theology. Contemporary Indian theology reflects a broad spectrum of very active theologizing within different traditions. The striking fact about theology in the period of World War II and the years immediately following is that most of the outstanding and creative theological thinkers had escaped a formal theological education. They had never been to seminary. They include the Madras jurist Pandipeddi Chenchiah (1886–1959), who had a lively encounter with Emil Brunner on the subject of the absolute priority for theology of Christology during the latter's postwar tour of Asia in 1949;[9] Vengal Chakkarai (1880–1958), who was also a Madras lawyer; and the ecumenist M. M. Thomas (1916–96). All these figures have in common an engagement with the issues of Indian society. Chakkarai was active in Gandhi's home rule movement and later, in 1951, became chairman of the All-India Trade Union Congress. M. M. Thomas, who came from the Mar Thoma Church in Kerala, was frustrated to find that he could not be recognized by the church because he was a Marxist and could not join the Communist Party because he was a Christian. Thomas and the more regularly theologically educated P. D. Devanandan did sterling work with the Christian Institute for the Study of Religion and Society and with the long-lasting journal *Religion and Society*. This, very much a product of independent industrializing India, set an example to Christian social thought in other countries, not least in the West.

Meanwhile, Stanley J. Samartha (1920–2001), a presbyter in the Church of South India and from 1971 to 1980 the first director of the World Council of Churches' subunit for Dialogue with People of Living Faiths and Ideologies, pioneered studies in dialogue with other faiths that are still with us today. The only means by which this creative work could be known in the West was through the mission networks. It was an early sign that the missionary movement, designed for one-way traffic, must learn to carry freight in both directions. The missionary movement was, after all, and perhaps still is, the only gateway that the Western church has to receive treasure from the churches of the non-Western world.

---

9. D. A. Thangasamy, *The Theology of Chenchiah with Selections from His Writings* (Bangalore: Christian Institute for the Study of Religion and Society, 1966), 6.

CHAPTER 14

Red Sky at Night, Judgment of God?

Missions and the China Experience

In the previous chapter, we described the years after the Second World War as a period in which the great beasts of new nations and world powers came forward as they do in Daniel 7, supplanting the great beasts who preceded them and apparently dictating the shape of events. We saw in relation to the vast new nation of India how missions found themselves caught up in these streams of world events, and how in this process—a process overseen by the Ancient of Days to the glory and permanent rule of one like a son of man, who in his mercy takes into himself the saints of the Most High—the whole church was transformed, so that the twentieth century became one of the most remarkable centuries for Christian expansion, probably the most remarkable since the first century. We have lived through an extraordinary period in church history that we are only beginning to understand.

In this present unveiling, we pursue the same theme in relation to China, a quest that will bring us almost to the present day. China has had a very complex Christian history. It has had three separate but partly overlapping phases of missionary history. The first of these began in the year AD 635 under the Tang dynasty when missionaries from the East Syrian church were received by the emperor, who after personal study of their books approved Christian teaching as suitable for publication throughout the empire. Of the church that emerged from this teaching we know very little. It persisted for several hundred years; then it seems to have disappeared, leaving perhaps some traces on Chinese Buddhism.

The second phase is a Catholic one. After some preliminary expeditions, the phase begins in earnest in the sixteenth century with a group of Jesuit missionaries who moved unusually deeply into Chinese language and culture but ultimately found their work rejected by the papacy. As the papacy set its face against the Jesuits' acceptance of the "Chinese rites" of ancestral veneration, periods of intense persecution followed for Chinese Catholics, who now appeared to be traitors to the fundamental Confucian principle of filial piety. Nevertheless, the Catholic faith in China survived before being reinforced in the nineteenth century when the Qing emperor finally allowed missionaries from the West after long forbidding their activity. For historical and linguistic reasons, Catholic and Protestant have been officially categorized as different religions, and in the eyes of the state, Catholicism is indeed a different religion from Christianity in China.

As described in chapter 8, the third phase begins in 1807 with the arrival of the first Protestant missionary, Robert Morrison, who worked at first in an entirely unrecognized forum and then unofficially, because his official position was as translator to the British East India Company.

The Catholic and Protestant phases of the missionary movement in China closed in the early 1950s when all Western missionaries were required by the newly victorious Communist government to leave China. Although the church in China retains the fundamental division between Catholic and Protestant, both Catholic and Protestant Christianity in China now wear a distinctively Chinese face.

Western Contributions to Chinese Anti-foreignism

Both the Catholic and Protestant missionary investment of personnel and resources in China was very considerable. Although British Protestant missions to China can be dated from Morrison's arrival in 1807, Protestant missions in general become significant in China only after 1842 following the First Anglo-Chinese or "Opium" War, in which Western navies bombarded Chinese ports, demanding and eventually receiving the liberalization of trade; part of that liberalization policy allowed foreigners to reside freely in certain named trading ports in China. Missions thus first gained their status in China as a result of Western military action, action in which China had been humiliated by people whom the governing and learned classes of the nation thought of as barbarians. It may be remarked that though Protestant missions were initiated by British missions, by the late nineteenth century, these were greatly outnumbered by Americans. China became the American mission field par excellence. As the United States became a Pacific power, so its Pacific horizons turned toward China and to Japan and Korea. This is reflected very much in the enormous American missionary investment in China in the early twentieth century, though as I have said, that investment reflected Protestant missionary enterprise as a whole. There is a further reflection here that China also tended to get the cream of the missionary offering, that there was certainly within British missionary societies a pecking order: China got the best candidates, India got some of the best, while Africa got the celestial cannon fodder; this implicit hierarchy was operating well into the twentieth century. So China had a tremendous proportion of the missionary investment, and therefore, what happened in China was significant not just for China but also for the missionary endeavor as a whole—one of the prime fields and the one to whom mission agencies had been sending their best people.

Second, because of the association of Christianity with foreigners—and foreigners who had caused national humiliation—missions have known a long history of hostility in China. For a long time, missionaries were simply unwelcome guests. Missionaries in other parts of the world were rejected or ignored because they were foreign: in African settings, it was common to be told, "Yes, God gave you your book, but he gave us something else. There is one way for white people and another for black people." But in China, the rejection went deeper. So a good deal of missionary effort went into removing prejudice, building bridges, and trying to open conversations.

The beginning of the twentieth century had seen the most violent outbursts against foreigners that the missionary movement ever knew, in the Boxer Rising of 1900, in which much foreign property, including large numbers of mission institutions, had been attacked, destroyed, and missionaries and their families had formed a high proportion of the foreigners who had been killed. The results of the rising had been the further humiliation of China. The Western powers had intervened and had required the Chinese government to pay indemnity for the lives and property that had been destroyed. Missions were divided as to how to respond to this initiative. Some, such as the China Inland Mission, who had suffered disproportionately, since their missionaries were often in the more remote locations with less chance of escape, refused any indemnity; and their spirituality, suffering, and death were to be part of the normal lot of the missionary, indeed of the Christian disciple. For others, indemnity was a work of justice. Others again (Timothy Richard, the famous Welsh Baptist missionary, was an advocate of this) argued for the Chinese government to be required to develop institutions such as universities that would bring enlightenment to China and improve the quality of its life. This was the sort of indemnity that should be required. This division was symptomatic of the wide range of outlook among missions in China.

Minimalists and Maximalists

Disagreements over the post-Boxer indemnities went deeper than differences in theology, although the whole theological spectrum can be found in China from the most liberal to the most conservative. There was in China, as has occurred many times in the history of the movement, a division between what one might call the maximalists and the minimalists in mission. The archetypal minimalist is James Hudson Taylor, of the China Inland Mission, whom we examined in chapter 8. Taylor called for the gospel, conceived as being expressed in words and in transformed lives, to be preached to every person throughout China until everyone in China in its remotest regions had had the opportunity to accept it personally—looking to the Lord's return as the climax of mission, and being suspicious of institutions, particularly large ones, as diverting resources and time from the urgent task of presenting the gospel.

The archmaximalist is Timothy Richard of the Baptist Missionary Society (1845–1919). He starts from a similar theological position to Taylor. Indeed, Timothy Richard had originally applied to the China Inland Mission himself. He had been rejected because they thought he was too denominationally Baptist and would be happier with his own crowd. Richard, starting from this similar theological position and beginning as an enterprising, innovative evangelistic missionary, finds himself in a place where he is present as an evangelist in the center of a famine. As an act required of Christians, he had successfully organized famine relief, had popularized the cause of famine relief in mission circles at home, and had won in his area of China great respect for missions in general. What is he to do now? Does he simply turn this to account as an evangelist? Rather, he finds himself thinking why famines take place in China, pondering the fact that they are not necessary or inevitable. They are caused, or made worse at least, by human error and by ignorance. As with most evangelical missionaries, his message had been essentially Christocentric: about what Christ has done, and done for *you*. A truly Christian theology of mission, he now argues, should take account of the work of God the Father, God the Creator; and a truly Christian contribution to China should include the spreading of the knowledge that would break the cycle of famine and deprivation and bring enlightened, effective government.

Many missions had followed this path. One result, as we noted in chapter 11 in relation to Dugald Christie, had been Christian colleges and Christian universities developing with entire medical faculties. As the twentieth century proceeded, the maximalists were seeing encouragement in China.

The old reactionary Qing Empire had fallen in 1911, and the new republic was seeing the value of modern learning and technology, prepared to make more use of the missions in order to provide it. Whole new opportunities were coming up, of service to the community; whole new numbers of missionaries were involved in providing these services. At long last, China appeared to be turning westward. Might this not mean that it would embrace Christianity as part of the modernity that it was now embracing in other spheres? When a declared Christian, General Chiang Kai-shek (Jiang Jieshi), emerged as leader of the Nationalist government in 1928, this view seemed to be confirmed. To many missionaries, a concern for Chinese culture now seemed misplaced. Old China was dying; new China would be modern. Inevitably there were those who took a different view, who took seriously the religious traditions of China, both the learned and the popular.

Christianity and the Communist Revolution

The whole history of China in the twentieth century is one of turbulence: revolution, war, division, controversy, and uncertainty. By the 1920s, a Communist political force was emerging alongside the Nationalist one, offering a pass to a new and more just China. It took its inspiration from the still young revolution in Russia of 1917. It demanded justice for the millions of China's poor and often hungry rural people. It decried the Western capitalist models of modernization, with the corruption and luxury of those who introduced them, as well as the greed of the landlords who lived in wealth while peasants starved. It is worth remembering that this message was appealing to many Christians, especially to students nurtured in the social gospel teaching of the Chinese YMCA. Many young people were open to both the Christian and the Communist message. Christianity and Communism alike appealed to people critical of the present social order, provided they could both be shorn of their "foreignness." It would be an exaggeration to claim that the people attracted to Communism were the people attracted to Christianity and vice versa, but among certain elite groups, this was sometimes the case.

World War II began early in China. In 1931, the Japanese cut off northeast China by installing a puppet government in Manchuria, which declared its independence of China. In 1937 came the Japanese invasion of China itself, with savage war and rapid Japanese progress in eastern China. The immediate impact of this on the West was limited. All eyes in the West were concentrated on Europe, on the developments in Germany and Italy and Spain with the new dictatorships there, and especially the threat of German expansion. The union of Germany and Austria had taken place just that year, the first sign of the nationalist plans in Germany. The first signs of the large-scale persecution of Jews were similarly taking place.

The missions through the Western churches played a major part in arousing sympathy for China and consciousness of what was happening there. The fact that Chiang Kai-shek and his wife were outspoken Christians was of major assistance here. I remember as a child in the early 1940s receiving books from the Edinburgh House mission press, little books, missionary booklets, and there was one on General Chiang Kai-shek and his deeply Christian wife, Soong Mei-ling, *Wings over China*;[1] I can see it to this day.

Missions recognized the truth in the Communist claim that the Nationalist government was riddled with corruption but tended to exempt Chiang Kai-shek of blame for this. A new dimension, of course, came with the Japanese attack on Pearl Harbor in December 1941 and the American declaration of war with Japan, followed by that of the Allies. At a stroke, the China war was part of the Western war, and China was an ally; Communist and Nationalist forces were now on the same side in opposition to the invaders.

For missionaries in eastern China, however, who had continued to work under the Japanese occupation, this meant internment as enemy aliens, and Western mission effort effectively ceased overnight. There were a few exceptions to this; the Church of Scotland had one missionary couple in Hulan in Manchuria, Alexander and Maria Babos, who were Hungarian nationals.[2] Because Hungary was an ally of Germany and thus of Japan, they were allowed to continue working when the rest of the mission closed down. That left missionaries in west China, now known as Free China, with its capital at Chunking/Chongqing. The year 1945 brought the dropping of the atomic bombs on Hiroshima and Nagasaki and the rapid ending of hostilities, the humiliation of Japan, and the appearance of the United States as the dominant Pacific power, with the flamboyant American general Douglas MacArthur

---

1. Basil Matthews, *Wings over China: Generalissimo and Madame Chiang Kai-Shek* (London: Edinburgh House, 1940).

2. The Rev. Alexander Babos (b. 1903) was a minister in the Reformed Church in Transylvania who in 1933 was accepted by the Foreign Mission Committee of the Church of Scotland for missionary service in Manchuria. In 1937, he married the Rev. Maria Loriner (1900–2006), one of the first women ministers in the Hungarian Reformed Church. They left China in September 1947 for the United States, serving various churches before moving in 1985 to Ontario, Canada. I am grateful to Rev. Sandy Sneddon and Rev. Ian Alexander of the Church of Scotland for this information. An obituary for Maria Babos may be viewed online: "Reverend Maria Babos," *Daily Bulletin*, https://www.legacy.com/us/obituaries/ivdailybulletin/name/maria -babos-obituary?pid=18122937.—Ed.

a potent symbol of how important this figure was going to be in relation to the Pacific powers.

From the point of view of the missions, the first task was to deal with exhausted or sick or traumatized missionaries who had been in internment or otherwise worn out with the extraordinary demands of recent years. Relief work was also immediately needed for distressed and hungry people in China. But beyond all this, there was the expectation that missions in China would restart more or less where they had left off. After all, China had been, as we have seen, a major focus of the missionary movement over all these years. But the political situation deteriorated into renewal of civil war between Nationalist and Communist forces. No compromise that the missions kept hoping for was ever reached. The economy was out of control. In 1948, three million Chinese yuan equaled one Hong Kong dollar. The government responded to this appalling inflation by changing the currency; within a few weeks, exactly the same thing had happened to the new currency. The Nationalist government had lost all credibility and any base of support in China. By October 1949, the Communists were effectively in control of the whole of the mainland. Chiang Kai-shek had set up his government in the island of Taiwan.

In the West, the former allies against Germany—the United States and Russia—had become rivals in the Cold War, and in terms of Western policy, China had to fit into the Cold War scenario. The United States insisted that Chiang Kai-shek was still the legitimate government of China and refused to recognize the Communist government at all. This had special significance since in the newly fledged United Nations, China had a permanent seat, along with the United States, the United Kingdom, France, and Russia, on the Security Council, the crucial governing body. For practical purposes, that seat now had to be held by Taiwan.

For the next two years, the position of missionaries in China remained unclear. Some of the remaining missionaries were impressed by Communist commitment to the poor and to the absence of corruption in the Communist administration after a long period when corruption had been endemic in government. Others were worried by student demonstrations and disruptive behavior. It is interesting to find a mainline mission, the London Missionary Society, proposing in November 1949 that missionaries should no longer be heads of institutions but should exercise unobtrusive roles designed to deepen church life, and doing so while Chinese methods of evangelism suited to the new context should be developed. This mission at least was seeing some of the ways in which the wind was blowing. It was being recognized that mission methods had to change radically, above all that missionaries should be less visible, less directive, and that old methods of evangelism were unlikely to work or perhaps even be permitted in the new situation and that therefore new ones must be found. Missionaries would continue to be "fathers in God" to their Chinese colleagues, but not in virtue of any office they might hold, simply by reason of their own faith and insight. The London Missionary Society passed these proposals to the church with which it was affiliated, the Church of Christ in China, which included Congregational, Presbyterian, and Methodist elements and made up almost a third of Protestant church membership in China. The senior staff of the Church of Christ in China met to consider the document on January 18, 1950, and were generally apprecia-tive of its tone, though the general secretary, H. H. Tsui (Ciu Xianxiang), warned that the term "fathers in God" might be misunderstood because some missionaries in the past had made the mistake of thinking of themselves as "fathers" and Chinese church workers as "children."[3] A more far-reaching reply came in another form a bit later.

The Chinese government had so far made no declaration about missionary work beyond greatly restricting missionary travel, and even this was care-fully explained as being for their own safety: there are air raids going on from Taiwan, and we do not want anybody killed. But during the year 1950, the government was making plain its terms for the survival of Christianity, and to do this it did not negotiate with the missions. It dealt with a group of Chinese Christians, members of the churches that it believed it could trust. This included members of the National Christian Council of China, to which the Church of Christ in China belonged. The National Christian Council of China had emerged from that enthusiasm for cooperation between missions that had been fostered by the Student Volunteer Missionary Union and given particular impetus by the World Missionary Conference in Edinburgh. It had been intended as all-inclusive, to represent the whole of Christian activity in China, all the churches. Edinburgh 1910 had indeed brought together a very wide spectrum of missions, and any theological differences between them related to High Church Anglicans who doubted whether their non-Episcopal colleagues were really part of the church. But things were different now. Many more conservative missions, including the large and prominent China Inland Mission, were not members of the National Christian Council of China.

---

3. The London Missionary Society document was written on November 9, 1949, by Ron-ald K. Orchard, the secretary for Africa and China; for its contents and the response of the Church of Christ staff, see George Hood, *Neither Bang nor Whimper: The End of a Missionary Era in China* (Singapore: Presbyterian Church in Singapore, 1991), 88-89.—Ed.

The Three-Self Principle Taking Root in China

The other bodies consulted by the Chinese leadership in 1950—and Zhou Enlai (Chou En-lai) seems to have been particularly involved in this)—were the YMCA and the YWCA, the Young Women's Christian Association. The YMCA had also been closely linked with the missionary enthusiasm of the student volunteers, especially those from America, and the YMCA had made a policy of appointing nationals to their executive posts, so that YMCA and YWCA secretaries were almost invariably Chinese. At the time, the YMCA was making use of the phrase "self-governing, self-supporting, self-propagating" as describing its aim. The phrase, as we saw in chapter 6, was an old one, coined in the middle of the nineteenth century by the English Anglican Henry Venn and the American Congregationalist Rufus Anderson to describe what in their different ways they saw as the object of mission policy: the emergence of self-governing, self-supporting, and self-propagating churches. Of course, this had not happened in China, or had happened only to a very limited extent. The YMCA was one of the few Christian organizations that could claim to be led by Chinese, and its executives were frequently and typically young educated people, more open perhaps to political radicalism than other parts of the church.

Three-self teaching had been renewed in China in the twentieth century through the Anglican Roland Allen (1868–1947). Allen, who was a missionary of the Society for the Propagation of the Gospel and who was involved in the siege of the legations during the Boxer Rising, was very aware of Chinese resistant feeling to foreign domination. Allen had stressed the requirement of national leadership, a nonprofessional ministry, missions not governing from the outside or building large structures unsustainable locally, and keeping within Chinese culture. These old elements from the mid-nineteenth century and the beginning of the twentieth were now incorporated into the thinking and the vocabulary of the Christians whom the new government was willing to accept as speaking for Christianity in future.

One of the most significant of these figures was Y. T. Wu (Wu Yaozong), born in 1893 (so he is a middle-aged man at the time that he becomes prominent) into a non-Christian family, converted in 1918 in his twenties at a YMCA rally addressed by the student volunteer leader Sherwood Eddy. He gave up his post in customs to work for the YMCA. He studied in the United States as YMCA officers often did, graduating from Columbia and from Union Theological Seminary. His theological position seems to have been liberal but not aggressively so. He had been influenced by American social gospel teaching but was certainly not a Communist in his earlier years. Indeed, he had been a strong pacifist until the Japanese attack on Manchuria changed his views. Like many other young radical Christians, he developed sympathy for Communist social aims and (he was a philosopher of religion by training) argued that the Communist *materialist* theory was fully compatible with belief in God. Matter is the means by which God reveals himself in nature.

Wu emerged as the leader of the movement that the government was ready to use as acceptable Christianity. He was the chief drafter of the document that is usually called the Christian Manifesto, which was sent in 1950 to all the missions and which is the real reply to the letter that the London Missionary Society sent in November 1949 to their partner body, the Church of Christ in China. The full title of the Christian Manifesto is *Direction of Endeavor for Chinese Christianity in the Construction of New China.*[4] The manifesto insists that imperialism has in the past made use of Christianity: we must purge imperialistic tendencies from within Christianity. It called on all Christians to sign; over time it was reported that four hundred thousand actually did. The outcome was the Three-Self Patriotic Movement, of which Wu was president from 1951, nominally until his death in 1979 but effectively until the Cultural Revolution in mid-1966, since the revolution effectively invalidated all the privileges given to the three-self movement.

The missions varied in their response to the manifesto and to the three-self movement, but there was soon no doubt as to what they should do. At first, it was assumed that the three-self development would come gradually as Chinese leadership replaced mission leadership. Any hope of that thought vanished in June 1950, when war broke out between North and South Korea and the United Nations named North Korea as the aggressor. For the Three-Self Patriotic Movement, patriotism was now redefined in terms of "resist America, aid Korea" (that is, North Korea). The missions realized that it was time to go. Consultations with local church authorities invariably resulted in the advice that it would be better to go. In December 1950, the Church of Christ in China delivered its message to the missions, indicating its determination to play a part within the new China. The message says, addressing the missions, "The church which you have helped to establish is now coming to a new position, being recognized by the new People's Government as a Chinese organization serving the Chinese people. In taking this political stand [and this is its own words], we would stress that the Chinese church is not breaking its ecumenical ties nor its friendly relations with older churches or its long

---

4. Wallace C. Merwin and Francis P. Jones, *Documents of the Three-Self Movement: Source Materials for the Study of the Protestant Church in Communist China* (New York: National Council of the Churches of Christ in the USA, 1963), 19.

and treasured associations with mission societies and missions." It goes on, "The banner of the Cross has never been easy to carry, and it will not be so in our new situation."[5] In 1958, the government abolished all denominations and recognized only one Protestant church for all purposes, and for practical purposes it was the Three-Self Patriotic Movement.

These developments have been variously interpreted. One interpretation can be seen in the writings of my late friend Leslie Lyall (1905–1996). In his various books, Lyall, formerly a missionary of the China Inland Mission, and latterly on the home staff of the China Inland Mission's successor, the Overseas Missionary Fellowship, depicts the Three-Self Patriotic Movement as a betrayal. Certainly, large sections of the Christian church never registered with the Three-Self Patriotic Movement and maintained Christian life without any official recognition—and subject to every form of harassment. By contrast, others have argued that the Three-Self Patriotic Movement enabled the organized Chinese church to survive the extraordinary pressures that Christianity faced as the new China tried to produce a new humanity.

Rethinking Missions

Our present concern, however, is the effect on missions. The China experience caused an immense degree of rethinking. In Britain, one deeply influential book was called *Christian Missions and the Judgment of God*.[6] It was by David Paton, who had served in China with Church Missionary Society from 1939 to 1945, and again from 1947 to 1950. Paton saw the enforced withdrawal from China as indeed an expression of God's judgment on missions for their desire to dominate, to direct, and to lay a pattern down for the indigenous church to follow. Paton called the missions of the 1950s and 1960s back to Roland Allen, to trust in the Holy Spirit and in the local church, to the principle of self-governing, self-supporting, and self-propagating churches. Paton indeed republished some works by Allen with an account of his life under the title *The Ministry of the Spirit*.[7] The principle of living under direction, living on other people's terms, and not being heads of institutions are all themes that come out in the book.

5. I have so far been unable to trace the source of this letter; the original may be in the Council for World Mission archives at the School of Oriental and African Studies in London.—Ed.

6. David M. Paton, *Christian Missions and the Judgment of God* (London: SCM, 1953).

7. David M. Paton, ed., *The Ministry of the Spirit: Selected Writings of Roland Allen; With a Memoir by Alexander McLeish* (London: World Dominion, 1960). The book was republished by Lutterworth Press in 2006, with an introductory essay by Lamin Sanneh.

A further result of the withdrawal from China was the presence of a large number of experienced but now surplus missionaries. Some of these were transferred to other fields, especially if they were serving with a mission that operated in several fields. My own predecessor in Sierra Leone in the 1950s had previously worked in China. But others opened new work, and the obvious new fields were among the overseas Chinese or among their neighbors. The result was the intensification of missionary work in Malaysia, in Singapore, in Indonesia, and in the Philippines, in each case starting with a Chinese population but moving beyond it. Hong Kong, now flooded with refugees, received many, and more problematically so did Taiwan. All this helped to create a vast China mission in waiting, Chinese Christians identifying with China, waiting for the reopening of its doors. This was in some ways a return to the situation in the nineteenth century when a China mission in waiting grew up in Malacca when missions were not allowed in China, where translations and printing and other literature for China was produced. The great difference between the two was that the missionaries in waiting in the new situation were themselves Chinese.

The main lesson, however, was that of a church without missionaries. It was a situation that was going to be repeated many times over the coming years, but in the 1950s, it was new. Would the church survive without missionaries? One of Leslie Lyall's works was called *Come Wind, Come Weather.*[8] You perhaps catch the quotation from the hymn in *Pilgrim's Progress.*

> Who would true valour see,
> Let him come hither;
> One here will constant be,
> Come wind, come weather.

The pilgrim, standing lonely, as the unregistered Christians were in China when betrayed, apparently by their brethren. They were dreaming "constant . . . , Come Wind, come Weather." This summed up a history that seemed to be depending on the unregistered believers in this view of China's history.

Lyall wrote another book called *Red Sky at Night.*[9] The red sky, of course, refers to the Communist night fallen on China, but it also relates to the proverb that a red sky at night is a shepherd's delight; it means fine weather

8. Leslie T. Lyall, *Come Wind, Come Weather: The Present Experience of the Church in China* (London: Hodder & Stoughton, 1961).

9. Leslie T. Lyall, *Red Sky at Night: Communism Confronts Christianity in China* (London: Hodder & Stoughton, 1969).

tomorrow. This was again expressive of the future. Of course, the church did survive. While estimates vary widely, not to say wildly, everyone agrees that there are now many more Christians—indeed many times more Christians—in China, registered and unregistered, than before the missionaries left. I wonder whether there is any parallel in Christian history to the church in China in what it has been through in the last fifty years, emerging as it has done, and clearly raising the question, What is its future? How will it fit into the rest of the church from which it has so long been isolated?

The pattern of closing missions was to take place many times. In the 1960s, it was the turn of Burma, and again on most estimates Christians have trebled their numbers in Burma since the exclusion of the missions. It was to happen under different circumstances in 1970 in what is now the Democratic Republic of Congo, where again Caesar, in the shape of General Mobutu Sese Seko, produced a church union, the Église du Christ au Congo, that no one else had been able to produce. But it was China that first taught some of us that we were dispensable.

CHAPTER 15

Winds of Change and Latter Rain

Christianity and the New African Nations

In chapter 7, we discussed Thomas Fowell Buxton's *The African Slave Trade and Its Remedy* (1840). Buxton's work could be described as the first systematic treatise on African studies, and probably also the first treatise on what we would now call development economics. Buxton argued that missionaries, the Bible, and the plow should go together, that Europe owed Africa reparations for the evil done by the slave trade, and that Africa could through calling out its own resources be saved from its present miseries and become an equal partner in trade and in the comity of nations. When this was written, European colonies in Africa were few and small, the Cape of Good Hope being the largest. It was the latter part of the nineteenth century that brought the parceling out of the whole of Africa, with the exception of Liberia and Ethiopia, among the European powers. Most of that expansion came after 1880, during the so-called Scramble for Africa, and much of it was preemptive: land was seized not because it was immediately desirable but in order to forestall its seizure by some other European power.

Missions had been involved in Africa, west and south especially, well before the scramble of the 1880s and 1890s, but the advent of territorial colonialism altered the dynamics. No longer were missions negotiating with independent African rulers who could give them entry or refuse it; they were dealing with a power that, while it might still refuse them entry (this often happened in areas where the colonial government feared Muslim susceptibilities) and while it might impose conditions and requirements, the missions appeared to be on the inside track, the local people and their rulers on the outside. The colonial governments found the missions immensely useful in providing an infrastructure of education and health care, which the missions did reasonably efficiently and extremely cheaply, the latter an important factor since colonial budgets were always small. Missions of the newer interdenominational faith type—which proliferated at the end of the nineteenth century and the beginning of the twentieth, missions that stressed the urgency of evangelism in the light of the Lord's return and feared institutional involvement as a distraction from this task—found themselves sucked into the system. Whether they talked to the chief or to the district commissioner, they were expected to provide schools.

The colonial ethos of the late nineteenth century had had another effect. In the precolonial era, inspired by the ideal of self-governing, self-supporting, and self-propagating churches, African leadership took charge in many missions. When Samuel Ajayi Crowther was consecrated bishop in 1864, he had already had charge of a mission for seven years, and a mission staffed entirely by African clergymen. Under colonial rule, this happened no more. African leadership, time after time, was bit by bit replaced by European.

African Prophets

In the second decade of the twentieth century, a movement took place in different parts of the continent—west, central, south, though not, as far as I am aware, in the east—the reasons for which are hard to explain. Powerful charismatic African figures arose, calling their people to repentance and faith. They were not usually on mission staffs; if they were, it was only at the most junior level, and they were certainly not commissioned by the missions. They claimed to hold their commission directly from God, given in dream or vision or voice. Vast numbers followed them. The first and most significant, the Liberian prophet William Wadé Harris (c. 1860–1929), can be regarded as the foundational figure in the Christianity of Côte d'Ivoire. All the churches—Catholic, Protestant, and independent—owe their prosperity to his walk across the then unevangelized French colony and over into the Gold Coast (Ghana), a journey he made on foot with two female companions between 1913 and 1915, in the course of which at least a hundred thousand people threw away their fetishes and cult objects and were baptized. Such figures were not working against the missions. Harris urged his converts to go to the mission if there was one near, and wait for one to arrive if there was not. But the work of missions was powerfully set forward as thousands came under their pastoral care as a result of the work of these people from nowhere.

The Movement for African Independence

During the First World War, owing to the presence of German colonies in East Africa and West Africa, much of the continent was a war zone. In World War II, that happened in sub-Saharan Africa only in Ethiopia. The end of the war left the colonial system intact. The Union of South Africa, as it was then called, was a self-governing dominion, formed in 1910; it remained part of the British Empire, or, as it was increasingly known from 1926, the British Commonwealth of Nations. Southern Rhodesia had a degree of self-government and its own Parliament, but this was entirely white, representing the white settlers. We noted in chapter 13 the saying of Arthur Creech Jones, colonial secretary in the British Labour government that gave India its independence in 1947, that there was only a century left in order to prepare the colonies for independence.

In reality, the movement for independence was already growing in many of the African colonies. In the French territories, it was inspired by intellectuals who had lived in France. In the British colonies, it was educated young men, especially those who had studied in Britain. Most had attended mission schools and drew their inspiration and their precedents from what they had learned there, both from the Bible and from history: the architect of Kenyan independence, Jomo Kenyatta, is a good example, having been educated in the Church of Scotland mission. In October 1945, a Pan-African Congress was held in Manchester, in England, which is often taken as a fountain of the new nationalist movement and as a landmark in the history of African government. Again we should notice that this was taking place in England, because it was students and others living in the country who were forming the backbone of this movement.

If independence for African colonies was not high on the government agenda in 1945, the colonies were at least not forgotten. Through colonial development and welfare acts passed in 1945 and 1950, the new Labour government sought to give a boost to colonial education and economic development. Some of these projects—the groundnut scheme in Tanzania, the Gambia egg scheme, and so on—crashed miserably; but there were signs of a new intention to invest in the colonies. Two of these developments at least had a marked effect on missions. One was a scheme that affected northern Nigeria in particular: to speed up education. And, again, the government turned to the missions. Instead of trying to recruit teachers directly, they offered the missions a sum that was based on the notional salaries of the teachers that they thought they needed. The task was essentially to train African teachers. Since the notional salary of one of these teachers was at least two and a half times a missionary salary, the missions saw this as a means of increasing their own investment in a vital area, for over the postwar years, the peoples of the central area of Nigeria, the high plateau, moved rapidly to the Christian faith. Since this region was administratively within northern Nigeria, which was dominated by a Muslim elite that looked to the Sultan at Sokoto as their spiritual and political guide, this was a development of both religious and political significance.

The Development of Scholarship on African Indigenous Religions

The first Colonial Development and Welfare project was the promotion of economic development in the British colonies; the second was the creation of new universities in East Africa and West Africa. This goal implied recognition that education must take its full course to the highest level; it was a tacit admission that these territories would indeed realize self-government one day. Two features of them are relevant to our purpose.

First, in Nigeria's oldest university, the University of Ibadan (founded in 1948 as University College, Ibadan), a department of religious studies produced and supplied the textbooks for the first academic teaching of a new subject called African traditional religion. Hitherto African indigenous religions had been classified under the catch-all of "animism" and given scant attention; they were thought of as part of a primitive outlook that people would grow out of as education improved. The person who invented the term "African traditional religion" and wrote the earliest books and treated the subject seriously as religion was a British Methodist missionary and academic called Geoffrey Parrinder, who died at the age of ninety-five in 2005. From Ibadan, the idea of the study of African religion spread to the other new African universities.[1]

The second feature to be noted is that a number of very able African scholars of religion and theology appeared in these new universities. They were for the most part committed Christians, usually ordained and committed to the church, and they had been trained in theology on Western lines, usually in the West. Instead, however, of doing what was expected of

1. Professor Walls was too modest to state that he played a major role in this process himself, notably at the University of Nigeria, Nsukka, where he taught African religious studies from 1962 to 1966. Professor Walls was greatly influenced by his fellow Methodist Geoffrey Parrinder.—Ed.

them and entering into the domain of the Western academy and producing work on form criticism of the Gospels or the nature of apostolic ministry, they began to concentrate their writing on African traditional religion, but treated theologically, seeking out what were the continuities between Africa's old religions and its new Christian one and considering how far they went. In effect, they were asking, What was God doing in the African past? Kwame Bediako (1945–2008), a very dear Ghanaian friend, was later to describe their activity as parallel to that of Justin and Tatian and the other second-century apologists who considered the relation of Christianity to the Greek past.[2] It was important for Christians educated in the Greek world to have an identity that was both Greek and Christian. It would be equally important now for African Christians to be sure of *their* identity, particularly since for so long, African identity had not been given much value. Now you must be able to be African and Christian. Here was the context in which African theology began addressing African issues, the ground in which an African theology might develop. I may say there was a great deal of disquiet in mission circles about this development, particularly in conservative circles.

African Independent (or Instituted) Churches

Something perhaps almost equally important and perhaps even more noticeable at the time was the discovery of the significance of what in the 1960s began to be called the African Independent Churches (the correct speech of today calls them African Instituted Churches; I personally do not think either term is really very good), but which up until then had been given names like "separatist," because their main characteristic from the mission point of view was that they had separated from and were no longer part of the churches directed by missions. The phenomenon had been known for long enough, right back in the nineteenth century. In the later part of the nineteenth century, as the colonial regimes took control and as colonial thinking became more typical in the missions, there was a great spread of these churches that were sometimes seeking to go back to an earlier phase of mission policy but that appeared to be simply about substituting African rule in place of European rule.

In the twentieth century, a new type of church appeared in various parts of the continent. We can see now that these grew from rereadings of Scripture by

2. Kwame Bediako, *Theology and Identity: The Impact of Culture upon Christian Thought in the Second Century and Modern Africa* (Oxford: Regnum Books, 1992).

people who read the Bible in a different way and saw things in the Bible that, in the type of European thinking we discussed in chapter 12, were bracketed out—in other words, the "non-Enlightenment" parts of the Bible. New forms of church were constructed in this way.

The first study of this type to become well known was the first edition of *Bantu Prophets in South Africa*, by the Swedish Lutheran scholar Bengt Sundkler, which appeared in 1948.[3] It was the first text to examine such churches closely and sympathetically and to produce an attempt to understand what they were and why they were. During the 1960s and 1970s, interest in this topic gradually increased, owing particularly to the work, first of the New Zealander Harold Turner, in his study called *African Independent Church*,[4] two volumes amounting to 608 pages in all, and then of the Briton David B. Barrett, in his book called *Schism and Renewal in Africa*.[5] Turner's study remains, I think, the fullest that has yet been done of any African Christian community. These works began to look at the rise of these churches and their nature and what they did, their concern with healing in particular, and began to raise the question, What is missing in mission Christianity? To what are these churches speaking that we are not doing? This led to a spate of studies in the 1960s and a cluster of conferences and had an effect on some missions. One American mission, the Mennonite Board of Missions, based in Elkhart, Indiana, came to define their special contribution in terms of these churches, of fellowship with them, of building bridges with them. That's another story. But just thinking of developments in scholarship: developments in scholarship *do* sometimes have an effect, and a positive effect, on what is actually done on the ground.

Implications of African Decolonization for the Missions

We need not describe in any detail the decolonization process that began in the 1950s, a decade after the war. The first new African nation was Ghana, the former British colony of the Gold Coast, which emerged in 1957 under the charismatic, confident, and ambitious leadership of Kwame Nkrumah. Other nations soon followed: Nigeria, the largest, Sierra Leone, and then the East

3. Bengt G. M. Sundkler, *Bantu Prophets in South Africa* (London: Lutterworth, 1948).

4. Harold W. Turner, *History of an African Independent Church*, vol. 1, *The Church of the Lord (Aladura)*, vol. 2, *The Life and Faith of the Church of the Lord (Aladura)* (Oxford: Clarendon, 1967).

5. David B. Barrett, *Schism and Renewal in Africa: An Analysis of Six Thousand Contemporary Religious Movements* (Nairobi: Oxford University Press, 1968).

African countries. France offered a different mode of independence, one that closely linked the new nations to France, especially for trade and commerce. The head of state of the Ivory Coast sat in the French cabinet for some years. Those colonies that refused this link, as the Republic of Guinea did, were harshly treated. All the new states were colonial constructs, with borders set by the colonial settlements. These borders bore scant relation to ethnic divisions and were sometimes arbitrary, and the new states had to build a national consciousness over the top of ethnic and regional consciousness. This was an issue that the Christian churches had long been addressing. The church in any one territory would typically bring together people of different groups who might be marginal or indifferent or even hostile to one another, and had to seek to develop a single consciousness of being Christians together. It had not been an easy matter, and the new states faced with the same problems found it no easier.

Two issues arising from the decolonization process as it affected missions may be noticed here. First, the missions, still in most cases heavily involved in education, saw nation building as part of their activity. They desired to identify with the new nations, to make a contribution to national life, and surely Christian teaching and Christian living were in themselves to be a contribution. But the programs were consciously addressed to helping build a new nation.

In the second place, the rapid move to independence highlighted the fact that the churches in particular countries were often led and governed by expatriates. Hardly anyone rejected the *theory* that churches should be self-governing; it was just that "they are not ready yet." But if the president or prime minister and all the cabinet could be nationals of the country, why could not the leadership of the church? Throughout Africa and in missions of different kinds, the coming of political independence was a signal to hand over leadership in the church. There was often a further process whereby the structures of the mission needed to undergo a sort of decolonization so that the real power was vested in the church rather than in the mission. In most cases, the restructuring was time-consuming; in some, it turned out to be painful.

The process of political decolonization was slowest in those colonies that had a white settler element in the population. It was complicated for home governments since not only did the settlers not wish to give up their cherished privileges, but also there was often a powerful lobby at home rousing public opinion in support of "our kith and kin," a cry that often had racist overtones. The first signs came in Kenya, where grievances about European land seizures gave vent in the 1950s to Mau Mau, a violent movement that used traditional institutions and traditional oaths as its methods. Many Christians resisted the movement, and some were killed for it. The British repression of the movement itself was brutal, involving incarceration in concentration camps. Nevertheless, Kenya did emerge in 1963 as an independent country, with the white population incorporated within it.

From 1953 to 1963, a political device known as the Central African Federation linked the territories of Nyasaland and Northern and Southern Rhodesia, the last named being, as we have seen, under white rule. The government tried to keep the federation intact, meaning that any form of independence would be under the leadership of Southern Rhodesia. Missionaries in Zambia and in Malawi and their parent missions were active in lobbying government and public opinion in Britain against this measure. This was notably the case in Scotland, which supplied most of the missions in Malawi. The pressure allowed Malawi and shortly afterward Zambia to become independent on their own without the Central African Federation, without the link to white Rhodesia. The Central African Federation was dissolved; Malawi and Zambia both achieved independence in 1964. This may have been the last occasion on which the churches had any influence in determining the policies of a British government. Southern Rhodesia, of course, went on to declare its own independence in 1965 and bring itself to a destructive war and eventually in 1980 to the emergence of Zimbabwe under the leadership of Robert Mugabe, which forms another tragic story.

The outstanding and most problematic case of white settlement was that of South Africa. In 1948, the National Party was elected with a commanding majority on a franchise that excluded most Black South Africans. It instituted according to its manifesto a policy of apartheid, legal separation of the races. Biblical justification was claimed, and the National Party set itself as the defender of Christian civilization. Under apartheid, South Africa became perhaps the most theologically active country in the world, seeing the growth of Black theology and the development of antiapartheid organizations such as the Christian Institute of Southern Africa.

The connected issues—the Central African Federation, Rhodesia, and apartheid—brought many missions into a new form of activity, seeking to inform their parent churches of the situation and keep the matter before the public. It was a return to the old days of the anti–slave trade campaigns, when missions became channels of information and public activity in support of the relief of suffering and oppression. It was a controversial role, and many conservative missions thought it was none of their business. Yet the churches in the West, taken as a whole, represented a body of public opinion that was both more concerned and better informed about Africa than the population at large. And the information was provided and the concern was fostered through their mission agencies.

Generally speaking, the colonial borders have been maintained since independence, but there have been at least two major challenges. One was Congo, where the Belgians had made no preparations for independence and the transfer of power in 1960 was done in a hurried and chaotic fashion, and an attempted secession of an eastern province, Katanga, followed. There were years of confusion. One result was an attack on foreigners during the Simba Rebellion in eastern Congo from 1963 to 1965, which led to the deaths of more missionaries, Catholic and Protestant, than any other single event since the Boxer Rising in China in 1900. A total exclusion of missions followed, and then a recall; foreign missions were an access port to Western resources and could sometimes deploy them more effectively than could broken-backed states themselves.

The secession of eastern Nigeria from the Nigerian Federation under the name of Biafra gave missions problems of another kind. The war, from 1966 to 1970, was long and bitter, and divided missions deeply. It gave rise to ethical debates about how far hunger and relief aid could be used as political weapons. Here the churches were at least informed by the missions, places of debate and sources of humanitarian aid.

The explosion of higher education gave rise to a phenomenon that needs to be considered under the heading of missions. The source lay in expatriate Christians, mostly British, mostly university teachers, though one of the most important was an old colonial officer who was now working for the colonial development and welfare. These people had been deeply influenced themselves by parachurch movements during their own spiritual journey, most notably the Scripture Union, an organization devoted to disciplined and organized daily Bible study, and what was then called the Inter-Varsity Fellowship, which coordinated the unions of Christian students, evangelical students in effect, in the universities. In the African situation, these expatriate teachers felt the lack of the fellowship and the ministry that they had known at home. They also felt a lack of these things in the African churches as they knew them. There was little sign of them in schools or colleges and no such organizations in the universities, nor did the churches offer anything like them.

A small group began in the University of Ghana, from where the movement spread to Nigeria and to Sierra Leone. In 1955, Scripture Union in Britain sent out a staff worker for West Africa, Nigel Sylvester, to be based in Ghana. Gradually the movement grew, establishing branches in schools and universities all over West Africa and holding occasional camps and conferences.

The history of what happened is still not properly recorded, though several doctoral theses have already appeared relating to different aspects of it.[6] These groups of young people do seem to have been the source of several major movements of Christian renewal. One was centered in eastern Nigeria, where the Scripture Union staff stayed throughout the civil war. The war brought appalling suffering and marked Ibo Christians in several ways. Cyril Okorocha notes how the characteristic theology before the war was a Deuteronomic one: in effect, honor God and he will honor you.[7] The postwar Christianity discovered a theology of the cross. It certainly developed an ascetic, sacrificial strain that had not been noticeable before, and these devoted young educated laypeople began to have an effect on church life, sometimes tending to disruption but often to enrichment.

In western Nigeria, which was involved in the war but suffered less, the effect was the same. The result was the emergence of new radical churches with names like Deeper Life Holiness Church, led by highly disciplined, highly educated, but not theologically trained younger people. The leader of the Deeper Life Holiness Church, for instance, was a former university lecturer in mathematics.

In Ghana, a chance contact with the Assemblies of God mission seems to have been a link in the chain that led to the charismatic or Neo-Pentecostal movement that is now the Christian mainstream in Ghana. It is a strange chapter of mission history, and the actual missionaries, though they were not usually called missionaries, were very few. The task of the missionary is often not to blaze with fire and smoke but to be the detonator of an explosion where the material is already to hand.

Chapter 10 described how the Commission I report on world evangelization that was considered by the World Missionary Conference of 1910 surveyed the continents one by one. It was optimistic about China and India and Japan, brief on Korea. On Africa, it said in effect that things are not as discouraging as one might expect. But it went on to indicate that as far as the interior of Africa is concerned, it is fair to say that the work of evangelization had hardly begun. And elsewhere, the report notes the possibility of Africa's becoming an Islamic continent, a prediction that now appears wide of the mark.

6. Since Professor Walls delivered these lectures, the history of this movement has received greater attention in published work: see especially Richard Burgess, *Nigeria's Christian Revolution: The Civil War Revival and Its Pentecostal Progeny (1967-2006)* (Carlisle: Paternoster, 2008), and Brian Stanley, *The Global Diffusion of Evangelicalism: The Age of Billy Graham and John Stott* (Downers Grove, IL: InterVarsity Press, 2013), 86-90.—Ed.

7. Cyril C. Okorocha, *The Meaning of Religious Conversion in Africa: The Case of the Igbo of Nigeria* (Aldershot: Avebury, 1987), 116-17.

We noted in chapter 13 the warning delivered to the South African Parliament in 1960 by the British prime minister, Harold Macmillan, that they should take note of the winds of change blowing through Africa, winds that had brought the new nations to birth and would make apartheid impossible to sustain. At that time, there were many who would have predicted that the winds of change that had blown away the structures of colonialism would take Christianity with them as part of the colonial detritus. It did not happen. Africans have come to faith in ever-increasing numbers since the dismantling of the empires. It is the homelands of the imperial powers where the faith has grown thin. The winds of change brought with them a refreshing, renewing latter rain.

CHAPTER 16

The Theological Challenge of World Christianity

New Questions and New Possibilities

We have watched the volcano erupt in the war of 1939 to 1945. We have considered the fallout for the Western missionary movement, looking first at India, where independence in 1947 was the first unmistakable sign that the Western empires were being dismantled. Vasco da Gama was sailing home. We saw how here, too, there were lessons for Western missions as the recognition developed of how far missions had actually been adopting an imperial outlook—still more, how the Church of South India and other signs were showing that the church in the non-Western world was prepared to innovate, open new paths, producing sometimes a fluttering in the theological dovecotes of the Western world.

We passed to China, the scene of some of the heaviest missionary investment, where missions found themselves totally excluded for the future. We saw that that event provided much heart searching within the missionary movement about some of its methods, and still more, some of its assumptions and attitudes. But the church in China not only survived, it expanded exponentially, and whole new fields were opened up, especially among the overseas Chinese.

Then, we explored aspects of new indigenous Christian movements, many of them outside the control or even the knowledge of missions as the new nations of Africa came into being. Across the world, a truly global church was born, growing, and maturing. The missionary movement in the West, now in its old age, had performed the task that it was called to perform. The movement could not be separated from the great migration of peoples from Europe to peoples beyond Europe, which began in the last years of the sixteenth century and concluded in the years following World War II—the migration that over centuries called into being the nations of the Americas, set up the empires, and controlled trade and the international order. But the missionary movement, though it sometimes shared the attributes, including the least desirable attributes, of this great European migration, was a semi-detached part and certainly a differently motivated part of the migration.

We noted that following World War II, the great European migration went into reverse. Vast numbers from the non-Western world began to come to Europe and North America, and this migration may determine the future course of world mission as much as the great European migration has affected mission in the last five hundred years. Our principal concern, however, was that inevitably the missionary movement had been shaped by the languages and cultures of Europe, and that a truly global church would reflect other influences as the Christian faith continued to interact with the cultures of Africa and Asia. It is this that I would like to follow up in this brief final chapter. I am inviting you to look at the implications for theology of the new Christian world, this global Christian world, which we began to glimpse in that first generation, that thirty-year period, following World War II.

Christianity's Accommodation with the Enlightenment

Western Christianity is a heavily contextualized, deeply acculturated product, soaked in European and American history and language. One of the factors that has determined its shape was the chapter of Western intellectual history that we loosely call the Enlightenment, that challenged the course of much previous European thinking and formed the outlook of the new country of the United States. The Enlightenment, with its exaltation of reason and science, its insistence on the autonomy of the individual self, threw down the challenge to traditional Christian thought. Western Christendom had long operated from the givenness of revelation, and the whole idea of Christendom implied the collective, corporate commitment of the whole community to the law of Christ. Western Christianity survived the Enlightenment by making cultural adaptations: in effect, it contextualized. It accepted the Enlightenment's insistence on a firm line dividing the empirical world—what we can see and feel, the realm in which science operates—and the world of spirit. But instead of saying, as the secular Enlightenment would have it, that there is nothing on the other side of the frontier—or if there is, we can know nothing about it—the Christian Enlightenment insisted that there were particular places at which the frontier could be and had been crossed.

Since, as we observed in chapter 12, the Bible is *not* an Enlightenment book, this meant in effect bracketing out some parts of the Bible as representing areas where the divine crossed into the empirical sphere in former times but does so no longer, or at least is not to be looked for. Tongues, prophecies, and works of power, therefore, are no more to be expected since the end of the apostolic age, being a special dispensation for the foundation of the church. This meant reshaping—contextualizing—theology to fit the smaller, shaved-down universe that constituted the Enlightenment, or, as we more often call it, the modern view of the world.

I am myself a lost child of the Scottish Enlightenment, and I do not despise it. It is part of my past, part of my identity. The trouble is that Enlightenment theology, conservative just as much as liberal, is theology for a small-scale universe, and most people in most of the world live in a larger, more populated universe than the Enlightenment allows for, with a permanently open frontier between the empirical world and the world of spirit, constantly being crossed in either direction. In other words, Western theology, Enlightenment theology, is too small for Africa and Asia. It has nothing to say on some of the matters of most practical concern. It has nothing to say for instance about witchcraft or sorcery: in an Enlightenment universe, witchcraft and sorcery do not exist. It has nothing useful to say about ancestors, for in an Enlightenment universe, we do not have ancestors other than in a historical sense. In so many areas, Western theology, coming out of its little universe, is disabled, lame, limping in the face of the problems of those who live in a larger universe. It has no answers, because it has no questions. I have never seen in any textbook or pastoral theology an answer to the question, "I am a witch, I kill people, I have killed three babies; how do I stop?" It is certainly no use saying, "Witchcraft is an imaginary crime."

So the church and the scholarship of the new age have to develop a theology for a bigger universe than the church of the old order has been using in recent centuries. Once again, the Western church stands to benefit from this if it is successfully done. The church itself in the West is finding Enlightenment theology insufficient for its own needs. I am still not sure that I know what postmodernism is, especially after a recent tour as an examiner for a course on it; but at the very least, it indicates dissatisfaction in the Western world with what we have taken to be the modern, that is, the Enlightenment, worldview.

Western theology cannot really cope with the principalities and powers, because essentially it cannot visualize them. The theology of the non-Western world may develop a genuine theology of the principalities and powers. If it does, I believe Western theology stands to benefit, for our theology finds it difficult to cope with the problem of evil and thus of salvation. It swings between individual guilt and responsibility and individual salvation, on the one hand, and, on the other hand, structural evil in the courses of the world. It quarrels over whether the gospel is intended for individuals or society; if the answer is "both," it cannot resolve the order of priority between the two. A theology that actually unlocked what Paul means by the principalities and powers, that unlocked what is that kingdom of God that frightens the demons, that demonstrates how Christ's cross became a triumphal chariot, dragging the evil powers behind it, could move us out of such unprofitable courses; and such a theology, I believe, is more likely to come from Christians in Africa or Asia with their larger universe.

The New Agenda for Theology Arising from Non-Western Christian Experience

Africa knows all about systemic evil. Systemic evil walks naked in broken-backed states where there is a war because there is a war because there is a war, and in the endless cycle of weekly funerals of AIDS victims. Western theology is still trying to come to terms with the Holocaust: how did the plan for the extirpation of the Jewish race and the partial execution of it take place at the heart of Christian civilization? African theology has to cope with the equally frightful genocide in Rwanda in 1994 and to consider how this happened in what by any standard was one of the most Christian countries in Africa.

We must hope and expect to see non-Western theologies developing, and many of them will mean breaking new ground, acquiring new skills that few now possess. We need a group of dedicated Christian historians who will cope with languages that few know, at least in combination, who know both Syriac and old Chinese, a combination that few scholars possess. Such scholars could recover for us a vital, almost lost, period of Christian history and an important interaction between Christianity and Buddhist thought. There is a huge amount of original research to be carried out in African and Asian Christian history, and it needs the fullest and most rigorous preparation. There is a vast work of synthesis to be done also. Over the past thirty years or so, hundreds of doctoral theses of varying quality have examined particular aspects of African, Asian, Latin American, and Pacific Christianity—and now gather dust, for no one has looked at them since. Forests of journal articles have been written, but we still lack the major works that have absorbed the labors of these sources, reflected on them, and brought them together.

The crucial fact is, African, Asian, and Latin American Christian history are not a matter of mere local significance; they are simply church history, the story of God's dealings with humanity. They belong to the whole church, and none of us can afford to be without them. Christianity has always been in principle global. The period that comprehended the great European migration, when Christianity was Western, was in fact the exception. So now in scholarship, as in Christian thinking as a whole, the new theological world of Africa, Asia, and Latin America must redress the balance of the old. The process could open new horizons for Western scholarship, letting oxygen into parts of the theological academy that are gasping for want of it.

There are so many theological workshops today, forcing new questions onto the theological agenda. India is probably the most testing environment in which the Christian faith has yet lived, and it *has* done for nearly two thousand years there. China is the great Christian enigma; it is hard to think of a parallel in Christian history to a church that has endured so much as it has in the past fifty years and emerged as it has done. Estimates of Christian numbers vary widely, not to say wildly, but one thing is certain: that there are many times the number of Christians there now than at the time when missions were expelled. China will clearly be a major player in the world league; we do not yet know what its position will be in the Christian league. Let's note, however, the degree of theological development that has taken place among the overseas Chinese.

In Latin America, as a much-rehearsed saying has it, "the theologians opted for the poor; the poor opted for Pentecostalism." The combination means that the sixteenth century has finally caught up with Latin America, which had the Council of Trent imposed without having to work for it. Korea has been the great surprise, the new missionary nation with its missionaries all over the world, a place where theologies of mission may yet develop. Theological developments in any of these could fill whole papers. But for the moment, let me think of developments in Africa.

African Readings of the Bible

Enlightenment thinking has shaped biblical studies in particular, and I suspect that in no area has the experience of African graduate students in Western universities been more testing than in the biblical field. Their desire has often been to establish relation between matters treated in the biblical text and some custom or institution in their own tradition: sacrifice, prayer, libation. But the demands of the literary historical method established by the Enlightenment greatly restrict the freedom of movement and can produce despair or, at best, two theses that do not really interact in a single dissertation. Yet Old Testament studies should be one area where Africa comes into its own. Western Christianity has always had difficulties with the Old

Testament. The extreme indigenizers among the Greeks wanted to remove it or reduce its importance.

European experience with the Old Testament was compromised by the often-fraught relationship with the Jewish community, and the Enlightenment decided that it needed careful explanation and special introduction as part of the bracketing process already described. In Western experience, the God of the Old Testament came from the outside. No Christian ever suggested that Zeus or Jupiter, or Odin or Thor, was the creator and moral governor of the world, or took their names for the God and Father of our Lord Jesus Christ. Instead of the Hebrew sacred name of Yahweh, they used the generic term "god" with some device, such as a capital to indicate his singleness. In Africa, the Old Testament is not a strange book needing complicated annotations. Customs, institutions, and relationships that need footnotes in the West are immediately recognizable to quite simple readers. The experience over the name of God, too, has been quite different from that in the West. Almost everywhere, African peoples already knew a being who was the creator and moral governor of the universe, and that being had a vernacular name—for example, Nyame among the Akan; Chukwu or Chineke among the Igbo; Modimo among the Batswana and the Sotho—a name that became the natural term to denote the God of the Scriptures.

This seems to me to open up new possibilities for African theological thinking that have been closed to Western biblical scholars and make it possible to bring a fresh appreciation of the Old Testament to the world church. Such dynamic thinking could break through the mental blocks imposed by the limitations of Greek philosophical thinking, which lacked a real equivalent in its background to the I Am that Moses met, the Yahweh of Sinai and Elijah's cave, the Mighty One that slew Rahab the dragon. Perhaps everyone has been waiting for Africa to bring the church to a richer understanding of the Old Testament and the liberation of theology to use Scripture without some of the cultural shackles formerly imposed on it.

Ethiopia has produced a unique integration of the Old Testament into its Christian life, but modern Africa almost invariably had the New Testament first, and a church grew up for many years with a New Testament as the Scripture, rather what Marcion would have wanted for early Christianity. What difference has the subsequent translation of the Old Testament made to churches so constituted? In 1968, David Barrett identified the availability of the whole Bible in vernacular translation as one of the indicators of the likely appearance of independent churches.[1]

---

1. David B. Barrett, *Schism and Renewal in Africa: An Analysis of Six Thousand Contemporary Religious Movements* (Nairobi: Oxford University Press, 1968), 127-34, 268-69.

A New Set of Theological Questions

Globally, the church requires theological pioneering. How and why did the creeds come into being? The creeds arose because of the cross-cultural transmission of the gospel into the Hellenistic world, raising new questions that could not be answered with the old, well-tried, proven theological equipment, and with such words and titles as "Messiah," questions about being and essence, which many old believers in Jerusalem might have thought irreverent, but which mattered deeply in a Greek intellectual context. There were questions about who Christ is. When today we use words such as these from the Nicene Creed, "begotten of his Father before all worlds, God from God, Light from Light, very God from very God, begotten, not made, being of one substance with the Father," we are drawn out in worship, and our hearts respond, "Yes! That is who Christ is."

The only way of getting there, however, was to ask Greek questions in the Greek language, questions that could not be answered by any single text of Scripture, using indigenous categories of thought, following indigenous methods of debate, making some indigenous mistakes along the way. What we think of as the classical doctrines of the Trinity and incarnation are made out of the intellectual materials available at the time, basically middle-period Platonism, converted by turning them toward Christ. It is the crossing of a cultural frontier that raises new questions of this kind: first, questions about what to do, then questions about what to think. Theology is about making Christian choices, about choosing to think in a Christian way. Just as Hellenistic culture raised questions about what to do and what to think that could not be answered in the old terms, just as the culture of my ancestors raised questions about sin and atonement, just as Enlightenment America raised still more questions, the old cultures of Africa and Asia will increasingly produce new crossroads, new places of Christian decision, where the word of the Lord will be "You have not passed this way before." Finding the answers will entail intense discipline, consecrated thought, using the indigenous languages, using indigenous categories of thought and ways of debate, using the intellectual materials to hand, converted to Christ's use.

That is how Christian theology has traditionally been done. Its proper home is not the library or the study but the living work and witness of the church. Dangerous, of course—doing theology *is* dangerous. When we do theology, we are talking of the high and holy one that inhabits eternity, the one whose word shakes the earth and heaven, Yahweh Sabaoth. Theology is an act of intellectual adoration of the Most High, but as with all talk about

God, it carries the risk of blasphemy. Active mission, then, creates new agendas for Christian theology, and theology learns new languages in order to take mission into the roots of identity.

Christian Encounters with Islam

Perhaps a brief excursus is appropriate here. One of the fundamental issues for mission in our contemporary world is surely the interface with Islam. This is a complex and many-sided matter; there is not a single interface with a single Islam but many different situations with different dynamics. Nevertheless, speaking very loosely, one may say that for a period of 1,400 years Muslims have not heard the gospel in any way that can profit them. They have heard the *words* of Christians, but they have not heard the gospel in those words because of what they think they know Christians are saying. Yet Muslims believe the Koran teaches that Jesus is the anointed Messiah of Allah. There have been situations in Africa where movement between the two faiths is possible, but in most places, the convert has no future. The stories of individual Muslim converts, wrenched out of their societies, are often tragic, indeed heartbreaking. If Muslims are to hear the gospel, it will surely not be one by one but by movements within the *ummah*, or community, and occasionally this happens. In various parts of Africa and of Bangladesh, to my knowledge, the stories continue of whole communities, often Sufi, followers of a particular sheikh, who have been studying what the Koran says of Jesus and have found the Messiah taking a more and more central place in their worship, often associated with a movement of moral reformation.

I was struck by the activity of one such community. How, I asked, do they pray? They prayed, as Muslims always do, with prostration. What, I asked, about the qiblah, the orientation of all Muslim prayer toward Mecca? Did they pray toward Mecca, as Muslims have done since Mohammed's early days when he had followed the Jewish custom and prayed toward Jerusalem? This community had decided to change the qiblah. They now prayed in a circle, since Jesus is in the midst of those gathered in his name.

There are yet other Muslim servants of Jesus who have remained as part of the Muslim community but pray to Christ. Perhaps we should remember and pray accordingly that the mission of God is not tied to the mission of the church, that we may yet see other movements whereby Christ becomes known in other faiths. But how is the church to relate to such movements? Can it see them as outside God's saving mission? I am sure that the nexus can never be something like the Nicene or Constantinopolitan Creed.

Two Ways of Being Christian in the New Testament

Diversity, cultural diversity in particular, was built into the church early in the apostolic period. It was the fruit of the first cross-cultural mission. And it was the outcome of the decision recorded in Acts 15 that gentile believers in Jesus did not require to be circumcised or to keep the torah. They were converts, not proselytes. From now on, there were two Christian lifestyles. There were old believers, who kept torah, circumcised their male children, kept the food laws, kept the Sabbath, washed before prayer, and attended temple when they could; and there were new believers, who did none of these things and had embraced the new Greek way of being Christian that we see being constructed in the New Testament epistles. The clash of lifestyles was obvious. But the two belonged to one Christian community. Antioch was its first center, the first bicultural church, and it is significant that it was in Antioch that the name "Christian" was invented. No one had needed a name before. It was the bicultural community that made it necessary. The development of this single community with two lifestyles runs through the New Testament. The Epistle to the Ephesians is full of it, after the rhapsodic opening about the *mystērion*, the now-open secret about the gentiles crowding into the people of God—a *mystērion* because while everyone knew in principle that the Messiah would bless the gentiles, no one could have guessed how important the gentiles were in God's plan.

Now came the solid instruction on relationship. The middle wall of partition is broken down. Jewish believers and gentile believers—not just two races but two cultures, two ways of living, two converted but quite differently converted lifestyles—are necessary to each other. This is how the new temple, which will replace the old one that gentiles cannot enter, is being constructed, and the two groups are building blocks in that temple; nay, they are organs in a functioning body of which Christ is the brain. In fact, only together, converted Judaic and converted Hellenistic, can we come to the full stature of Christ, for only in Christ is humanity complete. All our own representations of humanity are partial.

Paul is indignant when Galatian gentile believers accept torah and circumcision. Why? Were they not adopting the lifestyle of the best and most experienced believers? Were they not following the way of the apostles, nay, the way of the Lord himself? Paul cannot accept, even as an option, that someone born a Greek pagan should take on the lifestyle of even the best Jewish believers. "My little children," he cries out in Galatians 4:19, "of whom I travail in birth again until Christ be formed in you . . ." Christ is incarnated among those who receive him by faith in Galatia. He is a Galatian Christ who lives in Galatian society. Christ must become visible among the believers there. Becoming imitation Jews, becoming proselytes, in effect, and moving out of gentile society would negate that. And so, in the grand climax of Revelation 21, the new Jerusalem is foursquare, with gates pointing south, east, north, and west, with no main gate, no privileged point of entry. And the gates are never closed, and the glory of the nations, the special treasures of each nation, pass through those gates.

The bicultural church gave way in the end through the sheer success of the gentile mission and the growing rift in Mediterranean society, at least, between church and synagogue. But the idea continued of a church of different peoples. The early church was spread beyond Hellenistic society, as it spread not only through the Greek or Roman world but also through the Persian Empire among the Arab peoples. Further up the valley of the Nile, across to the Horn of Africa, into central Asia, the consciousness remained of a single church of many cultures and many languages.

The sixth century brings the great ecumenical failure that divided between those who did their theological thinking in Greek and Latin from those who did it in Syriac and Coptic. It developed the concept of an empire-wide rather than a worldwide church, cut off the Christians of Europe from the Christians of Africa and Asia, and divided the church along linguistic and cultural lines that made all the later such divisions easier.

The Contemporary Challenge

We come now to the particular context in which our own mission is set. The twentieth century saw the end of that great movement of population that had gone on for 450 years or so, that great European migration whereby millions of people from Europe had gone to the lands beyond Europe, set up new nations there using European languages and European cultural norms, setting up empires there, setting up a new world order politically and economically. The migration reduced to a trickle by the middle of the twentieth century, and the world order began to unravel. If we may adopt the language of the book of Daniel, which we did in chapter 13, we are now seeing a great beast, who had long dominated the stage, still roaring and lashing its tail, but being gradually moved from the center of things. It may be that beasts of a different stripe must have their day before the books are opened and the son of man comes with the clouds of heaven.

As the great European migration not only ceased in the middle of the century but actually went into reverse, millions of people from the non-Western world have poured into the Western. And that looks set to continue. Africa and Asia are now part of Europe. Africa and Asia and Latin America are part of North America, and they will never go away. The period of the great European migration and the beginning of the great reverse migration have seen extraordinary religious changes. Hinduism as we now know it, a coherent, confident faith adjusted to modernity and the scientific worldview, is largely a product of the British Raj in India, which also produced the conditions that created Pakistan, the first modern Islamic state. Colonial rule both facilitated the spread of Islam and built up a Muslim sense of grievance. And Christianity? Christianity began to recede in Europe and North America but to explode in other parts of the world, so that by the beginning of our century, the majority of the world's Christians were Africans, Asians, or Latin Americans, and again the process seems to be continuing. Christianity is now a predominantly non-Western religion, a fact that conditions all thought of Christian mission. Increasingly the people who carry it out will belong to Africa or Asia or Latin America.

There is another effect that transforms the nature of the ecumenical movement. We have at last bypassed the sixth century. We have once more the possibility of realizing a single world Christian community. We have the possibility, indeed, of realizing the conditions of the first century, the Ephesian moment as it were, of a church in which different segments of social reality, each converted to Christ, become building blocks in the new temple, organs in a body of which Christ is the head. And the great reverse migration brings the possibility to the congregational threshold. Perhaps the great ecumenical test, the litmus test of the church in this century, will be less the relations of what we call churches than the ability of African and Indian and Chinese and Korean and North and South American and east and west European Christians to work, to share meaningfully, within the body of Christ.

There are at least two great commissions in the New Testament. The one that is usually given that name is, of course, in the twenty-eighth chapter of Matthew, calling on the disciples of Christ to make disciples of all nations. We often read this as though it said, "make some disciples in each nation," but the words are "disciple the nations." We return to the thought of the conversion of culture-specific bits of social reality, turning each toward Christ, the things that make us distinctive, that give us our peculiarity, our nationality. Converted diversity will take us nearer the full stature of Christ, and only together, according to Ephesians, do we reach that stature. We cannot get there on our own.

The other great commission is in the Fourth Gospel, where the Lord, after showing to the disciples the marks in his hands and side, says, "As the Father has sent me, I am sending you" (John 20:21 NIV). The church enters God's mission through the Son: the mission to preach and to teach, certainly—a mission also to be and to do. A mission so that people may have life more abundantly. A mission to seek and serve those who are lost, to call people to judgment, to decision, to make up their minds, to preach good news to the poor and freedom for the prisoners, sight for the blind, release for the oppressed, and the Year of Jubilee where all debts are canceled, and the poor debtors find release. And with that, Jesus breathed on them and said, "Receive the Holy Spirit" (John 20:22 NIV).

Bibliography

Allen, W. O. B., and Edmund Mcclure. *Two Hundred Years: The History of the Society for Promoting Christian Knowledge, 1698–1898*. London: SPCK, 1898.

Anderson, Gerald H. "Peter Parker and the Introduction of Western Medicine in China." *Mission Studies* 23 (2006): 203–38.

Andrews, C. F. "Inter-racial Reconciliation." In *Addresses and Other Records*. Tambaram series 7. London: Oxford University Press, 1939.

Arndt, Johann. *True Christianity: A Treatise on Sincere Repentance, True Faith, the Holy Walk of the True Christian, Etc.* Edited by Charles F. Schaeffer. Philadelphia: Smith, English & Company, 1868. Available at Project Gutenberg. www.gutenberg.org/files/34736/34736-pdf.pdf.

Atkins, Gareth. *Converting Britannia: Evangelicals and British Public Life, 1770–1840*. Woodbridge: Boydell, 2019.

Azariah, V. S. "The Church and Its Mission." In *Addresses and Other Records*. Tambaram series 7. London: Oxford University Press, 1939.

Barrett, David B. *Schism and Renewal in Africa: An Analysis of Six Thousand Contemporary Religious Movements*. Nairobi: Oxford University Press, 1968.

Beaver, R. Pierce, ed. *To Advance the Gospel: Selections from the Writings of Rufus Anderson*. Grand Rapids: Eerdmans, 1967.

Bediako, Kwame. *Theology and Identity: The Impact of Culture upon Christian Thought in the Second Century and Modern Africa*. Oxford: Regnum Books, 1992.

Booth, William. *In Darkest England and the Way Out*. London: Carlyle, 1890.

Brown, Ford K. *Fathers of the Victorians: The Age of Wilberforce*. Cambridge: Cambridge University Press, 1961.

Burgess, Richard. *Nigeria's Christian Revolution: The Civil War Revival and Its Pentecostal Progeny (1967–2006)*. Carlisle: Paternoster, 2008.

Buxton, Charles, ed. *Memoirs of Sir Thomas Fowell Buxton, Baronet: With Selections from His Correspondence*. Cambridge: Cambridge University Press, 2011. Orig. 1848. https://doi.org/10.1017/CBO9780511751042.035.

Buxton, Thomas Fowell. *The African Slave Trade and Its Remedy*, 2nd ed. London: Murray, 1840.

———. *The Remedy: Being a Sequel to the African Slave Trade*. Cambridge: Cambridge University Press, 2012. https://doi.org/10.1017/CBO9780511783920.

Canning, George. "Address on the King's Message Respecting Portugal." *Hansard*, n.s., 16 (1826): 350–98.

Carey, William. *An Enquiry into the Obligations of Christians, to Use Means for the Conversion of the Heathens*. Leicester: Ireland, 1792.

———. *An Enquiry into the Obligation of Christians to Use Means for the Conversion of the Heathens*. New facsimile ed. Edited by E. A. Payne. London: Carey Kingsgate, 1961.

Carson, Penelope. *The East India Company and Religion, 1698–1858*. Woodbridge: Boydell & Brewer, 2012.

[Christie, Elizabeth Hastie]. *Dugald Christie of Manchuria: Pioneer and Medical Missionary; The Story of a Life with a Purpose, by His Wife*. London: Clarke, [1932].

Coleridge, Henry Nelson, ed. *The Literary Remains of Samuel Taylor Coleridge*. 4 vols. London: Pickering, 1836–1839.

Cranz, David. *The History of Greenland: Containing a Description of the Country, and Its Inhabitants; And Particularly, a Relation of the Mission, Carried On for above These Thirty Years by the Unitas Fratrum, at New Herrnhuth and Lichtenfels, in That Country*. 2 vols. London: Dodsley, [1767].

Cugoano, Ottobah. *Thoughts and Sentiments on the Evil and Wicked Traffic of the Slavery and Commerce of the Human Species*. London: Becket, 1787.

Cunningham, John William. *Sermon by the Rev. John William Cunningham, M.A. Vicar of Harrow, at St. Bride's Church, Fleet Street*. London, n.d.

Dasent, George Webbe. *The Story of Burnt Njal: Or, Life in Iceland at the End of the Tenth Century; From the Icelandic of the Njal Saga*. 2 vols. Edinburgh: Edmonston & Douglas, 1861–1862.

Dickens, Charles. *Bleak House*. London: Bradbury & Evans, 1853.

———. Review of *A Narrative of the Expedition Sent by Her Majesty's Government to the River Niger in 1841 under the Command of Captain H. D. Trotter*, by William Allen and T. R. H. Thomson. *Examiner* (August 19, 1848): 531–33.

Bibliography

Dwight, Sereno Edwards. *Memoirs of the Rev. David Brainerd, Missionary to the Indians on the Borders of New York, New Jersey, and Pennsylvania: Chiefly Taken from His Own Journal; Including His Journal, Now for the First Time Incorporated with the Rest of His Diary, in a Regular Chronological Sequence.* New Haven: Converse, 1822.

Edwards, Jonathan. *An Account of the Life of the Rev. David Brainerd.* Newark, NJ: Crane, 1811.

———. *An Account of the Life of the Reverend Mr. David Brainerd, Minister of the Gospel, Missionary to the Indians.* Boston: 1749.

———. *An Humble Attempt to Promote Explicit Agreement and Visible Union of God's People in Extraordinary Prayer.* Boston: Henchman, 1747.

———. *The Life of David Brainerd.* In vol. 7 of *The Works of Jonathan Edwards*, edited by Norman Pettit. New Haven: Yale University Press, 1985.

Eliot, John. *The Light Appearing More and More Towards the Perfect Day: Or, a Farther Discovery of the Present State of the Indians in New-England concerning the Progresse of the Gospel amongst Them.* London, 1651.

[Elmslie, Margaret Jackson]. *Seedtime in Kashmir: A Memoir of William Jackson Elmslie.* London: Nisbet, 1875.

"European Constitution." European Union. https://europeanconstitution.eu/wp-content/uploads/2019/05/European-Constitution-Full-Text.pdf.

Freeman, Thomas Birch. *Journals of Various Visits to the Kingdoms of Ashanti, Aku, and Dahomi in Western Africa.* 2nd ed. London: Mason, 1844.

Fuller, Andrew. *The Gospel Worthy of All Acceptation, or, the Duty of Sinners to Believe in Jesus Christ.* Clipstone: Morris, 1801. Orig. 1785.

———. *The Nature and Importance of Walking by Faith: And the Importance of a Deep and Intimate Knowledge of Divine Truth; Two Sermons, to Which Is Added Persuasives to a General Union in Extraordinary Prayer for the Revival and Extent of Real Religion, Addressed to the Northamptonshire Association.* Kettering: Fuller, 1815. Orig. Northampton: Dicey, [1784].

Gairdner, W. H. T. *"Edinburgh 1910": An Account and Interpretation of the World Missionary Conference.* London: Oliphant, Anderson & Ferrier, 1910.

Godwin, Benjamin, and Edward Steane. *Two Sermons Preached at Kettering on the 31st of May, and the 1st of June, 1842, before the Baptist Missionary Society, at a Special General Meeting Held in Celebration of Its Fiftieth Year: With an Account of the Meeting.* London: Houlston & Stoneman, 1842.

Gordon, A. J. *The Holy Spirit in Missions.* London: Hodder & Stoughton, 1893.

Gray, Richard. *Black Christians and White Missionaries.* New Haven: Yale University Press, 1990.

Gross, Andreas, Y. Vincent Kumaradoss, and Heike Liebau, eds. *Halle and the*

Beginning of Protestant Christianity in India. Halle: Verlag der Francke-schen Stiftungen zu Halle, 2006.

Harper, Susan Billington. *In the Shadow of the Mahatma: Bishop V. S. Azariah and the Travails of Christianity in British India*. Grand Rapids: Eerdmans; Richmond: Curzon, 2000.

Hastings, Adrian. *The Church in Africa 1450–1950*. Oxford: Clarendon, 1994.

Haweis, Thomas. *Sermons, Preached in London, at the Formation of the Missionary Society, September 22, 23, 24, 1795*. London: Barrett & March, 1797.

Haykin, Michael A. G. *One Heart and Soul: John Sutcliff of Olney, His Friends and His Times*. Darlington: Evangelical Press, 1994.

Henderson, G. D., and J. Bulloch, eds. *The Scots Confession 1560*. Edinburgh: Saint Andrew, 1960.

Hood, George. *Neither Bang nor Whimper: The End of a Missionary Era in China*. Singapore: Presbyterian Church in Singapore, 1991.

Horne, Melvill. "First Letter." In *Letters on Missions Addressed to the Protestant Ministers of the British Churches*. Bristol: Bulgin & Rosser, 1794.

———. *A Sermon Preached at the Parish Church of St. Andrew by the Wardrobe and St. Anne, Blackfriars, on Tuesday in Whitsun Week, June 4, 1811, before the Society for Missions to Africa and the East*. Philadelphia: Farrand, Hopkins, Zantzinger, 1811.

International Missionary Council. *Addresses and Other Records*. Tambaram series 7. London: Oxford University Press, 1939.

Jewel, John. *The Apology of the Church of England*. Edited by Henry Morley. London: Cassell & Company, 1888. Available at Project Gutenberg. www.gutenberg.org/files/17678/17678-h/17678-h.htm.

Johnson, Todd M., and Gina A. Zurlo, eds. *The World Christian Encyclopedia*. 3rd ed. Edinburgh: Edinburgh University Press, 2020.

Kagawa, Toyohiko. "The Meaning of the Cross." In *Addresses and Other Records*. Tambaram series 7. London: Oxford University Press, 1939.

Kamen, Henry. *The Spanish Inquisition: An Historical Revision*. 4th ed. New Haven: Yale University Press, 2014.

Koelle, Sigismund. *Polyglotta Africana: Or a Comparative Vocabulary of Nearly Three Hundred Words and Phrases in More Than One Hundred Distinct African Languages*. London: Church Missionary Society, 1854.

Koo, T. Z. "The Church and the International Order." In *Addresses and Other Records*. Tambaram series 7. London: Oxford University Press, 1939.

Kovács, Ábrahám. *The History of the Free Church of Scotland's Mission to the Jews in Budapest and Its Impact on the Reformed Church of Hungary, 1841–1914*. Studies in the Intercultural History of Christianity 140. Frankfurt am Main: Lang, 2006.

Kraemer, Hendrik. *The Christian Message in a Non-Christian World*. London: Edinburgh House, 1938.

La Chanson de Roland. Translated by Léon Clédat. Paris: Ernest Leroux, 1887. Available at Google Books. https://www.google.com/books/edi tion/La_Chanson_de_Roland/tZZcAAAAMAAJ?hl=en&gbpv=1&dq =La+Chanson+de+Roland+1887+L%C3%A9on+Cl%C3%A9dat&p g=PR3&printsec=frontcover.

Law, William. *A Serious Call to a Devout and Holy Life: Adapted to the State and Condition of All Orders of Christians*. London: Innys, 1729.

"The Lay of the Cid." Internet Sacred Text Archive. www.sacred-texts.com/ neu/cid.htm.

Legge, James. *The Religions of China: Confucianism and Tâoism Described and Compared with Christianity*. London: Hodder & Stoughton, 1880.

Lewis, Donald M. *The Origins of Christian Zionism: Lord Shaftesbury and Evangelical Support for a Jewish Homeland*. Cambridge: Cambridge University Press, 2010.

———, ed. *The Blackwell Dictionary of Evangelical Biography*. 2 vols. Oxford: Blackwell, 1995.

London Missionary Society. *Transactions of the Missionary Society*. London: Bye & Law, 1807–1810.

Lucas, Bernard. *The Empire of Christ: Being a Study of the Missionary Enterprise in the Light of Modern Religious Thought*. London: Macmillan, 1907.

Ludwig, Frieder. "Tambaram: The West African Experience." *Journal of Religion in Africa* 31 (2001): 49–91.

Lyall, Leslie T. *Come Wind, Come Weather: The Present Experience of the Church in China*. London: Hodder & Stoughton, 1961.

———. *Red Sky at Night: Communism Confronts Christianity in China*. London: Hodder & Stoughton, 1969.

MacNicol, Nicol. *A Shortened Version of Dr. Hendrik Kraemer's* The Christian Message in a Non-Christian World. London: International Missionary Council, 1938.

"Make Jesus King": The Report of the International Students' Missionary Conference, Liverpool, January 1–5, 1896. 2nd ed. London: Student Volunteer Missionary Union, [1896].

Martyn, Henry. *Journals and Letters of the Rev. Henry Martyn*. Edited by Samuel Wilberforce. London: Seeley & Burnside, 1837.

———. *The Letters of Henry Martyn*. Edited by Scott D. Ayler. Woodbridge: Boydell, 2019.

Matthews, Basil. *Wings over China: Generalissimo and Madame Chiang Kai-Shek*. London: Edinburgh House, 1940.

Merwin, Wallace C., and Francis P. Jones. *Documents of the Three-Self Movement: Source Materials for the Study of the Protestant Church in Communist China.* New York: National Council of the Churches of Christ in the USA, 1963.

Morrison, Robert. *A Dictionary of the Chinese Language, in Three Parts: Part the First, Containing Chinese and English Arranged according to the Radicals; Part the Second, Chinese and English Arranged Alphabetically; and Part the Third, English and Chinese.* Macao: Honourable East India Company, 1815.

Mott, John R. "The Possibilities of the Tambaram Meeting." In *Addresses and Other Records.* Tambaram series 7. London: Oxford University Press, 1939.

Müller, George. *Brief Narrative of Facts Relative to the New Orphan Houses, on Ashley Down, Bristol, and Other Objects of the Scriptural Knowledge Institution for Home and Abroad.* London: Scriptural Knowledge Institution for Home and Abroad, 1846.

Newbigin, Lesslie. *Unfinished Agenda: An Autobiography.* London: SPCK, 1985.

——. *Unfinished Agenda: An Updated Autobiography.* Edinburgh: Saint Andrew, 1993.

Niles, D. T. "Jesus, Whom God Raised Up." In *Addresses and Other Records.* Tambaram series 7. London: Oxford University Press, 1939.

Okorocha, Cyril C. *The Meaning of Religious Conversion in Africa: The Case of the Igbo of Nigeria.* Aldershot: Avebury, 1987.

Origen. *Homilies on Genesis and Exodus.* Translated by Ronald E. Heine. Washington, DC: Catholic University of America Press, 2002.

Paton, David M. *Christian Missions and the Judgment of God.* London: SCM, 1953.

——, ed. *The Ministry of the Spirit: Selected Writings of Roland Allen; With a Memoir by Alexander McLeish.* London: World Dominion, 1960.

Paton, William. "The Church and the World Community." In *Addresses and Other Records.* Tambaram series 7. London: Oxford University Press, 1939.

Records: China Centenary Missionary Conference Held at Shanghai, April 25 to May 8, 1907. Shanghai: Centenary Conference Committee, 1907.

Reichelt, Karl Ludvig, G. M. Rose, and A. P. Rose. *The Transformed Abbot.* London: Lutterworth, 1954.

"Reverend Maria Babos." *Daily Bulletin.* https://www.legacy.com/us/obituaries /ivdailybulletin/name/maria-babos-obituary?pid=18122937.

Robert, Dana L. *Occupy Until I Come: A. T. Pierson and the Evangelization of the World.* Grand Rapids: Eerdmans, 2003.

Schön, James Frederick, and Samuel Crowther. *Journals of the Rev. James Frederick Schön and Mr. Samuel Crowther: Who, with the Sanction of Her*

Majesty's Government, Accompanied the Expedition up the Niger, in 1841, in Behalf of the Church Missionary Society. London: Hatchard & Son, 1842.

Sharpe, Eric J. *Karl Ludvig Reichelt: Missionary, Scholar and Pilgrim*. Hong Kong: Tao Fong Shan Ecumenical Centre, 1984.

Sloan, George L. B. "Relation of the Christian Church to the Jewish Problem." In *Addresses and Other Records*. Tambaram series 7. London: Oxford University Press, 1939.

Smith, Reginald Bosworth. *Mohammed and Mohammedanism*. London: Murray, 1889.

Smith, Sydney. "Proceedings of the Society for the Suppression of Vice." In *Essays by Sydney Smith (Reprinted from the "EDINBURGH REVIEW") 1802–1818*. London: Routledge & Sons, [1874].

Stanley, Brian. *The Global Diffusion of Evangelicalism: The Age of Billy Graham and John Stott*. Downers Grove, IL: InterVarsity Press, 2013.

———. *The World Missionary Conference, Edinburgh 1910*. Grand Rapids: Eerdmans, 2009.

Stanley, Henry M. *In Darkest Africa, or, the Quest, Rescue and Retreat of Emin, Governor of Equatoria*. London: Low, Marston, Searle, & Rivington, 1890.

Stephen, James. "William Wilberforce." In vol. 2 of *Essays in Ecclesiastical Biography*, 212–13. 2 vols. 3rd ed. London: Longman, Brown, Green & Longmans, 1853.

Stock, Eugene. *The History of the Church Missionary Society: Its Environment, Its Men, and Its Work*. 4 vols. London: Church Missionary Society, 1899–1916.

Sundkler, Bengt G. M. *Bantu Prophets in South Africa*. London: Lutterworth, 1948.

Taylor, James Hudson. *A Retrospect*. London: China Inland Mission, 1894.

Thangasamy, D. A. *The Theology of Chenchiah with Selections from His Writings*. Bangalore: Christian Institute for the Study of Religion and Society, 1966.

Thelle, Notto R. "Karl Ludvig Reichelt 1877–1952: Christian Pilgrim of Tao Fong Shan." In *Mission Legacies: Biographical Studies of the Leaders of the Modern Missionary Movement*, edited by Gerald H. Anderson, Robert T. Coote, Norman A. Horner, and James M. Phillips, 216–24. Maryknoll, NY: Orbis Books, 1994.

Thomas, M. M. *The Christian Response to the Asian Revolution*. London: SCM, 1966.

Thompson, H. P. *Into All the World: The History of the Society for the Propagation of the Gospel in Foreign Parts, 1701–1950*. London: SPCK, 1951.

Thorogood, Bernard. *Gales of Change: Responding to a Shifting Missionary*

Context; The Story of the London Missionary Society, 1945–1977. Geneva: WCC, 1994.

Turner, Harold W. *History of an African Independent Church.* Vol. 1, *The Church of the Lord (Aladura).* Vol. 2, *The Life and Faith of the Church of the Lord (Aladura).* Oxford: Clarendon, 1967.

Venn, Henry. "On Nationality." In *Memoir of Henry Venn: The Missionary Secretariat of Henry Venn, B.D.,* by William Knight, 282–92. London: Longmans, Green, & Company, 1880.

Walls, Andrew F. *The Cross-Cultural Process in Christian History: Studies in the Transmission and Appropriation of Faith.* Maryknoll, NY: Orbis Books, 2002.

———. "The Ephesian Moment: At a Crossroads in Christian History." In *The Cross-Cultural Process in Christian History: Studies in the Transmission and Appropriation of Faith,* 72–81. Maryknoll, NY: Orbis Books, 2002.

———. "From Christendom to World Christianity: Missions and the Demographic Transformation of the Church." In *The Cross-Cultural Process in Christian History: Studies in the Transmission and Appropriation of Faith,* 49–71. Maryknoll, NY: Orbis Books, 2002.

———. *The Missionary Movement in Christian History: Studies in the Transmission of Faith.* Maryknoll, NY: Orbis Books, 1996.

———. "Missionary Societies and the Fortunate Subversion of the Church." *Evangelical Quarterly* 88 (1988): 141–55.

———. "Missions and Historical Memory: Jonathan Edwards and David Brainerd." In *Crossing Cultural Frontiers: Studies in the History of World Christianity,* edited by Mark R. Gornik, 185–202. Maryknoll, NY: Orbis Books, 2017.

Watson, Richard. "God with Us." In vol. 1 of *Sermons and Sketches of Sermons.* 2 vols. New York: Mason & Lane, 1840.

———. *The Religious Instruction of the Slaves in the West India Colonies Advocated and Defended: A Sermon Preached before the Wesleyan Methodist Missionary Society, in the New Chapel, City-Road, London, April 28, 1824.* London: Butterworth & Son, 1824.

Wesley, John. *A Collection of Hymns for the Use of the People Called Methodists.* London: Mason, 1784. Orig. 1780.

———. *A Collection of Hymns for the Use of the People Called Methodists: With a Supplement.* London: Mason, 1779.

———. "The General Spread of the Gospel." Sermon 63 in *The Works of John Wesley* (1872 ed.). Wesleyan-Holiness Digital Library. https://www.whdl .org/en/browse/resources/6881.

―――. *Journal of the Rev. John Wesley, A.M.* Edited by Nehemiah Curnock. New ed. 8 vols. London: Epworth, 1938.

―――. *Letters of the Rev. John Wesley, A.M.* 8 vols. Edited by John Telford. London: Epworth, 1931.

Wilberforce, Robert Isaac, and Samuel Wilberforce. *The Life of William Wilberforce.* 2nd ed. 2 vols. Philadelphia: Perkins, 1841.

Wilberforce, William. *A Practical View of the Prevailing Religious System of Professed Christians, in the Higher and Middle Classes, Contrasted with Real Christianity.* London: Cadell & Davies, 1797.

Williams, S. Wells. *The Middle Kingdom: A Survey of the Geography, Government, Education, Social Life, Arts, Religion, etc. of the Chinese Empire and Its Inhabitants.* 4th ed. New York: Wiley & Halsted, 1861.

World Missionary Conference. *The History and Records of the Conference together with Addresses Delivered at the Evening Meetings.* Edinburgh: Oliphant, Anderson & Ferrier, [1910].

―――. *Report of Commission I: Carrying the Gospel to All the Non-Christian World.* Edinburgh: Oliphant, Anderson & Ferrier, [1910].

―――. *Statistical Atlas of Christian Missions.* Edinburgh: World Missionary Conference, 1910.

Index

Abeokuta, 108, 189

Aberdeen, Scotland, 23, 96, 130

abolitionist movement, 66–71, 75, 87, 115;
British abolition of the slave trade (1807),
69, 113, 115; Wilberforce, 66–71, 75, 87, 116

Africa, 225–35; Cape of Good Hope, 6, 16,
31, 50, 111–15, 119, 140, 225; charismatic
prophets of the early twentieth century,
226; Commission I report of the 1910
Edinburgh conference, 157–58, 159–60,
166, 234; decolonization and independent
nations, 227–28, 230–35; decolonization
and missions, 230–35, 236; early Black missions to Sierra Leone, 64–65, 70–71, 112;
European colonialism, 6, 14–16, 31, 225–26,
227; indigenous religions, 228–29, 236;
Islamization and British colonial policy,
146, 158; mission and vernacular language
study, 121–23; the so-called Scramble for
Africa, 225; Watson's sermons on ancient
Africa, 71–73; World War I, 227; World
War II, 227. *See also* African Christianity

African American missionaries, 63–65,
70–71, 88, 112; British loyalists' missions to
Jamaica, 63–64; Nova Scotian missionary
settlers in Sierra Leone, 64–65, 70–71, 112

African Christianity, 226, 228–30, 233–34;
African Independent (or Instituted)
Churches, 229–30; charismatic or Neo-
Pentecostal movement, 210, 234; charismatic prophets of the early twentieth
century, 226; Christian growth in the
twentieth century, 166–67, 188–90; and
the International Missionary Council in
Tambaram (1938), 184–85, 188–90; new
universities and Christian movements,
228–29, 233–34; readings of the Old Testament, 240–41; theology, 228–29, 239

African Instituted Churches, 229–30

African National Congress (ANC), 185

African Slave Trade and Its Remedy, The
(Buxton), 110, 115–20, 225

Aggrey, J. E. K., 188

Ah Sou, L. T., 165n

Akrofi-Christaller Institute (ACI), xvii–xix

Algeria, 141, 200

Allen, Roland, 220, 222

All-India Trade Union Congress, 211

American Board of Commissioners for
Foreign Missions, 88–93, 141

American Civil War, 108, 147

American Revolution, 55, 63

Anabaptists, 19, 21, 28, 30, 45

Anderson, Rufus, 88–93, 96, 97; and the
American Board of Commissioners for
Foreign Missions, 88–93, 96; on the great
kairos and fulfillment of prophecies,
90–92; and New England Congregationalism, 89, 101, 105; on the Protestant

voluntary society, 92, 96; and three-self formula, 107, 220
Andover Seminary, 88–89
Andrews, C. G., 188
Anglicans. *See* Church Missionary Society; Church of England (Anglican)
Anglo-Chinese college at Malacca, 128, 130
Angus, Joseph, 95
Anne (queen), 29
Antioch, Syria, 3, 244
Antislavery Society, 71
Antony the Copt, 20–21
apartheid, South African, 232, 235
Apology for the Church of England (Jewel), 19
Apostles' Creed, 135
Arabic language, 11–12, 120, 123
Archbishop of Canterbury, 55, 68, 93
Arminianism, 37, 57n12, 84
Arndt, Johann, 28
Ashanti, 72, 189
Asia: Christian delegates to International Missionary Council in Tambaram (1938), 184–85, 186–88; Christian growth (twentieth century), 164–65; and the great European migration, 7–8, 31; medical missions, 164, 170, 171–80; Portuguese colonialism, 16, 31. *See also* China; India
Assemblies of God, 234
Associate Reformed Church, 89
Athanasius, 20
Atlee, Clement, 206
atomic bombing of Hiroshima and Nagasaki (1945), 217
Australia, 7, 141, 156
Azariah, V. S., 186–87, 204–5, 208, 209
Aztec Empire, 14

Babos, Alexander, 217
Babos, Maria Loriner, 217
Baltic states, 13
Banerjea, Krishna Mohan, 103
Bangladesh, 201, 243
Bantu Prophets of South Africa (Sundkler), 230
Baptist Magazine, 64
Baptist Missionary Society, 56, 64, 139, 165n, 215
Baptists: Carey's High Calvinist, 52–53,

55–59, 60–62, 99; China missions, 215; Jamaica missions, 63–64; opposition to slavery, 68; Particular Baptist Society for the Propagation of the Gospel amongst the Heathen, 61–62, 98
Barrett, David B., 230, 241
Baxter, Richard, 57n12
"Baxterism," 57
Bediako, Kwame, 229
Bengali language, 54–55, 129
Biafra, 233
Bleak House (Dickens), 121
Böhme, A. W., 29
Bonar, Andrew A., 94
Book of Common Prayer, 107
Booth, William, 146
Botswana, 169–70
Bowdoin College, 88, 89
Boxer Rising (1900), 133, 175, 214–15, 220
Brainerd, David, 35–43, 47–48
Bray, Thomas, 46
Brent, Charles H., 183
Britain: birth of evangelical missions, 52–62, 66–79; British Empire and India, 16, 17, 31, 200–207, 246; colonialism, 14, 16, 17, 31, 199–203, 227; eschatology and nineteenth-century missions, 83–95; nineteenth-century missions to non-Western churches, 96–108; race, culture, and society in nineteenth-century mission thinking, 109–11; voluntary society model of mission, 46–47, 52, 60–62; Wilberforce and the abolitionist movement, 66–71, 75, 87, 116
British Commonwealth of Nations, 227
Brunner, Emil, 210–11
Brunton, Henry, 94–95
Buddhism, 132–36, 146, 212, 239
Burma (Myanmar), 165, 201, 206, 207, 224
Buxton, Thomas Fowell, 70, 110, 114, 115–20, 121, 225
Calvinism, 30, 36, 45, 50, 86, 88, 94, 98, 107, 147; Carey's Baptist, 52–53, 55–59, 60–62, 99; Hopkins and evangelistic, 88
Cambridge Seven, 149–50
Cambridge University, 54, 67, 96–97, 123, 149–50

Canning, George, 181–82
Cape of Good Hope, 6, 16, 31, 50, 111–15, 119, 140, 225; Kemp and the London Missionary Society at, 112–14; Moravian mission to the Khoi, 111–12; slavery, 113, 114, 119
Carey, William, 48, 52–53, 54–59, 60–62, 66, 68, 73, 99; *An Enquiry into the Obligations of Christians*, 52, 56, 58, 61, 68, 87; evangelical eschatology and view of prophecy, 59, 87
Caribbean Islands, 5, 31, 46–48, 71–73, 88, 98, 102, 117, 140, 147, 158; Black British loyalists' missions to, 63–64; and the great European migration, 5, 31; Jamaica, 63–64, 102, 115, 117; slave trade, 69; Watson and British missions in, 71–73; West Indies, 29, 50, 70, 71
"Carrying the Gospel to all the Non-Christian World" (Commission I Report of the 1910 Edinburgh Conference), 157–62, 234
Catholic Church. *See* Roman Catholic Church
Celtic missionary movement, 4
Centenary Conference (World Missionary Conference of 1888), 155
Central African Federation, 232
Centre for Research Colleges in the University of Edinburgh, 180
Ceylon (Sri Lanka), 186, 201, 207
Chakkarai, Vengal, 211
Chalmers, Thomas, 76
Chao, T. C., 184
charismatic movement, 210, 234
Charnock, Job, 202
Chenchiah, Pandipeddi, 210–11
Chiang Kai-shek (Jiang Jieshi), 216, 217, 218
China, 212–24; Boxer Rising (1900), 133, 175, 214–15, 220; Buddhist monastic tradition, 132–36, 212; Communist, 213, 216–19, 221; Confucian tradition, 128–29, 131–32, 213; Cultural Revolution, 180, 221; European opium trade, 7; First Opium War (1839–1842), 130, 143, 170, 213; Japanese invasion and occupation, 185, 188, 216, 217, 221; Manchuria, 173–76, 216, 217, 221; Portuguese colonialism, 6, 16; Qing Empire, 140,

213, 216; World War II, 216–18. *See also* China missions; Chinese Christianity
China Centenary Missionary Conference (1907), 176–79
China Inland mission, 145, 149, 151, 214, 215, 219, 222
China missions, 34, 91, 125–36, 141, 212–24, 236; American, 213–14; and the Boxer Rising (1900), 133, 175, 214–15, 220; and the British East India Company, 126–27, 128, 202, 213; Catholic, 18, 25, 51, 127, 212–13; Catholic and Protestant phases, 212–13; Church of Christ in China, 219, 221–22; and the Communist government, 213, 216–19, 221; forced withdrawal and rethinking of, 222–24, 236; Legge, 130–32; medical missions, 164, 170, 171–80, 215–16; Morrison and the first Protestant mission, 55, 125–31, 169, 213; and the Nationalist government, 216–17, 218; Reichelt, 132–36; theological divisions between the minimalists and maximilists, 215–16; and translations of the New Testament into Chinese, 128, 129, 130–31; and Western contributions to Chinese anti-foreignism, 170, 213–15; World War II, 216–18. *See also* Chinese Christianity
Chinese Christianity, 164, 165, 219–23, 240; Church of Christ in China, 219, 221–22; growth, 164, 165; and new Christian theology, 240; Three-Self Patriotic Movement, 221–22; Wu and the Christian Manifesto, 220–21; YMCA and YWCA, 188, 216, 220
Chinese language, 126–31, 174, 175–76, 239
Christendom. *See* European Christendom
Christian Institute for the Study of Religion and Society, 211
Christian Institute of Southern Africa, 232
Christian Manifesto (*Direction of Endeavor for Chinese Christianity in the Construction of New China*), 221
Christian Message in the Non-Christian World, The (Kraemer), 184
Christian Missions and the Judgment of God (Paton), 222
Christian Response to the Asian Revolution, The (Thomas), 207
Christie, Dugald, 173–79, 180, 215

Church Missionary Society, 35, 37, 53–54, 68, 93, 94, 96–100, 107, 120, 222; and Church of South India, 208; founding by Anglican evangelicals, 97–98; medical missions, 171–72; mid-nineteenth-century missions, 142, 151, 171–72; Niger mission, 120, 151; Venn and, 96–100, 105-7, 123–24, 171
Church of Christ in China, 219, 221–22
Church of England (Anglican), 45–46, 49, 53, 98–100, 107; appointment of first Indian diocesan bishop, 204–5; Catholics (Anglo-Catholics), 159, 209; and the Church of South India, 208–10; and Dissenters, 50, 53, 55–56, 87, 99, 102; Edinburgh Conference (1910), 156–57, 158–59; English Book of Common Prayer, 107; mid-nineteenth-century missions, 142–43; nineteenth-century Jewish missions, 94; Oxford movement, 93, 142; Thirty-Nine Articles, 107. See also Church Missionary Society
Church of North India, 210
Church of Scotland, 19, 23, 56, 86, 94, 100–101; China missionaries during World War II, 217; Foreign Mission Committee, 217n; Mission of Enquiry to the Jews, 94. See also Free Church of Scotland
Church of South India, 208–10, 211, 236; ordinations, 209
Church of Zambia, 210
Clapham Sect, 64, 68, 70, 73, 75, 78, 97
Clarkson, John, 64
Coke, Thomas, 98
Coleridge, Samuel Taylor, 22–23
Columbus, Christopher, 12
Come Wind, Come Weather: The Present Experience of the Church in China (Lyall), 223
Communism, 213, 216–19, 221
Confucian tradition, 128–29, 131–32, 213
Congo, 14–15, 224, 233; medical missions and missionaries' health, 171; nkisi, 15
Congregationalists, 55, 57, 62, 88–89, 101–2, 142; Anderson and, 89, 101, 105; New England Congregationalism, 89, 101, 105, 147
conversion: European Christendom and patterns of, 8–11, 12–13; evangelical conversion movement, 21, 30, 40, 41–43, 76–77, 78–79; and the Jews, 86, 94; London Society for the Conversion of the Jews, 94

Cooper, Anthony Ashley (seventh Earl of Shaftesbury), 94
Coptic missionary movement, 4
Côte d'Ivoire (Ivory Coast), 226, 231
Council of Trent, 165, 240
Cowgate Mission (Edinburgh), 173
Cranz, David, 50
Crimean War, 171
Crisis of Missions, The (Pierson), 148–49
Cross-Cultural Process in Christian History, The (Walls), 155
Crossweeksung movement, 36, 37–41
Crowther, Samuel Ajayi, 102, 106, 120–23, 204, 226
Crusader States, 13
Cugoano, Ottobah, 64
Cunningham, J. W., 53–54

Dahomey, 72, 189
Dalits, 104, 203, 205
Daly, John Fairley, 155
Daniel (prophet), 198–201, 212, 245
Danish colonialism, 29, 48–50, 73; Tranquebar colony in India, 48–49, 98, 203
Dar al-Harb, 10–11
Dar al-Islam, 10–11
Darby, John Nelson, 93–94
Darkest Africa (Stanley), 146
decolonization and the Western missionary movement, 190–93, 201–11, 225–35; implications for Western theology, 192–93, 236–37, 239–45; Indian independence, 201–11, 227, 236; the new African nations, 225–35, 236. See also global Christianity
Deeper Life Holiness Church (western Nigeria), 234
Descartes, René, 51
Devanandan, P. D., 211
Dialogue with People of Living Faiths and Ideologies (World Council of Churches), 211
Dickens, Charles, 121
Dissenters (English), 50, 53, 55–56, 87, 99, 102
Dornakal diocese (Andhra Pradesh, India), 205
Duff, Alexander, 143
Dutch colonialism, 14, 16, 31, 111–14, 141, 207

Index

East India Company (British), 14, 35, 56, 73-74, 87, 126-28, 129, 139, 202-3, 213; in China, 126-27, 128, 202, 213
East India Company (Dutch), 111
East Syrian missionary movement, 3-4, 91, 212
ecclesiology and missions (nineteenth century), 96-108; Venn and the Church Missionary Society, 96-100, 105-7, 123-24, 171; Venn on the Christian significance of nationality (culture), 103-5, 109-10; Venn's idea of a national church, 100-108; Venn's three-self principle for new churches, 105-8, 220
ecumenical movement, 246; and Church of South India, 209-10; and the Edinburgh Conference (1910), 163, 209-10
Eddy, Sherwood, 220
Edinburgh Conference. *See* World Missionary Conference in Edinburgh (1910)
Edinburgh House mission press, 217
Edinburgh Medical Missionary Society, 172, 173
"Edinburgh 1910": An Account and Interpretation of the World Missionary Conference (Gairdner), 162-63
Edwards, Jonathan: and Brainerd's mission to the Native Americans, 34-43; and early British missions, 59-60, 67; eschatology, 87
Egede, Hans, 37
Église due Christ au Congo, 224
Egypt, 4, 185
El Cid, 11-12
Eliot, John, 33-35
Elmslie, William, 172
Emancipation Act of 1833, 116
Empire of Christ, The (Lucas), 153, 190-91
Enlightenment, xix, 30, 51, 192-93, 237-39, 241; and global, multicentric Christianity, 192-93, 237-39; and Old Testament studies, 241; roots of evangelicalism, 30, 51, 192; Western Christian theology's accommodation with, 192-93, 237-39, 241
Enquiry into the Obligations of Christians, to Use Means for the Conversion of the Heathens, An (Carey), 52, 56, 58, 61, 68, 87
Episcopalians, 62, 89, 183
Eritrea, 4

Erskine, John, 60, 87
eschatology and missions (nineteenth century), 83-95, 143, 144; Anderson and the early prophetic vision of the American Board of Commissioners for Foreign Missions, 88-93, 96; Anderson on the great *kairos* and fulfillment of prophecies, 90-92; Anderson on the Protestant voluntary society, 92, 96; book of Revelation, 86, 93-94; Carey's evangelical eschatology and view of prophecy, 59, 87; Darby, 93-94; the Evangelical Revival and evangelical eschatology, 85, 86-88, 93; Jewish missions, 94; Pierson's watchword ("the evangelization of the world in this generation"), 95, 150; premillennial eschatology, 93-95, 143, 144, 148; Wesley on the "general spread of the gospel," 83-86
Ethiopia, 4, 73, 124, 147, 225, 227, 241
European Christendom, 8-26; and American version of Christendom, 32-33; decline of, 22-24; encounters with Muslims and Jews in fifteenth-century Spain, 10-13; and the great European migration, 14-26, 31, 199-200; patterns of conversion, 8-11, 12-13
European Union, 23
evangelical humanitarianism (British), 66-79; Clapham Sect, 64, 68, 70, 73, 75, 78, 97; and evangelical conversion, 76-77, 78-79; India missions, 73-74; three legacies of, 77-79; Watson and British missions in the Caribbean, 71-73; Wilberforce and the British abolitionist movement, 66-71, 75, 87, 116; Wilberforce's social conservatism and moral radicalism, 70, 74-76, 77, 78
evangelicalism: Enlightenment roots of, 30, 51, 192; evangelical conversion movement, 21, 30, 40, 41-43, 76-77, 78-79; evangelical humanitarianism and early British missions, 66-79; Evangelical Revival, 85, 86-88, 93, 98-99; radicalism, 40, 93, 143
evil, systemic, 192-93, 239

Faith and Order Movement, 183, 209-10
"faith missions," 145, 151
Farmer, H. H., 184
Fiji, 7, 141

263

Finland, 13

First Opium War (1839–1842), 130, 143, 170, 213

Fourah Bay Institution (Sierra Leone), 122–23

Franciscans, 27

Francis of Assisi, 27

Francke, A. H., 29, 47

Free Church of Scotland, 172, 173–74

Freeman, Thomas Birch, 189

French colonialism, 31, 141, 199, 227, 231

French Revolution (1789), 55, 56, 74, 87, 93

Fuller, Andrew, 55–56, 57, 58–59, 60, 62, 67

"Fullerism," 58

Gairdner, W. H. Temple, 162–63

Gales of Change (Thorogood), 200

Gandhi, Mohandas K., 187–88, 203, 205–6, 207, 211

General Assembly of Massachusetts, 88–89

General Medical Council (Britain), 170–71, 173

"General Spread of the Gospel, The" (Wesley), 84–86

George (prince of Denmark), 29

George, David, 63–64

Germany: Confessing Church, 185; Pietists, 21, 28–30, 45, 46, 47, 48–50, 78–79, 83, 203; World War II, 185, 186, 216–17

Ghana: Akrofi-Christaller Institute, xvii–xix; charismatic or Neo-Pentecostal movement, 234; decolonization and independence, 230; as Gold Coast colony, 157, 189, 226, 230; Twi choruses, xx; University of Ghana, 233–34

global Christianity, 167, 192–93, 236–47; African readings of the Old Testament studies, 240–41; and the bicultural church of the New Testament, 3, 244–45; Christian encounters with Islam, 243; the contemporary challenge, 245–47; and the Enlightenment, 192–93, 237–39; new agenda for theological scholarship, 239–40; new theological questions, 242–43; and the theology of evil, 192–93, 238–39

Goa, 14, 16, 202–3

Gold Coast, 157, 189, 226, 230. See also Ghana

Gordon, A. J., 36

Gospel Worthy of All Acceptation, The (Fuller), 57

Government College of Fort William, 55

Granada, 11, 12–13

Grant, Charles, 56, 73

Gray, Richard, 15

Great Awakening, 34–35

Great Commission: Gospel of John, 246–47; Gospel of Matthew, 57–59, 100, 246

great European migration, 4–26, 31, 124, 147, 182–83, 199–200, 236–37, 240; consequences for Christianity, 17–18; crusading mode of Christian expansion, 13–17; and European Christendom, 14–26, 31, 199–200; missionary mode of Christian expansion, 17–18; and patterns of conversion, 8–11, 12–13; reversal of, 22–24, 154, 182–83, 190, 193, 201, 237, 245–46

Greenland, Moravian mission in, 50

Greenwich Observatory, 127

Guinea, Republic of, 231

Harris, William Wadé, 226

Hartenstein, Karl, 184

Harvard College, 88

Harvey Lane Leicester (pastorate), 52

Hawaii, 141

Haweis, Thomas, 53

Hayford, Mark Christian, 157

Haystack Prayer Meetings, 63, 88–89

healing missions. See medical missions

Heart Sutra (Buddhist), 133

Herrnhut, Germany, 29–30, 49–50

Hill, J. S., 106

Hinduism, 16, 17, 23, 48–49, 73, 85, 102, 146, 183, 203–8, 246

History of an African Independent Church (Turner), 230

History of Greenland, The (Cranz), 50

Hogg, A. G., 184

Holocaust, 185–86, 239

Hong Kong, 130, 141, 223

Hopkins, Samuel, 63, 88

Horne, Melvill[e], 53

House of Commons (England), 67, 119

Humble Attempt to Promote Explicit Agreement and Visible Union of God's People

in Extraordinary Prayer, An (Edwards), 59–60
Hungarian Reformed Church, 217n
Hungary, 217

Iceland, eleventh-century, 9–10
Incan Empire, 14
incarnation, doctrine of the, 20, 90, 193, 242
In Darkest England and the Way Out (Booth), 146
India: British colonial, 16, 31, 141, 200–207, 227; Commission I report of the Edinburgh Conference, 162; Danish colonies and missions, 48–50, 73, 98, 203; decolonization and independence (self-rule), 201–11, 227, 236; evangelical Protestant missions, 73–74, 102–3; and the great European migration, 7–8, 31; Hinduism, 16, 17, 23, 48–49, 73, 85, 102, 146, 183, 203–8, 246; Islam, 17, 102, 201, 206–7, 246; medical missions, 172; Mughal Empire, 14, 16, 31, 201–3; Mutiny of 1857 (First War of Independence), 202; partition and creation of Pakistan, 17, 206–7, 246; Portuguese colonialism and Catholic missions, 16, 202–3; Tranquebar colony, 48–49, 98, 203; Wesley and spread of the gospel to, 85; World War II and the "quit India movement" (1942), 206. *See also* Indian Christianity
Indian Christianity, 203–5, 208–11, 240; aspirations, 203–5; Church of North India, 210; Church of South India, 208–10, 211, 236; congregations and the *panchayat* (village council of elders), 105; contemporary Indian theology, 210–11; Dalits (Harijans), 104, 203, 205; delegates to the International Missionary Council in Tambaram (1938), 184–85, 186–87, 204; intellectuals, 103, 204; Kerala, 202, 203, 211; and new Christian theology, 240; the new secular state and effect on missions, 207–8; northeast state of Mizoram, 165; search for a national church (church union), 208–10
Indian Missionary Society of Tinnevelly (Tirunelveli), 208
Indian Mutiny (1857), 202
Indian National Congress, 205–6
Indonesia, 6, 7–8, 207, 223

International Missionary Council, 209–10; establishment of, 183–84; Jerusalem conference (1928), 190. *See also* International Missionary Council in Tambaram (1938)
International Missionary Council in Tambaram (1938), 181–90, 203; and the Edinburgh conference (1910), 183–88; the eve of World War II, 185–86; German delegates, 185; and Indian Christians, 184–85, 186–87, 204; and the indigenous church, 186–87; indigenous delegates from Africa, 184–85; indigenous delegates from Asia, 184–85, 186–88; neglect of the growth of the church in Africa, 188–90; on the persecution of Jews, 185–86; on topic of imperialism, 188
Inter-Varsity Fellowship, 233
Iraq, 3, 8, 199
Islam, 10–13, 91, 141, 146, 243, 246; Africa and British colonial policy, 146, 158; Commission I report of the 1910 Edinburgh conference, 158; fifteenth-century Spain, 5, 10–13, 27; global Christianity and encounters with, 243; India, 17, 102, 201, 206–7, 246; Ottoman Empire, 8, 91, 93, 141; Pakistan, 17, 206–7, 246; and post–World War I Middle East, 199; Wesley's spread of the gospel to Muslims, 85; in the West, 183
Israel, 182, 201

Jackson, Andrew, 89
Jamaica, 63–64, 102, 115, 117
Japan, 141, 175; invasion and occupation of China, 185, 188, 216, 217, 221; World War II, 200, 206, 217
Java, Dutch colonial, 141
Jesuits (Society of Jesus), 18, 25, 51, 61, 127, 203, 212–13
Jewel, Bishop John, 19
Jews: fifteenth-century Spain, 11–13, 27; German persecution and the Holocaust, 185–86, 239; nineteenth-century Anglican missions, 94; and the Tambaram meeting of the International Missionary Council (1938), 185–86; Wesley's eschatology and the conversion of, 86
Johnson, Andrew, 89
Johnson, Henry, 123

Jones, Arthur Creech, 200, 227
Journal of African Christian Thought (JACT),
    xviii, xxii

Kagawa, Toyohiko, 186
Kashmir, India, 171–72, 207
Keith, Alexander, 94
Kemp, Johannes van der, 112–14
Kenya, 227, 231–32
Kenyatta, Jomo, 227
Kerala, India, 202, 203, 211
Keswick Convention, 36, 151
Khoi of the Cape Colony, 111–15
Kimpa Vita, Beatrice, 15
King Philip's War, 33
Koelle, Sigismund Wilhelm, 123
Koo, T. Z. (Gu Ziren), 188
Korean Christianity, 164–65, 240
Korean War, 221
Kraemer, Hendrik, 184

Lagos, 102, 106
Langstane Kirk (Aberdeen, Scotland), 23
Latin America, 165–66, 240; Catholic Church
    in, 159, 165; and the Edinburgh Conference
    (1910), 159, 165; and the great European
    migration, 6, 14, 166; and the great reverse
    migration, 183; Pentecostal Protestantism in,
    166, 240; Spanish colonialism, 14; twentieth-
    century Christian growth, 165–66
Lausanne Congress on World Evangelization
    (1974), 198
Law, William, 46
Lebanon, 199
Legge, James, 130–32
Leicester Philosophical Institute, 58
Lesotho, 189
Liang Fa, 130
liberation theology, 166
Liberia, 124, 147, 225, 226
Liele, George, 63
Life and Work Movement, 183, 210
Livingstone, David, 124, 142, 169–70
Lockhart, William, 170
London Missionary Society, 50, 53, 54–55,
    89, 98–99, 107; Cape of Good Hope mis-
    sions, 112–15; China missions, 126–28, 130,

218–19, 221; founding, 98; Livingstone's
    service, 169–70; South India, 153
London Society for the Conversion of the
    Jews, 94
Lucas, Bernard, 153–54, 190–91
Ludwig, Frieder, 184–85
Lull, Ramon, 12, 27
Luther, Martin, 20, 28, 84
Lutheran church, 28, 47, 48, 49, 107, 135
Luthuli, Albert, 185
Lyall, Leslie, 222, 223–24

MacArthur, Douglas, 217–18
MacCarthy, Charles, 189
Mackenzie, Charles F., 142
Macmillan, Harold, 200, 235
MacNicol, Nicol, 184
Madison, James, 127
Madras Christian College (India), 203–4
Malacca, 14, 128, 130, 140, 223
Malawi (Nyasaland), 142, 155, 232
Malaya, 207
Malaysia, 223
Manchuria, 173–76, 216, 217, 221
Maori of New Zealand, 54, 141
Marcion, 241
Marrant, John, 63
Martyn, Henry, 35, 54
Mather, Cotton, 33
Mau Mau rebellion (Kenya), 231–32
Maurice, Matthias, 57
Mbanza Mbenga (Congo), 14–15
McCheyne, Robert Murray, 94
medical missions, 164, 168–80; China, 164,
    170, 171–80, 215–16; Christie and, 173–79,
    180, 215; Church Missionary Society,
    171–72; Elmslie, 172; and the healing
    ministry of Christ, 171, 176; hospitals and,
    172–73, 174, 175–79; medical training and
    the early Protestant missions, 168–70;
    and the professionalization of medicine,
    170–73, 179–80
Mencius, 131–32
Mennonite Board of Missions, 230
Methodism, 98–99; in Ashanti, 189; Black
    Methodists in Nova Scotia, 63; Tonga
    mission, 102, 141; Wesley on the spread

Index

of "scriptural holiness," 83–86. *See also* Wesley, John

Mexico, 5–6, 14, 27, 165

Middlebury College (Vermont), 88

Middle East: Ottoman Empire, 8, 91, 93, 141; post–World War I, 199

Mills, Samuel J., 88–89

Milne, William, 129

Milner, Isaac, 67

Ministry of the Spirit, The (Paton), 222

Missionary Movement in Christian History, The: Studies in the Transmission of Faith (Walls), 168

Missionary Review of the World (periodical), 148–49

mission societies, 97–100, 107–8, 184. *See also* Church Missionary Society; International Missionary Council; London Missionary Society; Society for Promoting Christian Knowledge; Society for the Propagation of the Gospel in Foreign Parts

Mobutu Sese Seko, 224

Mohammed and Mohammedanism (Smith), 146

monastic tradition: Buddhist, 132–36, 212; Christian, 20–21, 92

Moody, D. L., 149, 173

Moravian Brethren, 29, 37, 49–50, 111–12

Morrison, Robert, 55, 125–31, 169, 213; and the Chinese language, 126–28, 129; medical training, 169

Mott, John R., 150, 157, 162, 163, 183–84, 187–88

Mount Hermon conference (1886), 149, 150

Mugabe, Robert, 232

Mughal Empire (India), 14, 16, 31, 201–3

Mukden Medical College (Manchuria), 175–76, 180

Müller, George, 143–44, 148

Muslim world. *See* Islam

Mvemba a Nzinga, 15

Myanmar, 165. *See also* Burma (Myanmar)

Napoleonic War, 112

National Christian Council of China, 219

National Missionary Society (India), 208

Native American missions, 31–43, 46–48, 50,
88, 98; Brainerd, 35–43, 47–48; Crossweeksung movement, 36, 37–41; Eliot and the "Praying Indians," 33–35

Navigation School (Leith, Scotland), 174

Nazi Germany, 185, 186, 216–17

Nehru, Jawaharlal, 202, 207

Neo-Pentecostalism, 210, 234

Nepal, 165, 201

Netherlands Missionary Society, 112–13

Newbigin, Lesslie, 204, 208, 209

New College (Edinburgh), 173

Newman, John Henry, 93, 142

New Zealand, 7, 54, 99, 140, 141, 156

Nicene Creed, 135, 242, 243

Niger, 106, 120–24, 151

Nigeria, 102, 151, 200; civil war, 210, 233, 234; decolonization and independence, 230–31; Deeper Life Holiness Church, 234; efforts toward a national Church of Nigeria, 210; growth of the church in the twentieth century, 189–90; missionaries' cotton growing in, 77–78, 108, 143; movement for independence, 227–28; post–World War II universities and the study of African indigenous religions, 228–29

Niles, D. T., 186

Nkrumah, Kwame, 230

Nobili, Roberto de, 203

North America, colonial, 32–43, 46; Brainerd, 35–43, 47–48; Crossweeksung movement, 36, 37–41; Edwards, 34–43; Eliot and the "Praying Indians," 33–35; mission to Native Americans, 31, 33–43, 46–48, 50, 88, 98

Northampton Association of Particular Baptists, 60

North Korea, 164, 221

Norway, 132–33, 150

Norwegian Missionary Society, 132

Nova Scotia, 63, 64, 70–71, 84, 112

Nyasaland (Malawi), 155, 232

Okorocha, Cyril, 234

Old Testament studies, 240–41

"On Nationality" (Venn), 100–105, 107

Oppong, Samson, 189

Origen, 135–36

Ottoman Empire, 8, 91, 93, 141
Overseas Ministries Study Center (OMSC),
xviii
Overseas Missionary Fellowship, 222
Oxford movement (Church of England),
93, 142
Oxford University, 96–97, 130

Pacific Islands, 24, 84, 102, 140–41
Paine, Thomas, 56
Pakistan, 17, 201, 206–7, 246
Palestine, 94, 141, 199
Pan-African Congress in Manchester, England (1945), 227
panchayat (Indian village council of elders), 105
parachurch movements, 149, 233
Parker, Peter, 170
Parrinder, Geoffrey, 228
Particular Baptist Society for the Propagation of the Gospel amongst the Heathen, 61–62, 98
Paton, David, 222
Paton, William, 186, 187
Paul (apostle), 86, 90, 110, 133, 239, 244–45
Pearl Harbor, Japanese attack on (1941), 217
Pentecostals: Latin America, 166, 240; Neo-Pentecostalism, 210, 234
Persuasives to a General Union in Extraordinary Prayer for the Revival and Extent of Real Religion (Sutcliff), 60
Peru, 6, 14, 27
Peters, Thomas, 64
Philip, John, 114–15, 119
Philippines, 147, 223
Pierson, Arthur Tappan, 95, 147–49, 150, 151; premillennial eschatology, 95, 148; watchword, 95, 150
Pietism, German, 21, 28–30, 45, 46, 47, 48–50, 78–79, 83, 203; Halle, 29–30, 47, 48–50, 98, 203; Herrnhut, 29–30, 49–50
Pitt, William, 67, 69
Platonism, 242
Plütschau, Heinrich, 48
Plymouth Brethren, 93
Polyglotta Africana (Koelle), 123

Portuguese colonialism, 5, 6–7, 14–16, 31, 202–3
postmodernism, 238
Practical View of the Prevailing Religious System of Professed Christians, in the Higher and Middle Classes, Contrasted with Real Christianity, A (Wilberforce), 76
premillennial eschatology, 93–95, 143, 144, 148
Presbyterians, 46, 62, 89, 98, 100–101, 126, 147–48, 174, 176, 208, 219
Proclamation Society, 75
Protestant Reformation, 17–22, 27–30, 44, 47, 95, 107; English, 30; Scottish, 47, 95
Puritans, 21, 30–34, 45–46

Qing Empire (China), 140, 213, 216
Quakers, 32, 68
Quaque, Philip, 121
Queen's College, Cambridge, 67, 96
Quit India Movement (1942), 206

race and culture in nineteenth-century Western mission thinking, 109–24; abolitionist movement, 66–71, 75, 87, 115; Buxton and African missions, 110, 114, 115–20, 121, 123–24, 225; humanitarian evangelical missions and the African slave trade, 114–20, 225; idea of culture (civilization), 103–5, 109–11; theology of race, 109; Venn on the significance of "nationality," 103–5, 109–10
radical Christianity, 18, 21–22, 25, 28, 31, 32, 44, 45, 83; Catholic religious orders, 60–61; evangelical radicalism, 40, 93, 143
Red Cross, 175
Red Sky at Night: Communism Confronts Christianity in China (Lyall), 223–24
Reichelt, Karl Ludvig, 132–36, 184
Religion and Society (journal), 211
Revelation, book of, 59, 86, 93–94, 245
Rhodesia, 227. See also Zimbabwe
Richard, Timothy, 214, 215
Roman Catholic Church, 91; China missions, 18, 25, 51, 127, 212–13; early missionary movement, 17–18, 22, 58, 60–61; India, 202–3; Latin America, 159, 165; religious orders and missions, 60–61

Roman Empire, 10, 91, 110

Ross, John, 174

Roy, Ram Mohan, 103

Royal Africa Company, 121

Royal Institution, 146

Royal Proclamation against Vice and Immorality (1787), 75

Royal Society, 127, 129

Russia, 5, 7, 216. *See also* Soviet Union

Rwandan genocide (1994), 239

Ryland, John Collett, 57

Saga of Njal, 9

Saint John's College, Cambridge, 54

Samaj, Brahmo, 103

Samartha, Stanley J., 211

Samoa, 102, 141

Sangma, Thang Khan, 165n

Sanskrit language, 54–55, 129

Schism and Renewal in Africa (Barrett), 230

Schmidt, George, 111–12

Schön, J. F., 120–23

Scots Confession, 19

Scottish Reformation, 47, 95

Scottish revival in Cambuslang (1742), 60

Scripture Union, 233–34

Second Vatican Council (1962–1965), 198

Sermon on the Mount, 205

Sharp, Granville, 70

Siam, 147

Sierra Leone, 97, 102, 105–6, 115, 117–18; dangers to missionaries' health, 171; decolonization and independence, 230–31; early Black Nova Scotian missionary settlers, 64–65, 70–71, 112; Freetown, 64, 105–6, 120, 123; and language studies for African missions, 121–23; and the Niger expedition (1841), 120–23

Sierra Leone Company, 117–18

Simba Rebellion in eastern Congo (1963–1965), 233

Simeon, Charles, 78, 94

Simpson, William Young, 172

Singapore, 200, 223

slavery/slave trade, 7, 31, 66–71, 115–20; Baptist and Quaker opposition, 68; British abolition (1807), 69, 113, 115; Buxton on,

110, 115–20, 225; Cape of Good Hope, 113, 114, 119; Emancipation Act of 1833, 116; and the humanitarian evangelical missionary tradition, 114–20, 225; and Protestant missions to Jamaica, 63–64; Wilberforce and the British abolitionist movement, 66–71, 75, 87, 116

Sloan, George, 185–86

Smith, Reginald Bosworth, 146

Smith, Sydney, 75

social gospel teaching, 216, 220–21

Society for Promoting Christian Knowledge, 46–47, 49, 61, 98, 107

Society for the Propagation of the Gospel in Foreign Parts, 46–47, 50, 53, 61, 62, 97–99, 203, 208, 220

Society for the Suppression of Vice, 75

Society in Scotland for Promoting Christian Knowledge, 35, 47–48

Song of Roland, 10

Soong Mei-ling (Madame Chiang Kai-shek), 217

South Africa, 7, 156, 200, 227, 232; African National Congress (ANC), 185; apartheid, 232, 235; churches of, 166–67; Gandhi and the Indian community in, 188, 205; missions, 111–15. *See also* Cape of Good Hope

South Korea, 165, 221

Soviet Union, 200, 218

Spain: colonial Americas, 6, 14, 27, 31; colonial Philippines, 147; the great European migration, 5, 6, 31; Muslims and Jews in the fifteenth-century, 5, 10–13, 27; Spanish Inquisition, 12

Spangenberg, A. G., 29–30

Spanish Inquisition, 12

Spener, Jakob, 28–29

Spitalfields area (London), 115–16

Sri Lanka, 201, 210

Stanley, Henry Morgan, 146

Statistical Atlas of Christian Missions (1910), 155, 158

Steane, Edward, 139

Stephen, James, 68

Stock, Eugene, 35

Studd, C. T., 149–50

student missionary movement, 36, 149–51,

159; Liverpool conference of 1896, 150; Student Volunteer Missionary Union, 150, 219; Student Volunteer Movement for Foreign Missions, 36, 149–51, 159; watchword ("the evangelization of the world in this generation"), 95, 150; YMCA and YWCA in China, 216, 220
Student Volunteer Missionary Union, 150, 219
Student Volunteer Movement for Foreign Missions, 36, 149–51, 159
Sumner, John Bird, 93
Sundkler, Bengt G. M., 230
Sutcliff, John, 60, 67, 87
Sylvester, Nigel, 233–34
syncretism, 135
Syria, 3–4, 141, 199, 202, 244; birth of cross-cultural mission, 3–4, 244; East Syrian missionary movement, 3–4, 91, 212

Tahiti, 102
Taiwan, 218, 219, 223
Talbot, Edward, 159
Talbot, Neville, 159
Tambaram meeting. See International Missionary Council in Tambaram (1938)
Taylor, Abraham, 57
Taylor, James Hudson, 144, 145, 148, 151, 169, 215
Thirty-Nine Articles of the Church of England, 107
Thomas (apostle), 202
Thomas, M. M., 207, 211
Thorgeir (Icelandic elder), 9
Three-Self Patriotic Movement (China), 221–22
three-self principle, 105–8, 220–22; Anderson and, 107, 220; Chinese Christianity, 220–22; Three-Self Patriotic Movement (China), 221–22; Venn's principle for new churches, 105–8, 220; Wu and the Christian Manifesto in China, 220–21
Tinda, Moses, 39, 41
Tonga, 102, 141
Tranquebar, Danish colony of, 48–49, 98, 203
Transformed Abbot, A (Reichelt, Rose, and Rose), 135

Trinity, doctrine of the, 9, 242
True Christianity (Arndt), 28
Tsui, H. H. (Ciu Xianxiang), 219
Turner, Harold, 230

United Nations, 218, 221
United Presbyterian Church, 174, 176
United States of America: African American missionaries, 63–65, 70–71, 88, 112; American Board of Commissioners for Foreign Missions, 88–93, 141; American Revolution, 55, 63; American version of Christendom, 32–33; Christian decline, 24; Civil War, 108, 147; form of national church, 101–2; imperialism, 147, 213–14; missions in China, 213–14; Pierson and world evangelization, 95, 147–49, 150, 151; as postwar superpower, 200, 218; student volunteer missionary movement, 149–51; World War II, 217–18; YMCA and Mount Hermon conference (1886), 149, 150. See also North America, colonial
Universities' Mission to Central Africa, 142–43
University College, London, 130
University of Aberdeen, 130
University of Edinburgh, 154, 172, 173, 175–76, 180. See also World Missionary Conference in Edinburgh (1910)
University of Ghana, 233–34
University of Halle (Germany), 29–30, 47, 48–49, 98, 203
University of Ibadan (Nigeria), 228
University of Nigeria, Nsukka, 228n

Vedas, 193
Venn, Henry (1725–1797), 99
Venn, Henry (1796–1873), 100–108; and Buxton, 123–24; on the Christian significance of nationality (culture), 103–5, 109–10; and the Church Missionary Society, 96–100, 105–7, 123–24, 171; idea of a national church, 100–108; introduction of cotton growing in Nigeria, 77–78, 108; three-self principle for new churches, 105–8, 220
Venn, John, 68, 97
Victoria (queen), 8, 202
Virgil, 90
voluntary society model of mission: Ander-

Index

son and, 92, 96; and birth of evangelical missions in Britain, 46–47, 52, 60–62; student missionary movement, 36, 149–51, 159; Venn and the ecclesiological ambiguities of, 99–100

Wallis, Mrs. Beeby, 61–62
Warneck, Gustav, 162
watchword ("the evangelization of the world in this generation"), 95, 150
Watson, Richard, 71–73
Watts, Isaac, 64
Wesley, Charles, 46, 86
Wesley, John, 36, 38, 39, 46, 50, 83–87, 98–99; on abolition of the slave trade, 69; on evangelical conversion and "real Christians," 77; on the "general spread of the gospel," 83–86
Wesleyan Methodist Missionary Society, 71
Western Association (Bristol), 60
West Indies, 29, 50, 70, 71
Westminster Confession of Faith, 86
Whitefield, George, 98
Wilberforce, Thomas, 64
Wilberforce, William, 56, 64, 129; and the British abolitionist movement, 66–71, 75, 87, 116; and evangelical missions in India, 73–74; social conservatism and moral radicalism of, 70, 74–76, 77, 78
Wilder, Robert P., 149, 150
Wilkinson, Moses, 63
William Carey Memorial Church (Leicester, Scotland), 23
Williams, Samuel Wells, 147
Williams College (Massachusetts), 63, 88–89
Wilson College (India), 203–4
Wings over China: Generalissimo and Madame Chiang Kai-Shek (Matthews), 217
witchcraft, 192, 238
woman missionaries, 169
World Christian Encyclopedia, 155
World Council of Churches, 210, 211
World Missionary Conference in Edinburgh (1910), 150, 152–67, 183–88, 219; and

Catholic Anglicans, 159; Commission I report ("Carrying the Gospel to all the Non-Christian World"), 157–62, 234; the delegates, 156–57, 165n, 186; and the ecumenical movement, 163, 209–10; as the high point of the Western Protestant missionary movement, 154–55; on the home church and the unevangelized non-Christian world, 160–61; on the indigenous church (native church), 160, 166, 187; on mission theology, 162–63; on nationalism, 161–62; origins, 155; preparations, 156; and the Tambaram meeting of the International Missionary Council (1938), 183–88
World Missionary Conference of 1888 (so-called Centenary Conference), 155
World War I, 163, 185–86, 189, 199, 227
World War II: Africa, 227; China, 216–18; Holocaust, 185–86, 239; India, 206; legacy for the Western missionary movement, 197–201, 236; and the Tambaram meeting (1938), 185–86; and the Western missionary movement, 197–201, 236, 237
Wu, Y. T. (Wu Yaozong), 220–21

Xhosa people, 112, 113–14, 119

Yale Divinity School's Day Missions Library, 184
Yale University, 63
YMCA (Young Men's Christian Association), 149; China, 188, 216, 220; India, 208
Yorkshire Association, 60
Yorubaland, 101, 106, 108
Yoruba language, 106, 121
YWCA (Young Women's Christian Association), 220

Zambia, 210, 232
Zhou Enlai (Chou En-lai), 220
Ziegenbalg, Bartolomäus, 48–49
Zimbabwe, 200, 232
Zinzendorf, Nicolaus von, 29, 49–50

STUDIES IN THE HISTORY OF CHRISTIAN MISSIONS

Boone Aldridge
*For the Gospel's Sake: The Rise of the Wycliffe Bible Translators
and the Summer Institute of Language*

Alvyn Austin
China's Millions: The China Inland Mission and Late Qing Society, 1832–1905

Chad M. Bauman
Christian Identity and Dalit Religion in Hindu India, 1868–1947

Michael Bergunder
The South Indian Pentecostal Movement in the Twentieth Century

Judith M. Brown and Robert Eric Frykenberg, *Editors*
Christians, Cultural Interactions, and India's Religious Traditions

John B. Carman and Chilkuri Vasantha Rao
*Christians in South Indian Villages, 1959–2009:
Decline and Revival in Telangana*

Robert Eric Frykenberg
*Christians and Missionaries in India:
Cross-Cultural Communication Since 1500*

Susan Billington Harper
*In the Shadow of the Mahatma: Bishop V. S. Azariah
and the Travails of Christianity in British India*

D. Dennis Hudson
Protestant Origins in India: Tamil Evangelical Christians, 1706–1835

Patrick Harries and David Maxwell, *Editors*
The Spiritual in the Secular: Missionaries and Knowledge about Africa

Ogbu U. Kalu, *Editor*, and Alaine M. Low, *Associate Editor*
*Interpreting Contemporary Christianity:
Global Processes and Local Identities*

Donald M. Lewis, *Editor*
*Christianity Reborn: The Global Expansion of Evangelicalism
in the Twentieth Century*

Jessie G. Lutz
Opening China: Karl F. A. Gützlaff and Sino-Western Relations, 1827–1852

Stephen S. Maughan
Mighty England Do Good: Culture, Faith, Empire, and World in the Foreign Missions of the Church of England, 1850–1915

Jon Miller
Missionary Zeal and Institutional Control: Organizational Contradictions in the Basel Mission on the Gold Coast, 1828–1917

Andrew Porter, *Editor*
The Imperial Horizons of British Protestant Missions, 1880–1914

Dana L. Robert, *Editor*
Converting Colonialism: Visions and Realities in Mission History, 1709–1914

Jane Samson
Race and Redemption: British Missionaries Encounter Pacific Peoples, 1797–1920

Wilbert R. Shenk, *Editor*
North American Foreign Missions, 1810–1914: Theology, Theory, and Policy

Brian Stanley
The World Missionary Conference: Edinburgh 1910

Brian Stanley, *Editor*
Christian Missions and the Enlightenment

Brian Stanley, *Editor*
Missions, Nationalism, and the End of Empire

John Stuart
British Missionaries and the End of Empire: East, Central, and Southern Africa, 1939–64

T. Jack Thompson
Light on Darkness? Missionary Photography of Africa in the Nineteenth and Early Twentieth Centuries

Andrew F. Walls, Author, and Brian Stanley, *Editor*
The Missionary Movement from the West: A Biography from Birth to Old Age

Kevin Ward and Brian Stanley, *Editors*
The Church Mission Society and World Christianity, 1799–1999

Timothy Yates
The Conversion of the Māori: Years of Religious and Social Change, 1814–1842

Richard Fox Young, *Editor*
India and the Indianness of Christianity: Essays on Understanding—Historical, Theological, and Bibliographical—in Honor of Robert Eric Frykenberg